MAKING HOME
FROM WAR

MAKING HOME
FROM WAR

Stories of Japanese
American Exile
and Resettlement

EDITED BY
BRIAN KOMEI DEMPSTER

FOREWORD BY
GREG ROBINSON

Heyday, Berkeley, California

For those whose stories we've lost and for those with stories yet untold.

This book was made possible in part by a generous grant from the California State Library—California Civil Liberties Public Education Program.

Library of Congress Cataloging-in-Publication Data
Making home from war : stories of Japanese American exile and resettlement / edited by Brian Komei Dempster.
    p. cm.
Includes bibliographical references.
ISBN 978-1-59714-142-0 (pbk. : alk. paper)
1. Japanese Americans--Evacuation and relocation, 1942-1945. 2. World War, 1939-1945--Personal narratives, American. 3. Japanese Americans--Social conditions--20th century. 4. United States--Social conditions--1945- 5. Japanese Americans--Biography. I. Dempster, Brian Komei, 1969-
    D769.8.A6M325 2010
    940.53'17730923956--dc22   2010044107

Front cover photo, back cover photo, and frontispiece all from the War Relocation Authority Photographs of Japanese-American Evacuation and Resettlement collection, courtesy of The Bancroft Library, University of California, Berkeley.

Front cover photo: Mrs. Saku Moriwaki and her two-year-old daughter, Suga Ann, were the first Japanese American family to leave the Central Utah Relocation Center for California. Photo by Charles E. Mace, Topaz, Utah, January 3, 1945. WRA no. H-591.

Back cover photo: Mrs. Saku Moriwaki and her daughter, Suga Ann, are bid goodbye at the Topaz camp gate by her sister, Miss Suga Baba, and a Caucasian staff member. Mrs. Moriwaki, formerly of Berkeley, had accepted a position in the home of Mrs. R. A. Isenberg in Palo Alto. WRA no. -592.

Frontispiece: Roaring into Sacramento on July 30, 1945, a special train of seven cars brought 450 Japanese American residents back to their home state of California after three years of incarceration at the Rohwer War Relocation Center in McGehee, Arkansas. Photo by Hikaru Iwasaki. WRA no. -47.

Book Design: Lorraine Rath
Printing and Binding: Thomson-Shore, Dexter, MI

Orders, inquiries, and correspondence should be addressed to:

Heyday
P.O. Box 9145, Berkeley, CA 94709
(510) 549-3564, Fax (510) 549-1889
www.heydaybooks.com

10 9 8 7 6 5 4 3 2 1

CONTENTS

Our imprisonment during World War II has been documented by those rare filmmakers, authors, and skilled artists and poets whom those of us within this community have all come to know and love. Our project, now this book, provides a vehicle for the common folk to offer personal insights and to record their individual histories during and after that catastrophic mistake in American history that most of us are reluctant to discuss or fully acknowledge today. Our recollections give each story a face and a voice and add to our Asian American legacy.

Surviving the injustice, the prejudice, and the hardships during resettlement speaks volumes about the spirit that has led us to stand tall, to embrace our contributions that have made our country what it is today. Most of us, however, have remained silent, and now over half of us are not here to reveal our secrets of bouncing back from nothingness.

The following stories can inspire those who sit in waiting to tell their version of history and can aid them in the healing process. Our story is an American story, a portrait of others' mistakes, and our struggles to endure and overcome.

—*Toru Saito*
Public comment before the California State Library's California
Civil Liberties Public Education Program in 2007

FOREWORD

By Greg Robinson

World War II completely reshaped ethnic Japanese communities in the continental United States. During Spring 1942, army commanders—urged on by white nativists and by agricultural interest groups anxious to get rid of their economic competitors, as well as by opportunistic politicians—rounded up the entire population of Japanese ancestry on the nation's Pacific coast. Some 112,000 people, American citizens and longtime residents alike, were deprived of liberty without charge or due process, and on the basis of a blanket (and largely fictitious) claim of military necessity. In the process, they were forced to leave behind or dispose of the bulk of their property. They then were squeezed together into a network of so-called Assembly Centers, which were holding areas established under military rule in abandoned fairgrounds and racetracks. There they languished in hastily converted horse stalls and animal pens and were plagued by poor food and medical care, forced inactivity, and deprivation of basic liberties. After several months, military authorities transported the Japanese Americans to long-term confinement in "Relocation Centers," ten large-scale camps constructed in desolate areas of the Western states and Arkansas and managed by a new civilian agency, the War Relocation Authority (WRA). In these spartan camps, the inmates were housed in wood and tarpaper shacks, surrounded by barbed wire and military guards. The inmates worked hard, with help from some sympathetic administrators, to make the best of things for themselves within the camps, operating schools and cooperative stores and newspapers, among other activities. Still, the trauma of imprisonment, coupled with the harsh conditions, bred widespread discontent and sparked episodes of militant protest.

Most Japanese Americans remained confined in the camps throughout the war, even after their individual "loyalty" had been thoroughly examined and the War Department and the White House had privately agreed that there was no conceivable military necessity for their continued confinement. Although approximately one-fourth of the confined Issei and Nisei (first- and second-generation Japanese Americans, respectively) were able to gain official permission to leave the camps under a parole system and to resettle in the East and Midwest during 1943 and 1944, West Coast military commanders, seconded by anti–Japanese American politicians, still refused to reopen the excluded zone to people of Japanese ancestry. The restrictions remained in force until the end of 1944, when the Supreme Court ruled in the case of *Ex parte Endo* that the government had no authority to hold a concededly loyal citizen without charge. In response, the army lifted its West Coast exclusion orders in January 1945.

Once free to return to the Pacific Coast, most inmates from the camps began to migrate back. Resettlement east of the Rockies continued at a slower pace, but the Japanese populations of the Midwest and East Coast soon began to decline as those who had moved there from camp decided to return to their home regions in the West. In hopes of averting violent backlash from white racists, the WRA used various administrative devices to slow the flow of resettlers. Among their tactics, WRA officials automatically provided financial aid to all inmates settling outside the West Coast while demanding that any inmates wishing assistance to return to their prewar home regions submit detailed relocation plans, which the WRA then deliberately took extra time to process. Nevertheless, by the end of 1946, the majority of the mainland ethnic Japanese population was once again on the Pacific Coast, although significant pockets of Japanese American settlement remained in other parts of the country.[1]

The resettlers, already psychologically scarred by their confinement, attempted to rebuild their lives under difficult and trying circumstances. At first, despite the overall wartime economic boom, they faced widespread hardship. During the prewar years, Japanese Americans had been largely self-employed, most often as small shopkeepers or in agriculture, but they had been forced to give up their shops and the land they owned or leased at the time of removal, and most were not able to resume their former occupations once they returned. Instead, they were forced to move into urban areas and take whatever jobs they could get. This often meant that even those with high educational or professional experience were forced to take low-status jobs,

---

[1] U.S. Department of the Interior, War Relocation Authority, *The Relocation Program* (New York: AMS Press, 1975 [1946]).

sometimes involving menial labor. The majority were relegated to working for white families as gardeners or servants.[2]

Housing was an equally difficult problem. Japanese Americans who relocated to the West Coast were confronted by housing shortages, which were made worse by poverty and widespread racial discrimination. Furthermore, the war had brought a huge influx of war workers to the West Coast—primarily African Americans and white Southerners—and many of the newcomers had moved into the evacuated Japantowns, which then became overcrowded. The returning Japanese Americans often had no choice but to settle in temporary shelters and wait for the wartime leases on their old residences to expire. Hundreds more were forced into temporary housing in converted trailers; a large trailer camp, the Winona emergency housing project, grew up in Burbank (in Los Angeles County), and smaller camps—which were partly trailer camps and partly barracks—were created in El Segundo and Lomita, California.

To ease the housing problem, community groups formed hostels, and government officials attempted to steer resettlers, especially single Nisei, into domestic service positions, since they would thereby be provided rooms. Those with the means to buy homes and hotels opened space for lodgers in the old Japantowns. Even these combined efforts, however, could not absorb all the migrants. Instead, resettlers often huddled together in poor areas of cities such as San Diego, Los Angeles, Seattle, and San Jose. In particular, thousands of Issei and Nisei found permanent housing in black and Latino districts. For various reasons, some prewar Japanese neighborhoods, including the Old Town area of Portland, Oregon, and the Terminal Island district of Los Angeles, never regained their previous ethnic populations.

During the resettlement period, Japanese Americans took up some of their old community institutions and developed new ones. Resettlers were generally required to pledge not to congregate with other Japanese Americans as a condition of their "leave" from the camps and were warned by the War Relocation Authority and the FBI to "fit in" with the dominant society as much as possible. (They were even given little seminars prior to their release from camp instructing them on how to act on the outside.) Nevertheless, resettlers were often brought into close contact with other Japanese Americans,

---

2 Scott Kurashige, *The Shifting Grounds of Race: Black and Japanese Americans in the Making of Multiethnic Los Angeles* (Princeton, NJ: Princeton University Press, 2008), 195-7. For resettlement generally, see: U.S. Department of the Interior, War Agency Liquidation Unit, *People in Motion: The Postwar Adjustment of the Evacuated Japanese Americans* (Washington, D.C.: Government Printing Office, 1947); Dorothy Swaine Thomas, assisted by Charles Kikuchi and James Sakoda, *The Salvage: Japanese American Evacuation and Resettlement* (Berkeley: University of California Press, 1952).

both by internal factors, such as religious observance and common interests, and by external factors, such as racial prejudice and housing discrimination. One factor that kept the resurgent communities connected was the growth of local Japanese American newspapers and journals. Los Angeles's Japanese-language dailies *Rafu Shimpo* and *Kashu Mainichi* resumed publication (the latter entirely in Japanese), and San Francisco's prewar journals *Nichi Bei Shimbun* and *Shin Sekai* morphed into *Nichi Bei Times* and *Hokubei Mainichi*. Meanwhile, a new group of all-English weekly newspapers started up within the Japanese community, including *Crossroads* in Los Angeles, *Northwest Times* in Seattle, and *Progressive News* in San Francisco.

Another force bringing West Coast Japanese Americans together was a renaissance of community religious and social centers, such as Japanese Buddhist temples, Christian churches, and business and veterans groups. (The Japanese consulates that had anchored prewar communities, however, remained shuttered.) Hostels for resettlers doubled as recreational centers, providing libraries and game rooms for social events, while newly established multiethnic institutions such as the Pilgrim House in Los Angeles and the Civil Unity Committee in Seattle helped create youth programs and hosted public meetings to ease intergroup tensions. The Japanese American Citizens League (JACL), although resented by quite a number of camp inmates for its wartime policy of collaboration with the federal government's mass removal policy, was the sole remaining group of its kind in the postwar years, and large numbers of Nisei joined newly constituted JACL chapters along the West Coast. In addition to political advocacy, JACL chapters enthusiastically organized social events, dinners, and sporting leagues—particularly for basketball and bowling, the unofficial Nisei national pastimes!

State welfare and public assistance agencies generally refused to fund or direct the absorption and adjustment of the resettlers. Instead, the burden was taken up by local WRA offices, and then by private church and welfare groups after the dissolution of the WRA in mid-1946. The WRA was responsible for finding jobs and advocating for the newcomers, and its officials lobbied newspapers to offer positive coverage of Nisei, protested harassment and violence by hostile whites, and looked into charges of racial discrimination.

Both anecdotal evidence and official records testify to widespread patterns of ethnic-based hostility and exclusion by whites, although this attitude did diminish as the war period passed. In the cities especially, housing and job discrimination were common. Nisei often faced insults on the street and were refused service in stores. There were thirty-nine documented instances of terrorism against resettlers in the months after their return, including the torching of barns, sabotage of equipment, and shots fired into houses.[3] The most notorious case was that of Hood River, Oregon, where in November 1944 representatives of the local branch of the American Legion ordered the names of sixteen local Nisei servicemen stricken from the city's honor roll post, including that of Frank Hachiya, a Military Intelligence Service staffer killed while on duty in the Philippines. The incident was reported in *Life* magazine and soon attracted nationwide outrage. Under pressure from the national American Legion—as well as from locals who supported racial tolerance—the Hood River branch reversed its policy in April 1945.

The ugly social climate was reflected in official policy. Washington Governor Mon Wallgren said outright that Japanese Americans were not welcome in his state, and although California Governor Earl Warren called for full and positive public compliance with the return of the resettlers, the state government took several steps that contradicted that stance. Hoping to discourage Issei and Nisei from returning, California enacted a law forbidding Japanese immigrants to hold fishing licenses. On a larger scale, the state legislature allocated funds to enforce the long-dormant Alien Land Act, which barred property ownership by Japanese immigrants, as "aliens ineligible to citizenship," and unleashed a campaign to take away their property by means of "escheat" suits. (In an escheat proceeding, illegally acquired land is deemed vacant and reverts to state ownership.) California brought some fifty escheat suits against Japanese Americans within a two-year period, and dozens of families were stripped of their land or forced to pay settlements to quiet titles. Meanwhile, title insurance and mortgages became difficult to obtain. These suits continued until January 1948, when the U.S. Supreme Court struck down enforcement of the Alien Land Act in *Oyama v. California*, a JACL-sponsored test case. A year later, Oregon's Alien Land Law, newly strengthened in 1945, was in turn declared unconstitutional by the state supreme court in *Namba v. McCourt*.

Although much attention has been paid to the experience of Japanese Americans during World War II, the postwar years richly deserve further examination by historians. The resettlement era may lack the massive drama and pathos of the wartime confinement, yet as *Making Home from War* helps demonstrate, the resettlement period was just as important, if not more so, in shaping the lives of Japanese Americans, and their communities, social activities, and jobs. The pieces in this collection show that resettlement was by no means an entirely positive story; the damage of the war years was not so easily undone. The writers included here, who are mainly Nisei,

---

3   Audrie Girdner and Anne Loftis, *The Great Betrayal: The Evacuation of the Japanese Americans during World War II* (New York: Macmillan, 1969), 399 et seq.

experienced the difficult and largely unsuccessful struggle of their Issei fathers and mothers to pick up the pieces after their wartime trauma and to reestablish their prewar businesses and lives. Still, the personal stories in this anthology provide a window into the lives of the mass of Nisei who came of age in this postwar era, struggled successfully to acquire education, to find jobs and places to live, to open businesses, and to win recognition of their civil rights.

Greg Robinson is an associate professor of history and a research scholar at the Center for United States Studies at Université du Québec à Montréal. A longtime columnist for Nichi Bei Times/Nichi Bei Weekly, *he is the author of numerous scholarly articles on Japanese American history as well as the books* A Tragedy of Democracy: Japanese Confinement in North America *(Columbia University Press, 2009) and* By Order of the President: FDR and the Internment of Japanese Americans *(Harvard University Press, 2001). He is also the coeditor of* Mine Okubo: Following Her Own Road *(University of Washington Press, 2008) and editor of* Pacific Citizens, *an anthology of writings by Larry and Guyo Tajiri, due in 2011 from the University of Illinois Press. His study of postwar Japanese Americans, tentatively entitled* After Camp, *will be published by the University of California Press in 2012.*

PREFACE

I, the editor—in collaboration with members of the writing group and project administrator Jill Shiraki—have worked for three years to bring our project to fruition. The end product, *Making Home from War*, is meant to serve at once as a standalone book and a companion anthology to our first collection, *From Our Side of the Fence: Growing Up in America's Concentration Camps*. This new volume is accessible to all audiences, but it also offers several features that will be particularly useful for educators, students, and former camp prisoners. The structure and format of this book is modeled, to some extent, on our previous anthology, which includes an introductory section followed by a collection of stories and then a set of lesson plans, plus a bibliography and other background material. At the same time, there are notable differences.

First, the material in this book is by proportion more focused on the stories themselves, and some of them are quite long. This editorial choice was made for a variety of reasons: to honor the tremendous amount of quality writing that was produced; to acknowledge the depth, complexity, and continuous nature of the resettlement experience; and to supplement, but not repeat, materials from the first book.

Second, the amount and type of material each author wrote, and what we were able to include of that, varies. Although this was largely a choice made by the writers themselves, a number of interrelated factors also played a role, including the circumstance that all of the authors were in their seventies and eighties, and some of them were challenged or even restricted by health issues or other personal circumstances. To accommodate those working in multiple genres, we decided to be flexible and include other forms of artwork in addition to writing.

Third, we have included relevant visual aids to highlight the authors' experiences. Following the introduction, we have provided migration maps—skillfully designed by Ben Pease—that simultaneously track the journeys of all twelve authors before, during, and after the war. Individual maps then open each author section to immediately ground the reader and give a visual template that works in concert with the written pieces. Accompanying the lesson plans at the back of the book are further resources, including a migration chart pertaining to the authors in this collection and general information on the wartime imprisonment and postwar destinations of camp prisoners.

Fourth, new perspectives continue to emerge in our ongoing conversation about what language is most appropriate to describe the wartime imprisonment of Japanese Americans. Cognizant of this and, specifically, of what constitutes euphemistic language, we discussed the issue extensively in the "Note to the Reader" in *From Our Side of the Fence*. The stories in *Making Home from War* largely employ language similar to that of the first anthology, stringently avoiding the use of euphemisms to describe the concentration camp and postwar experience. An article titled "The Power of Words" by Mako Nakagawa in the August 20, 2009, edition of the *Nichi Bei Times* addresses two separate movements in the Japanese American Citizens League—at both national and regional levels—that aim to establish more specific criteria for what constitutes appropriate language in conjunction with America's concentration camps. This piece and the work of others, including researchers Aiko Herzig and James Hirabayashi, have made our writing group aware of and sensitive to this constantly shifting debate.

Therefore, we had difficulty reaching a consensus about certain terminology. Among the variety of opposing views, we acknowledge that the majority have valid rationale. Words like "internment" and "internee," for instance, are commonly understood in the Japanese American community and elsewhere to describe all Japanese Americans who were in camp; indeed, many of us utilized these words as such in our previous book, *From Our Side of the Fence*. After extensive deliberation and discussion, however, we chose terms in this new book that we believe are the most accurate from a legal and historical standpoint. For those confined in the War Relocation Authority concentration camps, we use the terms "incarceration," "imprisonment," and "confinement," and "prisoner" or "inmate." In describing those non-citizen Issei who were forcibly removed to Department of Justice (DOJ) internment camps, we use "detention" and "internment" along with "detainee" and "internee." As cited by Herzig, Hirabayashi, and other experts on the subject of Japanese American history, these are the proper terms to distinguish the DOJ group from others. For the sake of simplicity, however, we often use the terms "incarceration" and "imprisonment" as broader concepts that refer to all Japanese Americans—citizens and non-citizens alike—who were confined in any type of camp. While we reached our decision collaboratively to create consistency in the anthology, we recognize the need to continue the dialogue about appropriate terminology and the complex challenges of satisfying all perspectives. Ultimately, we hope the vital and ongoing debate about terminology doesn't divide the Japanese American community or deter us from the more important mission: to use language as a tool to empower Japanese Americans and to share our stories.

Fifth, we decided a historical overview was necessary to give proper background and context to our stories. We called upon Greg Robinson, a professor at the University of Quebec at Montreal and a respected historian on the Japanese American experience, who impressively stepped up to the task in writing a foreword for this book. While the majority of stories included here do focus on the postwar decade after incarceration, a period in which Robinson specializes, some begin earlier and some move into the later decades and up to the present. Moreover, in many of the stories, these writers use events from camp as reference points from which to compare and contrast their later situations. In reflecting upon and documenting resettlement, we have used the most liberal definition possible in order to acknowledge that this experience is a continuum. Indeed, the postwar experience cannot be extricated from the incarceration and vice versa.

Resettlement, in our view, continued into the 1960s, 1970s, and beyond, as former prisoners continued to come to terms with the magnitude of the injustice they had suffered. Part of resettlement, we would argue, were the landmark court cases of Gordon Hirabayashi, Fred Korematsu, and Minoru Yasui, along with the redress finally given to former prisoners in the 1980s— all of these events among the earliest examples of the U.S. government acknowledging and being held accountable for the wrongs it did to the Japanese American community. Only then did some former camp prisoners begin to feel a sense of closure and healing.

Finally, this book explores the ways in which resettlement is a process that continues even today. For the writers presented here, resettlement is many things: the shame of imprisonment, the silence held over the years, and, redemptively, the empowerment gained in the telling of their stories. For readers—both those inside and outside the Japanese American community— this collection emphasizes the importance of documenting our stories and connecting human faces to historical events, and it also demonstrates the capacity of art to both move and inform.

ACKNOWLEDGMENTS

Throughout this venture, I, along with our project team, have been sustained by the goodwill, commitment, and talent of many individuals, families, and organizations. This book project—ambitious in scope and collaborative in nature—could not have been realized without the constant personal, creative, editorial, and communal interchanges that happened between our dozens of participants.

First and foremost, we acknowledge the brave and committed writers included in this anthology: Florence Ohmura Dobashi, Kiku Hori Funabiki, Sato Hashizume, Fumi Manabe Hayashi, Naoko Yoshimura Ito, Florence Miho Nakamura (in memoriam), Ruth Y. Okimoto, Yoshito Wayne Osaki, Toru Saito, Daisy Uyeda Satoda, Harumi Serata, and Michi Tashiro. Throughout this massive undertaking, they never took their eyes off of the ultimate goal: to have their voices heard and their truths acknowledged through the stories they reveal in this book.

Our gratitude goes to special family members Sally Noda Osaki and Kristen Langewisch Marchetti, who, thrust into roles as coauthors, shone in their dedication and ability. The writers and I are also indebted to Jill Shiraki, our project manager, who has been helpful on numerous levels. Her genuine involvement during all phases and her steadfast, caring presence kept us nurtured and confident throughout the process.

In turn, we—I, the writers, and Jill—owe the California Civil Liberties Public Education Program (CCLPEP), State Librarian Susan Hildreth, and the CCLPEP Advisory Board a tremendous debt of gratitude for their generous grant, which funded this project. Former and current CCLPEP officers and staff Amy Sullivan, Christopher Berger, Linda Springer, and Colette Moody demonstrated unwavering support, flexibility, and integrity in their handling of the grant project that resulted in this book. We extend our appreciation to Diane Matsuda for her ongoing support. Thanks to the University of San Francisco (USF) Faculty Development fund for their additional assistance.

The producer of this book, the Japanese Cultural and Community Center of Northern California (JCCCNC), and Executive Director Paul Osaki, deserve significant credit for serving as our project sponsor and providing invaluable backing. We are grateful to Paul—along with JCCCNC staff members Marjorie Fletcher, Jennifer Hamamoto, Ruby Hata, Ken Maeshiro, and Lori Matoba—for offering a safe space for us to hold our classes and bring our stories to life.

Likewise, we thank the warm and vibrant staff at Heyday Books: Malcolm Margolin for his clear-headed direction, integrity, and belief in our project; Gayle Wattawa for her generous spirit, keen editorial skills, and lucid answers; she and Katherine J. B. Brumage for inviting us into their space; Lorraine Rath for the skillful layout of the book's text, images, and cover design; Lisa K. Manwill for wonderful and expert copyediting; Lillian Fleer, Natalie Mulford, Susan Pi, and Julian Segal for their energy and creativity in helping our book to reach a wider audience; Diane Lee for facilitating production direction; and David Isaacson for his capable administration. We also salute Patricia Wakida for opening eyes and paving the way.

Several individuals were instrumental to the realization of certain pieces in this collection. Shizue Seigel was the instructor of the Senior Women's Asian American Writing Workshop group at the JCCCNC, where some of the stories were first produced. Shizue provided valuable editorial feedback to three of the writers in her class who now appear in this book—Sato, Daisy, and Harumi. Cartographer Ben Pease showed skill and care in his design of our book's migration maps. Grateful mentions also go to: Greg Robinson, for his sharp, humane insight on all matters and for his generous help with the bibliography; he and Aiko Herzig for their consultation and written materials on terminology; the National Japanese American Historical Society—Rosalyn Tonai, Executive Director, and Ellen Sawamura, Executive Vice President of the Board of Directors—for recognizing our first anthology with a Nisei Voices Award, and for documenting the writers on videotape for posterity; the family of Florence Nakamura—in particular, granddaughter Kristen and son Scott—for their assistance with Flo's section; Gary Mukai of SPICE and Art Hansen, the founding director of the Japanese American Oral History Project at California State University, Fullerton, for their willing assistance; and Karl Matsushita of the Japanese American National Library for his help with the verification of resources.

We are grateful to the USF Asian American Studies Program and DeAnza College for their additional support in the form of campus events that showcased our work. Further appreciation is extended to USF's Department of Rhetoric and Language, the Martin-Baró Scholars Program, the Department of Communication Studies, the Department of English, the Asian Pacific American Student Coalition, the Dean's Office, and various other programs and departments for their cosponsorship and involvement.

Certain individuals and family members sustained me personally throughout this project. Anastasia Royal, a brilliant editor, close friend, and collaborator in art, gave me valuable feedback on numerous drafts of my introduction and other sections. Members of my Seventeen Syllables crew—Sabina Chen, Edmond Chow, Jay Dayrit, Roy Kamada, Caroline Kim, Lillian Howan, Grace Loh Prasad, and Marianne Villanueva—offered me ongoing creative sustenance and camaraderie. For the introduction, Jay, Caroline, Grace, and Marianne provided me with astute comments. Garrett Hongo, mentor and friend, deserves special recognition for his belief in my work and for his caring guidance. Dard Neuman, Eric Nikaido, James Tjoa, and Marc Wallis offered friendship and community along the way.

I give special thanks to my family members: to my wife Grace, whose love and care saw me through the many stages and hours of this endeavor; to Brendan, my brave little warrior son, whose fighting spirit teaches me the real meaning of courage and determination; to my parents, Stuart and Renko, and my brother, Loren, whose love and support are unconditionally present; to my Aunt Tae, whose mothering kindness keeps me grounded and who has shed light upon our family history included herein; and to the rest of the Ishida family and the Nichiren Buddhist Church of America, our family church, a place of creative, spiritual, and communal sanctuary.

—*Brian Komei Dempster*

INTRODUCTION

On a sunless day in the spring of 1947, my grandfather and his two eldest children stand in front of their former home. They take stock of the damage. Paint peels off the walls of the Victorian building; a front window is broken. The "Nichiren Buddhist Church of America" sign, once nailed down at the corners, no longer hangs beneath the balcony roof.

Only hours before, Grandfather, fearing the worst, had convinced his wife and their other five children to stay behind in the Richmond housing project where they had spent the last year. "Wait here. Don't worry. We'll call for you soon. I promise." He, with a son and daughter, had crossed the Bay Bridge and were now in San Francisco's Japantown. Once imprisoned by their own country, they are the first of the Ishida family to return home after six years.

They step forward and climb the concrete stairs to the walkway smeared with cherry blossoms and the dust of shriveled petals. Moving past the garden of overgrown bougainvillea, they haul their luggage up the wooden steps to the front door of their church home. There is no welcome but the squawking of crows and the glaring evidence of the work ahead. How long would it take them to fix up the church and make it livable? When would the rest of the scattered family find their way back and begin again?

This group of three—my weary ancestors—stand on the threshold of reentry, one part of the long and poignant story of resettlement that I have pieced together from family conversations.

Starting from scratch. Creating something from wreckage. Making home from war. The title of this book draws inspiration from the linked ideas of recollection and reinvention that form the connecting threads of the stories that follow. I am honored to edit this anthology, particularly in view of the personal stake I have in this period of history and the courage and commitment of all of those involved in this shared project. These twelve authors—just children, adolescents, and young adults when the war ended in 1945—were released from desolate desert camps in Utah, Arizona, Wyoming, Idaho, Colorado, and California, then taken by train to various locations and left to fend for themselves. The American government provided them with only meager stipends and War Relocation Authority directives that told them, "Assimilate. Blend in. Don't make waves."

Facing the unknown and a changed world, the authors, their families, and tens of thousands of other Japanese Americans—including my grandfather and his wife and children—arrived in places where they faced unwelcome attitudes and prejudice from current inhabitants, some of whom were brainwashed, or at least influenced, by the wartime propaganda machine. Such xenophobia made no distinctions between Imperial Japanese and Japanese who were born and living in America. It wrongly characterized Japanese Americans as traitors to their own country when, in fact, they were the ones who were betrayed. It also grossly discounted those Japanese Americans who had served in the military for the United States of America, and even died under its flag.

Cast out. Itinerant. Dispersed. Some of the authors included in this collection—Florence Ohmura Dobashi, Kiku Hori Funabiki, Fumi Manabe Hayashi, Sato Hashizume, and Harumi Serata—were forced to wait before they returned to the West Coast and their home states of California, Oregon, and Washington, in effect experiencing a second displacement in communities as far away as Eden, Idaho; Salt Lake City, Utah; Brecksville, Ohio; St. Louis, Missouri; and Manhattan, New York. Of those allowed to return directly to California—including Toru Saito and Michi Tashiro—many had lost their original homes and were left with no choice but to bide their time in makeshift lodgings, such as housing projects in the San Francisco Bay Area city of Richmond and tent camps in Cortez, a rural community in the San Joaquin Valley. While incarceration had uprooted them from their former homes and communities, their release and return from camp was, ironically, equally—if not more—difficult, requiring massive adjustment and the ability to cope with extreme transitions. There were homes to be found, jobs to be secured, lives to be rebuilt. Survival was a must, luxury an afterthought.

Forced into lives of hardship and menial labor in order to help support their families, the Japanese Americans persevered. They found the resilience they needed in the form of community, by gathering reserves of strength from family and friends, and by experiencing firsthand the depths of human resolve and faith. Certain key places throughout the West Coast—among them my grandfather's church, Daisy Uyeda Satoda's home at 410 Austin Alley, and the King Café her mother ran in San Francisco's Japantown—gave sanctuary to the dispossessed and isolated, acting as havens for the dispersed former prisoners to gather, build, and renew. Scenes of communal ritual appear throughout these stories, many of them centered on the sharing of food, conversation, and acts of loving kindness and restoration. Likewise, our church was healed by my own family and the members of its congregation working alongside one another.

Some released prisoners eventually turned to creative expression in art. In addition to writing, Naoko Yoshimura Ito and Ruth Y. Okimoto have used visual modes of discourse to document the injustices of incarceration. Samples of their quilts and paintings, respectively, are included in this book as well.

Others, however, were less able to cope with their experiences. Some forever struggled to start over, to reconnect with lost contacts, to trust in their neighbors, their communities, their country. The journey was made even more turbulent by the lack of support services for former prisoners. As one of the writers, Toru Saito, stated in a 2007 speech on behalf of our project: "In any current community crisis, we send out the therapists and mental health workers to help those in need. Back in 1945, we had no such intervention, and the results are kept in confidential files not open for public view."

This book is dedicated to those, like my uncles and countless others, who passed away rarely or never speaking about their experiences. It bears witness to those who weren't able to readjust or forget; indeed, certain characters and scenes remind us that the consequences of imprisonment can be devastating, sometimes leading to mental illness and even suicide. This volume can also shed light for those too young to remember—like my mother, who was only one year old at the time of the bombing of Pearl Harbor—who nevertheless bear the scars of this experience.

Facing pain. Seeking forgiveness. Making peace. Our first collection, *From Our Side of the Fence: Growing Up in America's Concentration Camps*, was the initial step toward spiritual closure and psychic resolution. In that anthology, published in 2001, we documented the incarceration experience and, to some extent, its consequences. The authors experienced empowerment, relief, and even catharsis from unearthing their memories, and their children and grandchildren expressed gratitude for finally knowing what had really happened during this time. Audiences in turn received a more complete picture of American history and were moved by the honesty and passion of the stories and the courage of the writers to voice their recollections. In 2007, the National Japanese American Historical Society bestowed the honor of a Nisei Voices Award upon our book, underscoring the value of storytelling as a mode of preserving history.

Yet these writers had so much more to say, so many more experiences that were not included the first time around. The journey was unfinished. We felt encouraged and eager to continue, and now we bring a second volume that begins where the first left off—at the end of imprisonment.

If the drama of the incarceration was an earthquake—concentrated and overt, marked by the bombing of Pearl Harbor and characterized by the camps strung with barbed wire and towers full of armed guards—then the drama of resettlement was the aftershock—drawn out and insidious, signified by abandoned barracks and irretrievable homes, blisters and sore muscles from picking fruit and washing dishes, insults and stares from suspicious bosses and neighbors, and the grating claustrophobia of being packed together in ramshackle living conditions.

For in any trauma, there is the aftermath, and some former prisoners were living in a permanent state of aftermath. Through reflection upon and understanding of later events—in this case the scar of resettlement—we can better come to terms with the violence of the original blow and its dark consequences. To finish the cycle of healing the wounds through words, we felt compelled to tell the sometimes neglected and often hushed story of what happened *after* the war.

Resettlement. Certainly writers, editors, filmmakers, and scholars have started to mine this rich area. Philip Kan Gotanda's play *After the War* looks at interracial dynamics in this era; John Okada's novel *No-No Boy* examines the postwar divisions between those Japanese Americans who served in the military and those who refused to do so in defiance of the Loyalty Questionnaire. Jeanne Wakatsuki Houston and James D. Houston, Hiroshi Kashiwagi, Toshio Mori, Mitsuye Yamada, Hisaye Yamamoto, and Wakako Yamauchi are among the writers and poets whose creative work addresses this experience. The dynamic editorial work of those like Garrett Hongo, Lillian Howan, and Patricia Wakida has been instrumental in bringing authors such as Yamauchi and Mori their due recognition. Dianne Fukami's *Starting Over*, Janice D. Tanaka's *When You're Smiling*, and other such documentaries, films, and programs capture the challenges that Japanese Americans faced after camp. Greg Robinson and others have done valuable scholarship on this period (roughly focused on the decade from 1945 to 1955), including his historical overview that opens this book.

Our collection, *Making Home from War: Stories of Japanese American Exile and Resettlement*, builds upon this growing body of work about World War II and the postwar era. To our knowledge, it is the first book to relate stories of resettlement from both a personal and collective viewpoint. Through the process of hearing these stories and realizing this book, I have shifted my own idea of what resettlement is—I used to think it was a fixed point in time (1945–1955), but now I believe it is an ongoing process that continues even today—and the stories and accompanying photos presented here help define resettlement not in terms of "when" but of "who." Here, resettlement is the displaced self forging a new path from the ashes of war, adapting to unfamiliar and uncomfortable places, living a migrant existence in transitional spaces, and inventing community from broken ties.

These brilliant writers bring us scenes of forced removal and, later, the shock of reentry. They describe the indescribable: the bodies of their neighbors drowned in floods and damaged by back-alley abortions, the wrecking ball destroying neighborhoods, flattening Japantowns. They dissect racism: the scrutiny of their Asian American faces. They touch on the rudeness of in-your-face slurs and taunts alongside the brave advocacy by attorneys and priests to reinstate rights that had been stripped away. Here we see a grandmother breathing her last breath right after the Redress Act is signed by President Reagan in 1988, there we see a Sansei child—me—being born in a more just and tolerant—though still imperfect—United States. Our words in *Making Home from War* ride the wave of the future, in sync with President Obama's message of hope and transformation. Yes, we can change anger into forgiveness, pain into strength, silence into story.

This time around, almost a decade later, the challenge was greater, the task even more urgent. With the writers now all in their seventies and eighties, we adapted our methods to their physical limitations, and a spirit of loving collaboration and integrity informed every phase of this project. Sally Noda Osaki served as coauthor to her husband, Yoshito Wayne Osaki, asking him pointed questions, filling in the blanks, and helping to shape his own voice and story. Their son, Paul Osaki, the executive director of the Japanese Cultural and Community Center of Northern California, graciously provided space for our writing classes and also sponsored our project. The family of Florence Miho Nakamura, who sadly passed away during our project, shared her writings, along with their own, so we could again bring her stories to life. For over two years, our writing group met and engaged in fruitful dialogue, and the writers invited me into their homes for conferences during which we undertook the daunting and rewarding task of revising their drafts into finished pieces.

It was crucial that I—a Sansei mixed-race poet and university professor trained in writing and literature, and someone who had not lived through the camp and resettlement experience myself—maintain a delicate balance as editor. I needed to be gentle, supportive, and respectful as I tried to elicit stories from a generation who had come before me, most of them Nisei. Yet I had to be tough, honest, and constructive in my criticism in order to make the best book possible. Another challenge I sometimes faced with the writers was the unreliability of their memories and their struggles to recall exact details, people, dates, and times. I encouraged them to recreate their own experiences in the most truthful way possible and yet not be completely bound by facts or the absence thereof; although these stories primarily draw from the realm of autobiography, they use creative license when needed. A few of the writers draw from outside sources in their pieces so that they can provide relevant context and crucial information. As laborious and long as the process was, I am honored to have worked with these courageous writers and to have seen, with them and through them, the completion of this book.

The finished product in your hands, *Making Home from War*, is one of dynamic intergenerational exchange, the synthesis of creative and editorial energies, raw emotions and experiences crafted into scenes. On one hand, it is a mythic parable defined by a universal trope, speaking in honor of any culture that is oppressed and colonized, changed by war, and forced to remake itself from destruction: the Filipino people who were "freed" by General McArthur after the conquest of the Japanese, the Vietnamese who immigrated to America after the fall of Saigon, the Iraqis who attempt to navigate the complex nature of American military occupation and its slow withdrawal. On the other hand, it is a specific odyssey of Japanese American resettlement. Collectively, its authors explore—on geographical, psychological, and metaphysical levels—how resettlement displaced their families, fractured their concepts of home, and reshaped their identities. This book's chapters—each organized chronologically—allow us to intimately re-live the authors' journeys in the order they occurred. Its anthology format creates a holistic picture in which we see not only the distinct details of each experience but also how each individual story overlaps and intertwines with others. The lesson plans at the end of the book act as both an invitation and a template for other former prisoners to write their own resettlement stories.

I sit down in my family's Buddhist church, our home for generations. In the first row, in front of the altar, I face the table, the black marble pot of ash anchoring the tablecloth of red silk, the fabric embroidered with gold flowers. Behind this, I see the red wooden chair where my grandfather once sat, chanting from the gold-leafed sutra book now frayed at the edges. This history-filled place still remains, and the spirits and stories animate it even now.

Making Home from War reaches far into the past, melding together what was once forgotten—or silenced—and what was deeply embedded into the fabric of new, brave lives.

Listen, the voices tell us: Once we were torn away. Through the years of war, we built homes out of imagination. When we returned, we began again. We remade ourselves. We gathered and shared. Now, in words, we have found our way back.

—*Brian Komei Dempster*

A. Pre-WWII Residences

Fife, WA
Harumi Serata

Portland, OR
Sato Hashizume

Berkeley, CA
Fumi Hayashi

Clarksburg, CA
Wayne Osaki

Oakland, CA
Daisy Satoda

Turlock, CA
Michi Tashiro

San Francisco, CA
Kiku Funabiki
Naoko Ito
Florence Nakamura
Toru Saito

Riverside, CA
Florence Dobashi

San Diego, CA
Ruth Okimoto

0   100   200 Miles
0   100 200 Km

B. Temporary Detention Centers

Puyallup, WA
Harumi Serata

Portland, OR
Sato Hashizume

Tanforan, CA
Fumi Hayashi
Florence Nakamura
Toru Saito
Daisy Satoda

Merced, CA
Michi Tashiro

Santa Anita, CA
Ruth Okimoto

Pomona, CA
Kiku Funabiki
Naoko Ito

0   100   200 Miles
0   100 200 Km

Florence Dobashi and Wayne Osaki
went directly to incarceration sites.

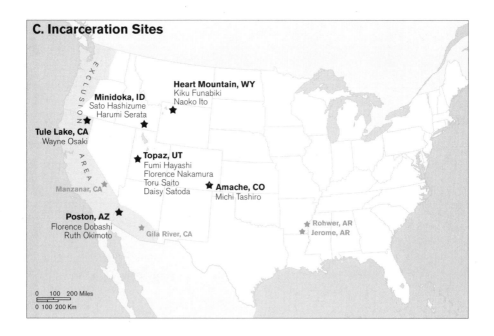

C. Incarceration Sites

Heart Mountain, WY
Kiku Funabiki
Naoko Ito

Minidoka, ID
Sato Hashizume
Harumi Serata

Tule Lake, CA
Wayne Osaki

Topaz, UT
Fumi Hayashi
Florence Nakamura
Toru Saito
Daisy Satoda

Amache, CO
Michi Tashiro

Manzanar, CA

Poston, AZ
Florence Dobashi
Ruth Okimoto

Gila River, CA

Rohwer, AR

Jerome, AR

0   100   200 Miles
0   100 200 Km

D. Transitional Housing

Portland, OR
Sato Hashizume

San Francisco, CA
Kiku Funabiki
Naoko Ito
Florence Nakamura
Wayne Osaki
Toru Saito
Daisy Satoda

Eden, ID
Harumi Serata

Cortez, CA
Michi Tashiro

Salt Lake City, UT
Sato Hashizume

Brecksville, OH
Florence Dobashi

Manhattan, NY
Kiku Funabiki

Richmond, CA
Toru Saito

**St. Louis, MO/
Kirkwood, MO**
Fumi Hayashi

San Diego, CA
Ruth Okimoto

0   100   200 Miles
0 100 200 Km

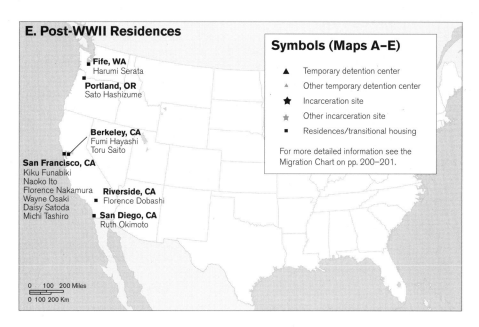

E. Post-WWII Residences

Fife, WA
Harumi Serata

Portland, OR
Sato Hashizume

Berkeley, CA
Fumi Hayashi
Toru Saito

San Francisco, CA
Kiku Funabiki
Naoko Ito
Florence Nakamura
Wayne Osaki
Daisy Satoda
Michi Tashiro

Riverside, CA
Florence Dobashi

San Diego, CA
Ruth Okimoto

Symbols (Maps A–E)

▲   Temporary detention center

▲   Other temporary detention center

★   Incarceration site

★   Other incarceration site

■   Residences/transitional housing

For more detailed information see the
Migration Chart on pp. 200–201.

0   100   200 Miles
0 100 200 Km

Florence enjoys a Sunday picnic after church. Cleveland, Ohio, mid-1945.

FLORENCE OHMURA DOBASHI

Florence Ohmura Dobashi, born and raised in Southern California, was imprisoned in 1942 at the Colorado River Relocation Center in Unit I (Poston I) near Parker, Arizona, at the age of fourteen. From there, she was allowed to relocate in August 1944 to Brecksville, Ohio, for her senior year of high school. In late September 1945 she rejoined her family in Riverside, California, for one week and then hurried on to attend the University of California, Berkeley, as a public health major. Four years later, she graduated from the University of California, Los Angeles, with a Bachelor of Arts degree from the Department of Political Science, having majored in international relations with an emphasis on the Far East.

Fresh out of school, Florence thought that social and political conditions throughout the world were deplorable, and she wanted to help improve them. Admiring the American Civil Liberties Union (ACLU) of Northern California for its courageous stand against the arbitrary mass removal and incarceration of Japanese Americans during World War II, she applied for an opening in its office and went to work there. At that time, she and Ernest Besig, the director, comprised the Northern California branch's entire staff.

After six years of assisting in legal cases and participating in the organization's growth, Florence obtained a part-time position with the ACLU's General Counsel, Wayne M. Collins, with whom she worked for another two years. During this period (the 1950s), she was active in and served on the boards of the Young Democrats Club of San Francisco, the Japanese American Citizens League, the Buchanan Street YMCA, and various local Nikkei political groups.

Later, she was employed for twenty years at the School of Medicine at the University of California, San Francisco, where her background in public health, political affairs, and business was useful in her job as an administrative analyst. Now retired, she volunteers for a few service-oriented organizations within the Japanese American community and participates in creative writing workshops that have encouraged her to articulate her experiences and to learn about those of other individuals.

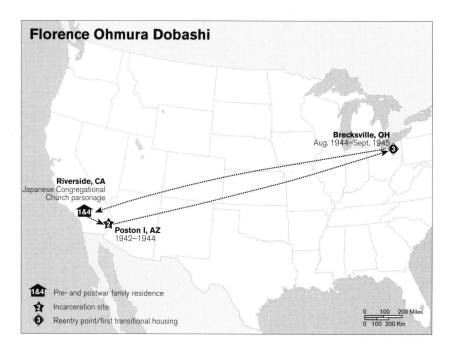

OUTSIDE THE FENCE

The hot sun beat down on the dry desert earth, and dust swirled around me and my friends as we milled about, preparing to board army trucks that would take us to the train depot miles away. We had come from our barracks to this staging area near the camp gates. Once we boarded the truck and it started moving, the breeze helped to cool me, only sixteen years old, seated in the uncovered vehicle with other students. I braced myself on the bumpy truck as Poston vanished from view. Only years later would I laugh at the irony of the official name—the Colorado River Relocation Center—a euphemism for the concentration camp that housed us Japanese Americans in the bleak Arizona desert during World War II. But then, on that scorching day in August 1944, I thought what any teenage girl might: *Egads, I took so much time combing my hair just right, and now it's a mess! Oh well, the other girls on the truck are in the same boat.*

When we boarded the train, the still air inside grew stuffy. The windows were locked, and an armed, scowling soldier stood guard at the front of the car. He commanded loudly and gruffly in a deep voice, "Do not, I repeat, do not try to open the windows."

I whispered to Rita, my traveling companion, "I don't dare ask why. The guard looks so scary."

"Oh well," said Rita. "We should be used to the heat after roasting in Poston."

Even worse, during the seemingly interminable journey across the continent—from western Arizona to eastern Illinois—I felt frustrated by the blackened windows, a barrier between me and the awe-inspiring scenery that my fellow students and I had sung about countless times throughout our school years: "O beautiful for spacious skies, for amber waves of grain, for purple mountains' majesty, above the fruited plain. America! America!"

I'm so glad Rita is with me. I glanced at my two hometown schoolmates sitting across from me, the handsome and highly intelligent brothers Edwin and William. *Thank God, they're here, too.* Edwin, about five feet, six inches tall, was a year ahead of me and had been vice president of the senior class. Although William was a year younger than me, he was in the same grade and was my height at about four feet, ten inches. Both brothers were fair-complexioned with prominent, strong, square jaws and thick shocks of black hair.

Commenting on the shutters blocking our view, Edwin ventured, "It's to protect us from bigots who might see our Japanese faces."

William pulled at the shades, retorting, "It's to conceal our release from camp. And we know our destination, so what's the point of preventing us from seeing where the train goes? Just more despicable malice toward us so-called Japs."

"Well, whatever the reason," I replied, "the armed guard and the blackened windows make me feel confined—like a prisoner. I wonder if this is how convicts are escorted to penitentiaries."

I scanned the railway car filled with fellow students and others, all going east. Rita added, "I'm glad we were labeled 'loyal' and allowed to leave the camp."

Somebody else remarked, "But it's too bad we can't return to the hometowns in California that we were evicted from."

Rita and I looked at each other as another guy said bitterly, "Who wants to go back to where we're not wanted?"

Despite all the fear and mixed emotions of friends and strangers, I was delighted at the prospect of going east across the continent: *I am so excited I get to see more of the huge United States than just Southern California.* I envisioned my home, then a quiet, small town named Riverside, fifty miles east of Los Angeles. For a moment, I yearned for Riverside, its extensive green groves of luscious oranges and grapefruit, and then I smiled at the irony of my situation. When we moved inland to Riverside from the coastal town of Chula Vista, I used to complain that it was too hot during the summers; now, compared to Poston, it was cool.

My thoughts wandered on. *Someday, when the war is over, my family will return to Riverside and pick up where we left off. And so will I.*

Like everybody else, I felt elated about leaving camp behind. I was amused at how we joked and laughed about it, using sarcasm to ease our pain. "Thank God, we're out of that godforsaken desert." But then I heard someone else, without irony, express our real bitterness: "It was a goddamned prison camp."

"Yeah, he's right," I said quietly to myself.

When the popular brothers from my hometown casually said, "So long. Good luck," and then left the train at Grand Junction, Colorado, I thought, *Uh oh. There goes my last connection with home. That sure was an abrupt goodbye, considering we might never see each other again.* Although William and I had attended the same school and the same church in Riverside and had also gone to the only high school in the Poston concentration camp, we had rarely spoken to each other until then. Still, it felt like a loss, because in Riverside, William and I had been the only Japanese Americans in our class. I had been annoyed by my classmates' occasional attempts to fix me up with him, urging, "You should become a couple and go to parties together." Besides, I had a secret crush on Jerry, a blond classmate.

How could I know then, as the train doors closed and we pulled away, that I would see both William and Edwin fifty years later? That, at a Poston Class of 1945 reunion, William, who had grown about a foot taller, would seek me out to chat about old times in Riverside? At an even later reunion, I finally told him, "You know, I used to kind of avoid you in Riverside— because people were always trying to push us together. Sorry about that."

"Yeah, they kept telling me to ask you out and to school parties," he responded.

I laughed, "It certainly took me a long time to explain why I was snubbing you. I guess exceedingly slow motion is better than none."

But back there on the train in 1944, I wasn't thinking about that. Only where I was going and who I was going with. I reflected, *I'm so shy and reserved I feel lucky to be traveling with Rita. She makes friends easily with her relaxed and warm, chatty manner.*

COLORADO RIVER WAR RELOCATION PROJECT
Employment Division

PROJECT AUTHORIZATION NO. 9

SCHOOL PRINCIPAL - UNIT 1   Date 8/16/44   194___

This is official notification to prepare for the departure of children of

OHMURA, FLORENCE HISAKO _____ Project Address   4-7-C
(Name)

Forwarding Address c/o Baptist Hostel, 2429 Prospect Ave, Cleveland, Ohio
R.F.D. or Street No.   Town   State

Who will depart Aug. 22 P.M. 194 4   on Indef.   Leave No. ____
(Date)   (Type)

Accompanying Family Members   Signature
Name   Age   Unit ___ Leave Manager

Routing: Unit Leave office transmits
this form directly to
appropriate unit school
principal

(2515)

A Permit to Leave provides clearance for Florence to attend school in Brecksville, Ohio.
August 1944.

Before we realized how much time had elapsed, the train had wended its
way from western Arizona to Chicago, where Rita and I transferred to another
train destined for Cleveland, Ohio. Finally, without blackened windows or
an armed soldier watching us, we looked out at the blue sky, white clouds,
and gray factory buildings outside of Chicago, then farmland and lush green
forests, and I momentarily felt overjoyed. *I'm finally free!*

Well, sort of free, I thought. I turned to Rita and said, "We still have to check in
with the War Relocation Authority in Cleveland as soon as we get off the train."

"That's so they can help us get resettled," Rita answered. "Let's go and get
it over with."

As the train slowly glided to a stop, I looked forward to seeing where I
would spend my senior year in high school. Rita and I grabbed our luggage
and stepped off the train into a new world. I wondered if Rita felt what I
did—if she, too, dreamed of a real school, in a real stucco or brick-and-
mortar building unlike the makeshift school in Poston's black tarpapered
barracks. During our first year of confinement, we had to tramp all over
camp to attend various classes in barracks designated as "Recreation Halls"
for different blocks. My friends and I had also participated in church services

and Sunday School lessons there and, despite the other inconveniences, I was pleased that all of the Protestant Christian denominations had united to form one church. Later, our school would be housed in adobe structures built by adult "evacuees," as the government called us inmates to enhance its public image—*as if we had been removed from our homes for humanitarian reasons,* I would think years later.

Not until 1999, when I read Jeffery F. Burton's *Confinement and Ethnicity,* did I realize that Poston's proximity to the Colorado River, only about two and a half miles west, is what caused the location to be humid—very humid. People who had never lived in the Arizona desert asked, "But wasn't it dry heat?" to which I replied, "Dry or not, 100 degrees is 100 degrees. It is HOT!" Outside the fence, here in Cleveland, we would get a reprieve from the sometimes 120-degree summer heat. For the first time in two years, we would see green lawns, unlike the parched, barren soil we had endured at camp. No longer would we have to walk through blinding, choking dust storms to the classrooms housed inside flimsy barracks; no longer would we have to sit in desks where we sweated while trying to concentrate on politics, world problems, the history that was being made.

REORIENTATION

As we got off the train at Cleveland, Rita and I stood, bewildered. Hordes of people walked down the long covered walkway beside the equally long train, toward the station's waiting room. "Everyone seems to know where they're going; do you know where *we're* going?" I questioned.

"I sure hope somebody from the WRA is at the gate to meet us," Rita said.

"Yeah," I replied. "Otherwise, we're in trouble."

To our relief, inside the station we found a tall, slender middle-aged woman with wavy light brown hair holding aloft a large placard bearing the initials "WRA." As we approached, she smiled and asked, "Are you from Poston? I'm Mrs. Dooley of the War Relocation Authority."

"I'm Rita, and this is Florence," my friend said.

"I'm glad each of you is carrying a suitcase," Mrs. Dooley remarked. "That way you'll have a change of clothing. You'll stay overnight at the WRA hostel, and your employers will pick you up tomorrow. It will take a while for the baggage cars to be unloaded, so we'll come back later to get the rest of your things. Assuming you have other things."

Oh my gosh, I thought. *Does Mrs. Dooley think the government stripped us of all our belongings except for these meager suitcases?* "Oh, yes. We do," I quickly replied.

Once we were in the WRA car, Rita and I tentatively leaned back into the plush seats and looked out the windows. It felt strange getting into an automobile again. As Mrs. Dooley drove us through Cleveland, I glanced at Rita, who had grown up in a small farming community and was agog at the sights and sounds of the city. I, having lived in Los Angeles, was at ease with the hustle and bustle of countless cars and the crowds. As men in suits and women in hats and dresses scurried about on sidewalks among big buildings, I thought, *Boy, am I glad to be back in civilization! Guess what? We're no longer concentration camp prisoners!*

At the same time, I wondered if Rita was just as apprehensive as I was about other things. *What will we face in this new place? Will others treat us well? Will they be hostile?* After all, our parents' native country was now an enemy of the United States.

Mrs. Dooley drove us until we reached our first stop: the WRA office. She disappeared once we entered the well-lit room to undergo orientation and training for reentry into our lives as ordinary citizens. Here, the counselor advised all of us, "Keep a low profile. Obey all rules, regulations, and laws. Do not congregate in groups of more than two other Japanese Americans in public. Be quiet and well-behaved. In other words," the counselor said, "you must be inconspicuous and exemplary citizens!"

That's what Mom and Pop always told us—to be good citizens. So that part shouldn't be hard. But Mom and Pop didn't say a thing about not congregating in groups of Japanese Americans. That may be difficult for those in Cleveland, where many of us live. I'm glad that in Brecksville, where Rita and I are headed, we'll be the only Japanese Americans. So it shouldn't be a problem for us.

As the counselor continued her endless list of dos and don'ts, I fidgeted in my chair, bored, staring at the slow hands of the clock. These warnings were like a broken record, repeating the advice given to us by the school counselors before we had left Poston. They had also told us that we would work as "schoolgirls" in separate homes, twenty hours per week, doing housework and perhaps taking care of children in exchange for room, board, and ten dollars per month. With her voice droning on and on, I tuned her out, anxious thoughts slowly overtaking my mind: *Ten dollars every month is a lot of money. That's more than I've had at one time during all of my life! But winter is only a few months from now. By then I hope I have saved enough to buy a heavy coat to wear when it snows. I'll need snow boots, too. We're no longer in the Southwest desert. I wonder how much money I'll need for winter clothes. Oh well, so what else is new? At home we've always had to scrimp and save.*

When the counselor finished, Rita nudged me and I snapped back to attention. We quickly rose from our seats and joined Mrs. Dooley, who was waiting for us near the entrance. At a brisk pace, she walked ahead of us as we trailed behind; as soon as we closed the doors to the car, she started the engine and pulled away from the curb. In the backseat, Rita and I fell silent. *Where are we going? Who will we live with? What will they be like?* The counselor's words echoed in my head: "Your hosts will be kind and good people." I sure hoped she was right.

DETOUR

The new baby was overdue. In mid-September 1945 Mr. Klein told me one day, "The baby should have been born by now, but for some reason it doesn't want to come out."

I was excited for them and wanted to support them. I had grown fond of Mr. and Mrs. Klein and their three children, who had been my host family since I'd arrived in Brecksville. Mrs. Dooley had dropped Rita and me off at the hostel, and shortly afterward, the Kleins had picked me up and driven me to their house. There, I helped with dishes, did laundry, made beds, and performed other ordinary chores, as my mother had me do at home before the war. The Kleins not only gave me a room and a bed to sleep in as well as food to eat, but they took me to Cleveland and bought me a heavy woolen coat along with snow boots. They also had taken me to their jeweler to select a gold watch, which I paid for with money my father had sent. He had mailed me one of his stipend checks from the Congregational Church headquarters so I could buy myself the watch as a graduation gift from him and my mother.

So while I had enjoyed my time with the Kleins, I was also anxious to leave and move on with my life. Although I wanted to help them, I dreamed of starting college, where I would expand my horizons. *I certainly wish the baby would hurry up. School starts at the University of California in October, and I want to spend a few days in Detroit visiting my mother's sisters, whom I've never met before. And I want to stop in Chicago for a couple days to visit friends from the Poston concentration camp who have settled there. I probably won't be able to visit the Midwest again once I get home to Riverside.*

"Can you stay until the baby is born?" Mr. Klein asked as my first day of college neared. "Could you please watch the kids for a week while my wife recovers in the hospital?"

I pondered my dilemma. I felt obligated to Mr. Klein who, at six feet tall and husky, was a softy who ran a newspaper agency in Cleveland. He worked a lot and drove twenty miles north to Cleveland each day from his house in Brecksville, so most of my dealings were with his wife. Mrs. Klein was also tall, about five foot ten and heavyset. Because of her generous size, I had not even realized she was pregnant at first.

Yet I was irritated at having to curtail or possibly even cancel my planned stopovers before I reached Berkeley. I had packed my suitcase and trunk—a wooden box made in Poston—so I could leave on short notice. Mr. Klein had thoughtfully offered to ship the trunk to my parents in Riverside, so most of my belongings were already on their way home. I thought ruefully then, *I shouldn't have kept out only three sets of clothes. Now I have to wear the same things day after day.*

As the days in September came and went, I grew more and more anxious for the baby to arrive. A week stretched out into a month. I knew nothing of pregnancy, so I had to rely on what I was told. "The baby was due on a certain date, but it didn't want to come out. God only knows when it will," Mr. Klein would say, seemingly calm. Still the well-behaved Nisei, I smothered my feelings and tried to put on a brave face.

Finally, the baby was born. As promised, I stayed and took care of the house while Mrs. Klein recovered in the hospital, her husband alternating between her bedside and his office. Meanwhile, I cooked all the meals, fed and took care of the kids, did even more dishes and laundry than usual, made all the beds, and dusted and cleaned the house, making up for the absence of both parents. By the time Mrs. Klein came home, after about a week, I was exhausted.

At the time, I was also just relieved because I was finally able to leave. Truthfully, I was also annoyed that I could then spend only a day or so in both Detroit and Chicago visiting family and friends. Upon reflection months later, I thought, *In my anxiety to get away, did I express my gratitude to the Kleins enough? They had been so kind. I hope Pop wrote a letter of thanks to them. He's usually so polite and efficient.* In my immaturity, it didn't occur to me to write the letter myself. Now, I wonder what they did after I left. I hope they hired somebody to help Mrs. Klein, who was still recovering.

Although I worried about my departure from the Kleins and getting to California on time for the start of school, the trip did give me the chance to visit my maternal grandmother and aunts in Detroit. We had never met before, but they welcomed me with hugs. "We're so happy to finally meet you!" they exclaimed. I was overwhelmed, and even moreso when they surprised me with a lovely pink cashmere sweater. Although the Kleins had been generous, I had never owned something so luxurious. With my aunts urging me, "Try it on. Try it on," I eagerly slid my arms into the cardigan and buttoned it up. Even though it was the smallest size available, the sleeves were too long, the body was too wide, and the bottom edge of the sweater almost reached my knees. I was utterly disappointed. Since I was scheduled to leave the next morning, we had no time to go shopping for a replacement. Regretfully, I left it behind with my aunts, who must have felt as disappointed as I did.

Soon, I forgot about the sweater. And eventually I stopped worrying about the Kleins too and immersed myself in the routine of school in Berkeley. Later—too late—I realized that I should have kept the sweater. At first, I reasoned I could have sent it to one of the Klein daughters, but I brushed aside the thought because then I would have felt bad about giving a gift to only one child. The true destiny of the sweater should have been for my mother to receive it. A few inches taller than I, she probably would have been delighted with the gift from her half-sisters. She had left Northern California while they were still young children and had not seen them since the 1920s. For a day, it was as if I had stood in for my mother, enjoying their lavish attention and donning their almost-fitting gift.

A Homecoming of Sorts

I try to go home, but it's gone, changed, barely recognizable. It's 2001, and many of the streets that were two-way are now one-way, and streets that once crossed the railroad tracks are dead ends. I stop the car. I look at the map again. How do I get to the intersection of Fourteenth and Vine Streets, where my family lived from 1938 until 1942, the year we Japanese Americans were taken from our homes to the WRA camp on an Indian reservation in the desolate Arizona desert? The rest of my family returned to this home after their release in 1945 and lived there until my father was transferred from his church in Riverside to another in Santa Barbara in 1948. If I study the map and drive around, maybe I can find it.

As I enter the town, it's not all gone, but my view has changed. The train station is still where it used to be, but it looks larger than I remembered. It looks clean, as if the exterior has been maintained. Perhaps it's been renovated. I wonder if it is still in use. My life has been defined by the trains I have boarded and deboarded. In Riverside before the war I sometimes sat at my desk upstairs beside a window and, across the vacant, weed-covered lot, watched the long freight trains pass by on the tracks a block away. Late at night, I listened to the clickety-clack of their wheels on the rails and the mournful sound of their whistles as they crossed the residential streets. Then in August 1944, when I was released from Poston, I boarded a train and rode eastward across the country, finally ending up in Brecksville, just twenty miles south of Cleveland.

And now it's 2001 and I'm back in my car, driving through my hometown. Fifty-nine years have elapsed since our departure for Poston, and I see that Riverside has grown from a population of about sixty thousand to a city of hundreds of thousands. I see it's no longer a small, sleepy small town but a sprawling metropolis.

I see the beautiful, ornate Spanish architecture of the courthouse in Riverside now surrounded by ungainly, boxy stucco structures. I see the stately Gothic-style Congregational Church downtown still at its old location, so blackened with soot, probably from all the traffic on the street, that it reminds me of old churches in Europe. Should I enter the famous Mission Inn, its Spanish mission–style building also still standing there across the street? I am repulsed by a garish neon sign over the ivy-covered entrance that detracts from this historic building's dignity.

Riverside is my home, and my friends have made their mark here. Junkichi Harada is commemorated in a plaque embedded in the front lawn of his former home in Riverside. This house—the object of a lawsuit—has been designated a Cultural Heritage Landmark. The building has been well-maintained and looks much as it did during the 1940s: a pale yellow, boxy house. The entire front of the second story overhangs the first floor and forms a porch along the width of the building, and across the front of the second story are four evenly spaced rectangular windows, the same number of windows as along the sides of the house. In 1916, Harada, an

The existing north wing is part of the original building of Central Junior High School. Riverside, California, 2001.

Issei (first-generation immigrant from Japan) restaurant proprietor, placed the title to his house in the names of his three American-born children and mounted the first successful legal challenge to the 1913 Alien Land Law, which prohibited land ownership by alien Japanese.

Riverside is our home, the home we were uprooted from, home to the junior high school where I enjoyed good times before World War II, where my teachers described me as "happy, popular, efficient—a leader" on the official record sent to the high school at Poston. A school is on Magnolia Avenue exactly where Central Junior High used to be, yet the sign in front says "Central Middle School." *But what has happened to my lovely school in the past fifty years?* From the street it looks like a group of nondescript white, wooden temporary barracks that, except for their color, remind me of the black tarpapered barracks in the Poston concentration camp—quite a contrast to the classical Spanish-Moorish architecture of the Central Junior High that I remembered. The green lawn in front of the school looks much smaller than I thought it was, and the groves of trees on each side of the lawn are still there but appear less dense. The trees are so tall and their trunks so

Florence sits between friends, Mary (left) and Martha (right), at the edge of the lily pond at Central Junior High School on a Sunday afternoon. Riverside, California, 1942. Photo by Tomiko Ito.

Flo's aunt and younger sister Ruthie stand in front of the Japanese Congregational Church and parsonage, where the Ohmura family lived for several years, both before and after the war. Riverside, California, 1948.

thick that I wonder if they are the same ones that stood there fifty years ago.

I keep searching for home, recalling what is gone. I drive around the block to see the rest of the school. The playing field is still there and covers the rest of the entire block, but it's surrounded by an ugly cyclone fence.

As I come around to the third side of the block, beyond a black wrought-iron gate near the street, I see a familiar white Spanish-style building, its roof bordered in aquamarine. I get a glimpse of the ornate variegated red ceramic tile set diagonally on the lower quarter of its walls. Through a gate I can see that what was once a circular white water-lily pond—located in front of the former entrance to the original school building and also lined with the same diagonal red tile—is now a huge planter filled with greenery and flowers. It's time to get out of the car for a closer look!

This reconstituted school brings back memories of the prison where I was confined during World War II. It was an unusual prison—one that required no iron fences or gates, just one solitary string of wire attached to flimsy two-foot-tall posts to mark the boundary of the camp. With nowhere for us to go, nobody tried to escape. We were surrounded by a bleak, desolate desert and the wide, swiftly flowing Colorado River approximately two and a half miles west of our camp.

The front of my former Riverside school is now encircled by ugly barracks—but at least they are painted white. The buildings at the perimeter are connected to each other by tall, black wrought-iron fences and locked gates, which give the impression that the school is an impregnable fortress—or is it a prison, a place of confinement? I wish the ugly new structures had been placed *behind* the beautiful original buildings, but then I suppose it would be more difficult to keep out present-day vandals and other bad characters who seemed nonexistent before the war. The school looks smaller than I remembered it. I half wish I could get inside the gates, and I'm half glad that today is a holiday and I cannot.

Maybe home is not a place but a path, the route I used to walk home from school. As I reach Fourteenth Street, where Magnolia's name changes to Market Street, I look down Market and see the De Anza Theatre, where my friends and I used to see movies on occasional weekend afternoons, when our parents could spare the children's admission fee of ten or fifteen cents. (Shirley Temple, the famous child actress, was my all-time favorite movie star—my heroine. I tried to see all of her movies and avidly collected pictures of her from newspapers and magazines that young-adult members of the church gave to my mother.) The building looks well-maintained and the tall vertical sign and marquee still say "De Anza," but it now houses other business establishments.

The Riverside Marketplace sign at Fourteenth and Vine Streets marks the former site of the Japanese Congregational Church. Riverside, California, 2001.

Or maybe home is a corner, the crossroad that I reach at last: Fourteenth and Vine Streets. The intersection has been reconfigured so the rectangular lot where our home once stood is now a large triangular traffic island comprising a small park. I take a picture of the spot where I think we lived. It appears to belong to a nearby commercial shopping center called Riverside Marketplace, according to a large sign facing Fourteenth, the principal street. The green trees and grass in this peaceful area belie the heavy traffic on Fourteenth, which now leads to a freeway on-ramp. No freeway ran through town in the old days. Now cars, cars, hundreds of cars whiz by. It's a wonder the greenery survives their poisonous exhaust fumes. Luckily, there are traffic signals at this intersection now. Otherwise, I could never cross the streets to take more pictures of my old home ground.

Although I try to capture home in photos, the images cannot bring me back to what it was. Home is no longer there, but my memories remain.

Kiku holds up her father's prisoner uniform as she testifies at the redress hearings in San Francisco in 1982. Photo by Isao Isago Tanaka.

Kiku Hori Funabiki was born on July 4, 1924, in San Francisco's Japantown. She resided there until 1942, when she was incarcerated in the Heart Mountain concentration camp, in Wyoming. After her release from camp, Kiku attended Queens College in New York. When she and other prisoners were finally allowed to return to the West Coast in 1944, Kiku and her family resettled in their home in the San Francisco Bay Area and she then matriculated at UC Berkeley.

Even after her release from camp, Kiku experienced an intensely hostile, racist society, and after graduation she became an active participant in the Redress and Reparations movement. One of the high points in her life was her selection by the National Coalition for Redress and Reparations to represent former inmates and challenge the injustice of the forced removal of Japanese Americans. In 1984 she went toe to toe with the white male establishment in the form of the House Judiciary Committee in Washington, D.C.

Fast forward to now, when, as Kiku states, "We face yet another challenge: that of aging, as we find ourselves in our seventies and eighties. In these vintage years, we are forced to face unrelenting reality as we slow down into dotage—the spring now a shuffle as we favor our aches, everything an impressionistic blur as we can't see well with glasses or without them. We creak; we leak." Kiku is on a strict daily ninety-minute workout routine. She exercises her mind in Brian Komei Dempster's writing course, where, she says, "we are forced to journey into the layers of our inner selves." As Kiku gets to know who she truly is, she is reminded of the comic character Popeye and his simple soliloquy: "I am what I am." Kiku's goals are still to grow, to connect, to give back some of the blessings in her life, and to be playful in the process.

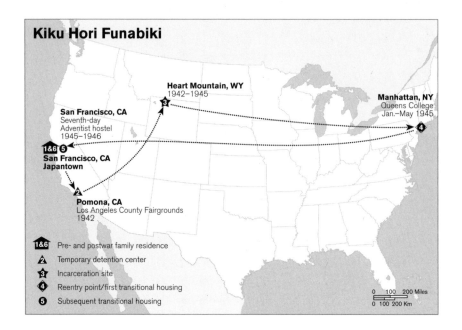

Kiku Hori Funabiki

Heart Mountain, WY
1942–1945

Manhattan, NY
Queens College
Jan.–May 1945

San Francisco, CA
Seventh-day
Adventist hostel
1945–1946

San Francisco, CA
Japantown

Pomona, CA
Los Angeles County Fairgrounds
1942

1&6 Pre- and postwar family residence

2 Temporary detention center

3 Incarceration site

4 Reentry point/first transitional housing

5 Subsequent transitional housing

0   100   200 Miles
0 100 200 Km

THE CHAIR

The first day we arrived at the Heart Mountain concentration camp, we entered our quarters: barracks with four bare walls and four army cots, one for each of us. Next, we wandered around our block to orient ourselves, discovering empty crates and cartons around the mess halls; taking a few of them, we elevated the interior décor to "orange-crate contemporary." For the next two and a half years, our modus operandi would be Resourcefulness.

Close habitation breeds rumors, and a very popular one was that lumber was stored next to the administration area, officially available only to contractors who constructed barracks according to camp blueprints. My brother Tats and other prisoners took this as a challenge. When night fell, their traffic teemed at the lumber yard as they pilfered the wood. We called it "Midnight Inventory." How they dodged the curfew and the guards is still a mystery. In any case, my brother brought back enough lumber to build real furniture. As an engineer, Tats was meticulous in any undertaking. He drew a sketch of a handsome armchair with a high back and arms that smartly slanted inward. Then he built the chair, a designer piece reserved for special guests.

Soon after, we had such a guest in Reverend Kaneko, the pastor at a church my mother had attended in San Francisco. A dignified figure, tallish and quite portly, he was making a visitation to members of his church, the

First Reformed. When he arrived at our barracks, Mama happened to be the only one there and received him warmly. "I feel so blessed for his concern," Mama told us after his visit. He knew she had suffered a stroke before our forced removal, and she was grateful he was checking in with her.

After a short prayer, Reverend Kaneko rose to leave…and so did the chair! Its inwardly slanted arms clung to the good reverend's generous girth like a fond embrace, as if to say, "Don't leave; stay a while." Mama agonized as she apologized to a very embarrassed pastor, suppressing laughter as she tried discreetly to help this good man of God dislodge himself from the chair's tenacious grip.

After the big war ended and the West Coast began to open up, finally allowing the return of camp prisoners, my brother Tats, who had left camp before us, took a short leave from his job in New York to help my parents make the move. One of my mother's highest priorities was the disposition of the chair, which she had become attached to because of its association with Reverend Kaneko. "*Natsukashi,*" she said. "Nostalgic." Our barrack neighbors, the kind Reverend Nozaki and his wife, offered to take in my parents at their church hostel in San Francisco, but crating such a cumbersome piece across the West and into the city was unthinkable. With heavy hearts, we left the chair behind in the barren barrack room with the bare army cots. We hoped that some looter would take the loving chair to grace his patio, as it had always received our guests warmly.

RELEASE

My breakthrough to the "free" world occurred in 1944. We had been confined for the entire war in a desolate desert habitat where we were enclosed by a barbed wire fence. I hadn't seen Papa for nearly three years.

It was understood: even before Papa was reunited with us, my brothers would leave as soon as they were granted release, and I would remain behind at camp to care for my aging parents. My eldest brother, Tats, left immediately upon his acceptance of a teaching position in New York, and my second brother departed soon after to resume his education. When Papa was finally returned to us, for the first time since the FBI seized him from our home, I relished every moment with him, my gentle friend, counselor, support, and confidante. Papa never lectured me; he simply let me be.

I never questioned my caregiver role, being the youngest sibling and the only female. On a basic level, I made sure Papa and Mama got their meals from the mess hall, but even more critical, I made sure she got adequate medical attention for her stroke. But as much as I had accepted my position as caregiver, I needed to get on with my life. And my stoic parents, who deeply valued education, knew that I had to continue my schooling at any price. My decision to accept entry into Queens College was an easy one, especially since my brother Tats and his wife had already settled in New York.

After arranging for a very kind church pastor and his wife, who lived a few barracks away, to check in on my parents, I made final plans to leave. As I boarded the bus, I took a last glance at my parents, still exiled within their prison, one infirm, the other just beginning to reacquaint himself with his family. Misty-eyed, I could hardly look back at the two frail figures waving to me while I rode away on the bus bound for "freedom."

REENTRY

I was a wide-eyed "podunk" clinging to my brother Tats with trepidation as I entered New York City, bustling metropolis, crossroads of the universe, of congestion, of shiny autos, a cacophony of blasting horns daring the stampede of humanity to enter the rushing traffic. I was traumatized. Why were these sophisticated New Yorkers in such a frenzied rush? No one dared to saunter or pause to smell the flowers.

My brother stopped in his tracks on Fifth Avenue. "Look up," he said. The Empire State Building! Over one hundred stories high, the world's tallest! I leaned back in disbelief, so far that I nearly toppled over. Such was my initiation to modern civilization.

The shock of my reentry had been gradual until this moment. Only ten days ago, I had taken a bus from the Heart Mountain concentration camp in Wyoming to the train station in Billings, Montana. The train we boarded was not exactly Amtrak, more Toonerville Trolley Local, and at every whistle stop, the train screeched to a halt. We were loaded beyond capacity, mainly with servicemen on leave, and some of us were forced to sit on our luggage in the aisles. I tried to doze through a long night as passengers stepped over me to use the facilities. I was overwhelmed—overwhelmed yet grateful to depart the desert, in awe of the unknown that lay ahead.

After chugging on between stops, we finally arrived at Grand Central Station, New York. I was soot-covered from having ridden in an open-windowed car through tunnels. Totally exhausted, I welcomed the sight of Tats and his wife, who had waited there all night and almost into dawn for my very delayed arrival. They had to report to work in a few hours, but they had waited. I counted my blessings. Given their generosity, I was mindful not to wear out my welcome.

Tats felt responsible—he'd become caregiver to me, a just-released prisoner, isolated for three years—and he took time off from work one day so we could go to Manhattan, where the War Relocation Authority (WRA) helped former prisoners find living quarters and employment. Tats and I entered the Empire State Building and stepped into the express elevator. The doors closed, the elevator gathered speed, and my ears popped as we climbed what must have been sixty or seventy floors. When it abruptly stopped, I felt relief. The doors opened, and I expected a red carpet welcome, but instead the WRA office was very businesslike and run with expedience: no tarrying—rush, rush, rush. Their processing of former camp inmates was quick and practical, but not much more beyond that; they had experienced a heavier demand from camp arrivals than they were prepared for, and in response the staff made no allowances for the licking of wounds, instead displaying a strictly Take It or Leave It attitude. They admonished, "You need to decide quickly about lodgings. They won't be available for long." But they were not unwelcoming, they were simply New Yorkers.

For a student like me, the only lodging and board available was to be employed as a "schoolgirl," a euphemism for a servant who performed menial jobs in a household in exchange for a closet-sized room, meals, and a pittance for spending money. From the WRA files, I selected an address on Park Avenue, since the household only comprised a widow and her adult daughter. With this, I could leave behind the prison of barbed wire where we were deprived of privacy, the mess hall where we lined up three times a day, the latrine with no partitions between toilets that rendered me chronically constipated. Now I would have freedom of movement and could call my own shots.

PARK AVENUE

I had just settled in the modest servant quarters, the size of a large walk-in closet. I had not been informed of my roommates, the original New Yorkers—cockroaches—and I soon learned that these critters indiscriminately inhabited Manhattan, from the squalor of metropolitan ghettos to posh Park Avenue penthouses. Worse yet, I was instructed by the doorman, "All domestics are to enter and exit through the side door that leads to the service elevator." I was taken aback. Other than for us servants, this door was used for garbage collection. I was struck with further disbelief when the woman of the house, Mrs. Levy, said to me with incredulous audacity, "You should consider yourself fortunate that I'm providing you with as prestigious an address as Park Avenue, Manhattan." I muttered under my breath, "Where I enter through the garbage entrance."

As a schoolgirl, I was expected to do light housecleaning over the weekend and to help with evening meal preparations each night. For dinner Mrs. Levy always cooked the entree while I set the grand dining table. I would lay out her fine linen, china, crystal goblets, silver flatware, and elaborate candlesticks, and then I would go into the kitchen to make the vegetables and salad and pour the beverages. When the meal was ready, Mrs. L. would remove her apron and take her place at the head of the dining table. With her foot, she would depress a bell affixed under the Oriental rug to summon me from the kitchen. Only after I served her and her daughter could I take my meal in the kitchen, helping myself from the stove. Later, I would make the mistake of reporting this to my mother upon my return to San Francisco, and she burst into tears. "*Ashi de, ashi de?* With her foot, with her foot?" she murmured. In Japan any expression made with the feet is considered the most uncouth insult in any social situation.

Since classes at Queens College were beginning just a few days after I arrived in New York, I had no time to look for a less degrading living situation, and so I stayed. The first weeks at Park Avenue had been unsettling as I wondered about my status—expendable and expected to be in total compliance to "white rule"—and even though I resented Mrs. Levy's demeaning attitude, I felt compelled to fulfill my duties. It seems even though I was no longer in camp, I was still expected to live by the rules of others. Upon our release, for instance, we had been given official directives: "Keep a low profile. Limit congregation with Asians to a minimum. Never converse in Japanese in public." The government's rationale: times were volatile; we would be associated with the enemy. Meanwhile, I tried to concentrate on my studies, anxiously looking forward to the day of real liberation, when the West Coast would open, my parents would be released from camp, and I could rejoin them and the human race in San Francisco.

The misery over my dehumanization was broken temporarily one day when I discovered, by accident, that a friend from San Francisco, Masako, was employed by a family only a block away from where I was staying. When I met up with Masako, her family stood in stark contrast to Mrs. Levy's: Masako had been placed as a caregiver for two young children in a wonderful family who treated her like one of them. I felt so privileged to meet the father, Dr. Benjamin Spock, a caring person, total gentleman, world-renowned pediatrician, and outspoken peace activist. Unfortunately, the good doctor's schedule was heavily committed beyond his medical practice for speaking engagements, and neither I nor my friend found the time or opportunity to speak in depth with him.

I spent free afternoons with Masako, weeping on her shoulder at times,

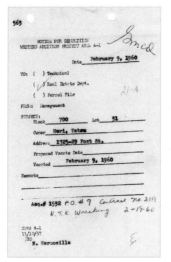

Left: Notice for the demolition of 1725 Post Street dated Feburary 9, 1960, during the redevelopment of San Francisco's Western Addition. Courtesy of the San Francisco Redevelopment Agency.

Right: 1725 Post Street (fifth building from the right) was a residence and office built by Sojiro Hori, Kiku's father, in the 1930s. Courtesy of the San Francisco Redevelopment Agency.

but other times making the best of our stay in the city. On our afternoon walks we occasionally strayed from our route to the children's playground in Central Park, where Mrs. Spock had asked us to take the baby, instead veering in the opposite direction to Fifth Avenue. We would cautiously slip into the very fashionable shops, like Saks Fifth Avenue, risking a run-in with Mrs. Spock herself. We were two kids in a candy shop with no money. The Spock baby whom we walked in his stroller was not yet talking. He'd never snitch on us.

At long last, the West Coast opened to released camp inmates. Mama and Papa were free to return home. Papa once again occupied the home office on 1725 Post Street in San Francisco, where he slowly restarted his business and contact with old clients. At the time, we never could have known that less than a decade later our Japantown neighborhood would be demolished. Back then, I was just a student, cautious with hope, and the semester at Queens was winding down. I couldn't pack my bags for San Francisco fast enough.

I remember vividly my last day at the "prestigious" address on Park Avenue; I had worked there for six months. Fortunately, my employer was out. I left a note and the servant's key in the foyer and departed for the last time, taking

Demolition of Project A-1 for the Geary Expressway, c. 1962. After the dramatic razing of several blocks in San Francisco's Japantown, Post Street (shown in the upper right) was next to be demolished and replaced by the Japan Trade Center. Courtesy of the San Francisco Redevelopment Agency.

the main elevator down to the front entrance. There stood the white-gloved doorman in his snappy uniform of navy blue serge with gold braids and buttons who constantly gestured at me to take the garbage elevator. I had taken his insolence long enough and had reached my boiling point. I flung my mild disposition to the winds and gave him the finger, albeit *verbally:*

"I've just come out of the door for the last time, and I'm carrying my bags to return home to California, where I'm entering my house through the *front* door, while you'll be opening the door for others, forever."

ISN-23-4-552-C1

This serial number was assigned to my father after he was seized by the FBI with more than two thousand other Japanese nationals suspected of sabotage. Declared "enemy aliens" and "prisoners of war" by the government, all internees, including Papa, were made to wear denim prisoner uniforms that bore serial numbers. My father, Sojiro Hori, was, in 1941, a forty-year resident of the United States and a productive, hardworking taxpayer of stellar character. He was not a U.S. citizen because the law prevented all Issei, including my father, from becoming citizens.

Following the seizures, the Department of Justice (DOJ) detained and interned these Issei from two to six years without charges, without due process. After three years of internment, Papa was released to yet another prison, Heart Mountain Relocation Center, in Wyoming. There, he joined the rest of his family, bringing with him the denim prisoner's jacket that he had purloined as a way to share his experience. He showed us the jacket and then told us about the trousers, which he didn't have. "The seat of my pants were stenciled in large white letters—P W—standing for Prisoner of War. It was like a target." It may as well have been a bull's-eye. I shuddered in rage and frustration.

Several years after Papa's release, when the Freedom of Information Act went into effect, I examined transcripts of the interrogations of Papa by the federal agents. Demonstrating their ignorance, prejudice, and blatant lack of humanity, the FBI could only come up with the baseless accusation of "Potentially Dangerous Enemy Alien" as a reason to incarcerate my father. The only evidence they could muster? Papa was an officer in the Japanese Association, a benevolent organization to help new arrivals into the Japanese American community establish themselves in a white-dominated society.

Kiku views her father's prisoner jacket on display for an exhibit by the National Japanese American Historical Society, September 12, 2001.

The transcripts corroborated what I already knew: that no documented acts of sabotage had been committed by my father, our family, or any U.S. residents of Japanese descent. In 1982, Aiko Herzig, a longtime activist, accidentally discovered a document in the Federal Archives in Washington, D.C., that reaffirmed our innocence, something that was further confirmed, around the same time, by the research of Peter Irons, an attorney and political science professor at the University of California, San Diego. Despite these incredible discoveries, however, far too little documentation exists about the detention and internment of the Issei by the DOJ. Other than some brief reports from government files, I only know of two books that address this subject: *My Six Years of Internment: An Issei's Struggle for Justice* (1957, 1990) by Reverend Yoshiaki Fukuda, a Konko priest who gives a personal account of his own December 7, 1941, seizure by the FBI and subsequent six-year internment; and *Judgment Without Trial: Japanese American Imprisonment during World War II* (2003) by Tetsuden Kashima, a third-generation Japanese American and a professor of American ethnic studies who documents the Issei experience of internment.

Through these books and anecdotes from friends whose fathers were interned like mine, I became aware of the staggering acts of torture inflicted on them. Reverend Fukuda writes of Issei men in their late fifties and sixties who "were made to work on the construction of roads and airfields…clean army stables…and even…transport ammunition." Fukuda documents how camp officials enforced this type of labor in the below-zero temperatures of Montana and the extreme heat of Lordsburg, New Mexico, blatantly violating the Geneva Convention Agreement, which "clearly states that prisoners shall not be exposed to such extremes of climate."

Fortunately, since my father was taken in several months after December 7, the day Pearl Harbor was bombed, conditions had improved somewhat due to the knowledge and wisdom of Reverend Fukuda himself. In accordance with the Geneva Convention Agreement, Fukuda argued for the rights of himself and his fellow internees by negotiating with camp authorities.

Others, however, suffered unconscionable abuse. Yuri Nakahara Kochiyama, another frontline activist and longtime friend, related to me the story of her father's mistreatment and later documented the experience in *Passing It On* (2004), a memoir in which she describes the wartime saga of her father, Seiichi Nakahara, the owner of a wholesale fishing industry in San Pedro, California. His short-wave radio, a necessary tool for staying in contact with fishermen of Japanese descent, was deemed evidence enough for someone to accuse him of being a spy. At the outbreak of the war, Mr. Nakahara was bedridden with tuberculosis and diabetes, and by midday of December 7, FBI agents rushed in and forced him out of bed, threw a robe over him, and hustled him away, refusing to advise the family why, where, or for how long he would be gone. I identify with the family's terror and helplessness of that moment; the image of my father being taken away in shackles has not faded. I was too terrified to even bid Papa goodbye.

During his internment, Mr. Nakahara's condition deteriorated rapidly because he was refused essential medication. He could no longer speak, see, hear, or even recognize his own family members, and he died a lonely and tortured death.

When this kind of racially motivated injustice and abuse resurfaced after 9/11—this time directed at Middle Easterners in the United States—I was driven to express my outrage in writing. Almost seventy years have elapsed since the parallel experience imposed on our community.

What do we do? Agha Saeed, professor of political science and ethnic studies at UC Berkeley and head of the American Muslim Alliance—with over seven thousand members and ninety-five chapters—stated after September 11, 2001: "This crisis has made it necessary for America to know who we are and what we are." Americans needed to know who we were and what we were in 1941 too. At the same time *we* have the responsibility to make it known to Americans who *we* are and what *we* are today. Even now, we still hear the daily rhetoric, the term "Muslim" associated with terrorism. Families are still being split, children are losing their fathers, innocent people are being falsely accused. Are they, too, branded with numbers?

Author's note: Quoted and paraphrased material is taken from page 40 of My Six Years of Internment, *by Reverend Yoshiaki Fukuda, and pages 6 and 7 of* Passing It On, *by Yuri Nakahara Kochiyama.*

KANSHA

The word *kansha* conveys a deep expression of appreciation that is not easily translated into English, since it is based so strongly on Japanese culture. "Profound and humble gratitude" is as close as I can get. This piece expresses my *kansha* to very special human beings who acted with compassion, integrity, and truth, no matter the consequences.

Upon our release from camps and return to American society at large, we faced a volatile climate of hate, including screaming messages on buttons that said things like *JAP HUNTING LICENSE, OPEN SEASON, NO LIMIT* and *LET'S BLAST THE JAPS CLEAN OFF THE MAP.*

Hate propaganda badges like this one were worn visibly during and after World War II.

Before the war, I could go into a shop and expect to be waited on like any consumer. Not so when we returned. Housing was the most critical. Sections of San Francisco were closed to us. The Salvation Army, whose large building in Japantown was built with funds from the Japanese community, rejected our pleas for temporary housing. The rationale they gave us: they needed to reserve it for their Officer Training. Consequently, the gymnasium of the Buddhist Church became the only shelter for many resettlers. Those in rural areas experienced even more extreme overt bigotry, including drive-by shootings and the torching of their homes.

Yet I will always hold profound *kansha* for the heroes who, at great risk to themselves, reached out to us and gave us hope. One of them was Father Edward J. Whelan, a Jesuit priest who headed St. Ignatius College, now the University of San Francisco. My father's relationship with him began in 1925, when, as proprietor of an employment agency, he provided custodians for the college. Upon hearing about the FBI's seizure of my father and other Issei, Father Whelan wasted no time in sending out several affidavits on my father's behalf. He even sent one to the United States Attorney General, Francis Biddle. Confirming my father's "exemplary character" in his extended association with him, Father Whelan declared that there was no basis for my father's internment. Father Whelan received this written response from an assistant: "In the case of Sojiro Hori, now interned as a dangerous alien enemy, it has been referred to this office for consideration." Such was the mentality of authorities.

Father Whelan placed himself in the crossfire of those contentious times. He was one of the several hundred righteous Americans who acted on their consciences and stood up for our rights. Shizue Seigel, working with the Kansha Project, has compiled a book of interviews, *In Good Conscience: Supporting Japanese Americans during the Internment* (2006), and reading each testimonial, I am humbled with gratitude. The commitment of Father Whelan and others gave me hope then and gives me hope now. Likewise, President Barack Obama's message of hope is no longer an abstraction. I can feel it. I can embrace it. It has become a part of my life.

Hashizume family photo, taken in 1949. Back row: Tom, Sato, Shigeko (Arlene), George. Front row: Kiyoko, Norman, Papa. Photo by Gladys Gilbert Studio, Portland, Oregon.

Sato Hashizume was born in Japan in 1931, raised in Portland, Oregon, and incarcerated during World War II in the Minidoka War Relocation Center, in southern Idaho. Without work or a home to return to after the war, her family relocated from camp to Salt Lake City, Utah, and after one year there, Sato's father started a hotel business back in Portland. There, Sato received her nursing education at the Providence School of Nursing and her baccalaureate degree at the University of Oregon (now Oregon Health Sciences University). Later, during her graduate studies at the University of Minnesota (UM), she was inducted into Sigma Theta Tau, the nursing honors society.

Following her time at UM, she came to San Francisco and was employed by the University of California, San Francisco (UCSF), where she retired after twenty-six years of service as a teacher, administrator, and nurse practitioner. While at UCSF, she took a leave of absence to serve as a nurse educator aboard the hospital ship the USS HOPE at Sri Lanka. In her retirement years, she has been surprised and delighted with the unfolding of her life as she develops the craft of writing. An excerpt from her story "The Food" was first published in Only What We Could Carry: The Japanese American Internment Experience, *edited by Lawson Fusao Inada (Heyday Books, 2000).*

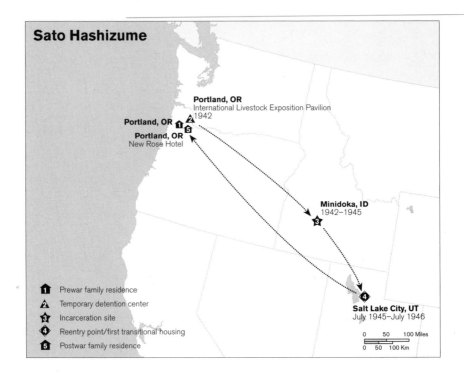

Sato Hashizume

Portland, OR
International Livestock Exposition Pavilion
1942

Portland, OR

Portland, OR
New Rose Hotel

Minidoka, ID
1942–1945

🏠 Prewar family residence
🏚 Temporary detention center
✪ Incarceration site
④ Reentry point/first transitional housing
🏠 Postwar family residence

Salt Lake City, UT
July 1945–July 1946

0   50   100 Miles
0   50 100 Km

LEAVING

The mess hall line was becoming shorter each day. Instead of the snaking queue along the side wall to the back door, the line had shrunk to about one third of what had been its usual length over the past four months. Last night about thirty people were ahead of me, including my neighbor Mary and Mr. and Mrs. Koike. Mrs. Sawada with her three small children stood behind me. I realized that I might never see these people again, so I wanted to linger and chat with them. We moved unhurriedly as we approached the "hash" tables.

"Where are all of you going?" I turned and asked Mrs. Sawada.

"I guess we're going back to Portland," she answered. "But I don't know where all five of us will live. We'll probably stay with my brother and his family in his two-room apartment until Fred can find a job. I can't imagine how ten of us will fit in their tiny apartment," she said with a half-laugh. "Maybe we'll stay at the Japanese Methodist church. Toshie Muira, who works in administration, was saying that the churches were housing a few people from camp until they could get settled."

I wish I were going to Portland with you, I thought to myself. *I wouldn't mind staying at the Methodist church. At least I would be back in Portland and know the people staying there.*

"Aren't you going to Portland too?" Mrs. Sawada asked Mary.

"I guess so, but I haven't heard from Dad since last week," Mary said. "So far, we don't know where we'll live either. We heard housing is scarce, and everyone is doubling up or living in basements. Someone said one couple was sleeping in a closet. Dad is helping a farmer in Troutdale, and hopefully he'll have a place for us there. Who knows, we may have to stay in the farmer's barn. We don't know what we're going to do, but Dad told us to get ready—we are leaving next week for sure."

Well, at least Papa found a place for us to stay and had a job waiting for him, I thought.

"I'll talk to Toshie this evening," Mrs. Sawada said. "She seems to have more information than anyone else. She told Yuki that there might be openings not only in churches but in a housing project near the North Portland Assembly Center where we were forced to stay. The place is called Vanport or something like that. I'll let you know what she says."

As I reflected on the uncertainty of housing for the people returning to my hometown, I looked toward the Koikes, who had been quiet during our conversation.

"I don't know what we're going to do either," Mrs. Koike said as she cast a worried look at her husband.

"Goddamn them!" Mr. Koike exploded. "I'm not leaving! They forced us in here and now they're forcing us out. Where are we supposed to go? I don't have anyplace to go to. They made me lose my grocery store, my home—everything. I don't have money—no job—nothing. What am I supposed to do? I'm seventy-two years old. I'm not a kid anymore. What am I supposed to do? Goddamn those bastards. They'll have to kick me out! I'm not leaving!"

While Mr. Koike's bursts unsettled me, I think he expressed an anger that some other Issei must have felt but were uncomfortable giving voice to. After Mr. Funatake, the block manager, announced the closing of Minidoka at dinner one evening, Mr. Koike had bitterly complained to his neighbors. "How's an old man like me supposed to find a job to support my family? How come no one from administration is helping us?" he would say. "Where are we supposed to live? Who's going to pay for the rent and food?" Now, with the camp closure imminent, he could no longer contain himself. Questions swirled in my head: *What will happen to Mr. Koike and his family if they refuse to leave camp? Will they be arrested? And if the mess hall closes, how will they get food?*

I hesitated for a moment, allowing Mr. Koike to finish, then took my opportunity to say farewell to the neighbors in my block. "We're leaving for

Salt Lake City early in the morning before the mess hall opens," I said. "So I want to say goodbye. Good luck, everyone. I hope we meet again someday." As we separated to our different tables, I worried about how these people were going to manage. *How unfair it is to force us out of camp without any help with jobs and housing,* I thought. *And with just twenty-five dollars each from the government for resettlement, what is going to happen when the money runs out?*

I joined Kiyoko, who was sitting alone at a table that was once filled with our friends. As we ate our last watery, tasteless camp stew, my sister and I, lost in our thoughts, said very little for some time. I thought about "the Hermit." No one had seen him for two or three weeks, and back when he would come to the mess hall from his desert tent, dirty rags hung from his gaunt frame. His eyes, glazed and vacant, stared at us all without recognition. "Have you heard anything about the Hermit?" I asked. "I wonder if he knows he has to leave?"

Kiyoko shook her head. "He looked so bad the last time I saw him, I don't think he'll make it if they send him back to Oregon. I hope someone helps him. He's going to die if he stays in the desert much longer."

"Talking about sick people, Mr. Tanaka's been in and out of the hospital with a very bad heart and barely gets around," I said, concerned, wondering how any of us with mental or health problems would manage the journey home and receive appropriate care. "What do you think Mr. Tanaka and his daughter will do?"

"Jean thought that she and her dad would take the train to Portland, where her uncle is staying," Kiyoko said. "But I wonder if Mr. Tanaka can make the overnight trip. When he's home he gets so out of breath taking a few steps that Jean brings his meals to the barracks. It's a lot of responsibility for a seventeen-year-old."

"When do you suppose they'll leave?"

"I don't know. I can't keep track of people anymore," Kiyoko said. "Everyone is so busy packing and moving that half the time they leave without telling anyone except their next-door neighbor. That's how I found out about the Handas. They left so quickly, they didn't drop by to tell us where they were going, and we've been friends for years. I don't know where they went and when we'll see them again, either."

Kiyoko's words rang true. It was a whirlwind of people leaving and scattering across the United States to places far from Portland. The changes were happening too fast, and I felt scared that I would never see this community again. I wondered, *Will we ever see our friends again? How will we find them? And will they be able to find us?*

My appetite gone, I pushed my tray away.

OUR BARRACK ROOM

In the early light of dawn, I took my final look around the barrack room, our home for the last three and a half years. Papa's well-used, handcrafted bench would be left behind, along with the orange-crate shelves and the print fabric closet cover. Now faded and hanging askew, it revealed the empty shelves and wooden clothes-hanger pole. Kiyoko stripped down the four army cots to the mattresses. The other two beds, dusty and unused for the two years after my sister Shige and brother George had each left camp for Cincinnati, were left folded against the side wall. I smiled at the dull, discolored potbelly stove that made perfectly browned toast as we warmed ourselves. The crisp, fragrant bread was such a treat compared to the pale and soggy mess hall fare.

"Com'on, Sato, hurry up. The army truck is here," Kiyoko called from outside, interrupting my thoughts.

"I'm coming," I yelled back. I headed toward the entry and, bending slightly, patted the smooth surface of Papa's bench. I was going to miss this room, a comfortable place where Tei and Mary had patiently taught me how to knit mittens. I remembered how the second mitten grew two sizes larger than the first but they profusely complimented my effort anyway. I now put on the hand coverings I had labored over and then worn just once, having hidden them in the bottom of the closet. I was more successful with the shells from Tule Lake that Mrs. Ogura shared so I could create my own shell corsage. "I can't believe you made it," Shige said in a letter when I sent the corsage to her for her birthday. I was pleased.

I was going to miss all my sister's friends who stopped by with the latest gossip or to chat about old times in Portland. I felt a pang of loneliness when I thought of my friends, Jean and Setsuko, who lived in my block and recently moved away. We would while away many hours just hanging out and talking about the boys in our class. But mostly I was going to miss my buddies, Frances and Lucy, childhood friends since we were five years old. Frances had already left camp for Portland and Lucy went off to far-away St. Paul, Minnesota. And now I was headed without my friends to Salt Lake City. A little shiver went up my spine.

I stepped outside, closed the door, and hurried to the waiting transport truck.

MAKING ENDS MEET

"Tomorrow, Papa is going to start working at a dry cleaning place," Kiyoko said with a smile. "He's lucky to get a job where he knows the ropes. And he's a good tailor, too."

Papa stands in front of his dry cleaning business. Portland, Oregon, 1921.

"Yeah, in camp he remade all those rejected army riding pants into straight-legged trousers," I said. "And they looked pretty good with those sharp creases. The younger guys didn't want anything to do with them, but the older men lined up with their jodhpurs for Papa's makeover. Where did he learn to sew like that?"

"Before he went into the apartment house business full-time—about the time you were born—he had three small businesses: a dry cleaner, a cigar stand next door, and a ten-room apartment house above both of them," Kiyoko answered. "He didn't know anything about tailoring but learned from a client who showed Papa how he wanted his pants altered. Papa was amazed that the man paid for the alteration and then returned to have more trousers fixed."

"I'm excited about him starting his new job," I said. "I know he will do well."

The following day Papa surprised us when he returned home before noon. We—Father, Kiyoko, Tom, and I—had moved into this house after our release from camp in July of 1945. Here, we rented two rooms from the landlord, a man of German and Jewish descent, and his wife. "Why are you home so soon?" I asked.

"Someone else took the job," he said with a mirthless chuckle. "The Japanese owner was surprised to see me and said the job had been given to another man from a camp in Utah the day before. He apologized over and over as he explained that he wasn't sure when I would return, and the new employee was already available."

A knot formed in my stomach. I felt hurt and disappointed for Papa.

He didn't waste any time focusing on his bad fortune, though. "*Shoganai,* it can't be helped," he said with a shrug and then combed the newspaper want ads. Since he had had his own businesses for much of his life, looking for employment was new to him. With limited English, and now in his late fifties, the task of finding a well-paying job would be daunting, but he was optimistic. The best position he found in the want ads was as a cook at the University Club. He had never cooked anything except rice before, but he thought he could learn on the job, as he had done in the past with railroad work, dry cleaning, tailoring, and managing an apartment business. *After all, what could be so difficult to learn,* he must have thought.

When Papa came home around noon on the day he had applied for the cook position, my heart sank. I thought he had lost another job, but he said that he was only on his break and would return to work at 3:00 p.m. for four more hours, this time as not a cook but a dishwasher. He laughed as he told us about his morning. "*Ii ohanashi no tane.* It's a seed for a good story." He would say this to us before launching into a funny story about himself.

"I arrived promptly at seven in the morning to prepare breakfast at the restaurant," he began. "The first order was two eggs, 'sunny-side up.' I didn't know exactly what to do, so I picked up the first egg and tried to crack it. My big, clumsy thumbs crushed the shell and broke the yolk all over my hands." He chuckled. "I tried again and again, five times before the manager took me aside and asked if I had ever cooked in a restaurant before. I had to answer 'no.' The manager was very kind. He said, 'I know you need work,' then transferred me to dishwasher." I laughed with Papa but felt he deserved a better job.

From late summer until winter, we settled into our German-Jewish landlord's rental space. During this time, Kiyoko married George Hata, a returning army veteran from the 442nd infantry regiment. Papa worked a split shift, 7:00 a.m. to 11:00 a.m. and then 3:00 p.m. to 7:00 p.m. He spent the intervening four hours riding the bus to and from home and resting for a couple of hours. One day when I came from school, Papa was in bed, unable to move. "What happened?" I asked anxiously, and he began his story.

"I hurried to return for the last hours of my workday. I didn't notice that the drop in temperature had frozen the slushy snow to slippery ice." Papa went on to describe how he lost his footing and fell hard as he crossed the busy street to catch his bus. He tried to stand; pain seized his groin. The traffic lights changed and cars rushed by. His concern increased with each passing moment. Then, unexpectedly, a car pulled over to the curb and stopped.

"Can I help you?" a stranger asked.

"Yes, yes. No moobu…Go homu. (Yes, yes. I can't move…Go home.)" The over-six-foot, brawny man in a plaid lumber jacket and knit cap pulled over his sandy-blond curls loomed over Papa. He slipped his large, sure hands under Papa, cradled him in his arms, and effortlessly picked him up. Then, he positioned him in the car and drove to our house, where he placed him on the bed.

"Sankyu, Sankyu (Thank you, Thank you)," Papa said.

"Thank you so much," Kiyoko added with heartfelt gratitude. "We hope it wasn't too much trouble for you." She must have wondered what she could give the man as a token of our appreciation, but she came up empty-handed.

"It wasn't a bother," the Good Samaritan said. "It wasn't out of my way. I hope he'll be better soon." In the flurry of activity, he left without giving his name. For several days Papa spoke about the amazing ōkii hito (very large man) who had lifted him like a baby, so gently and easily, and brought him home.

Papa had no health insurance, and with limited funds he had to receive his care at home without the benefit of x-rays or hospitalization. Dr. Aoki came to the house just once to diagnose Papa's fractured pelvis. He ordered a pelvic sling attached to a rope that went straight up to a pulley on a frame above the bed, then ran overhead past the foot of the bed, where it hung down with weights. The counterweights held Papa's hips just above the bed to avoid unnecessary painful movement and bed friction. Although the contraption was awkward, Kiyoko quickly learned how to raise his head for meals, turn him for bathing, and provide personal care.

The sight of Papa lying helpless in bed worried me. *Would he be okay and walk again?* I wondered. *And if he wasn't working, how would we pay for the rent and food?* Papa and my oldest sister, Kiyoko, who had become our surrogate mother after Mama's passing when I was two, never asked Tom and I, ages sixteen and fourteen, to find employment, but we felt the need to contribute to the family's income, especially until Papa regained his health. In order to work, Tom gave up wrestling, a sport he loved, and his position as the team captain. Tom, like Papa, hid his disappointment with a shrug of his shoulders. "It can't be helped," he'd said quietly. He worked after school in the produce market where Kiyoko's husband was employed.

I searched the ad section of the *Utah Nippo* and found a position for a "schoolgirl." Mrs. Poole, a thirtyish, sun-weathered socialite and the wife of an upscale clothier, interviewed me. "Aren't you a little young for this job?" she asked in a cool, condescending tone between puffs on her cigarette.

"No, I'm fourteen," I replied confidently. I knew the child labor laws only kept children who were under fourteen from working. Now that I was old enough to work, I thought I was no longer a child.

"Do you know how to cook?" asked Mrs. Poole, blowing cigarette smoke around me.

"Oh yes," I answered without hesitation. "I learned how to cook in the eighth grade in Minidoka." I had made both muffins and white sauce in my home economics class. I assured Mrs. Poole that I also knew how to babysit and clean house.

Appraising me with narrowed eyes, she took a long drag on her cigarette before saying unenthusiastically, "Oh, all right." With the severe shortage of domestic help during the war years, she must have felt she had little choice.

She offered me ten dollars a month plus room and board, with time off on Sundays and a half-day on Thursdays. I was expected to dust the entire main floor every day, vacuum twice a week, and squeeze three glasses of fresh orange juice with a hand-crank juicer, all before school. When I returned, I was to do the washing or ironing, watch the children, help prepare dinner, set the table, and clean up the dining room and kitchen after the evening meal.

After settling in my basement room, I donned my blue and white pin-striped uniform and was ready to start. Mrs. Poole told me to set the dining room table for dinner with the placemats from the buffet. Feeling pleased because I had just learned how to set a table with flatware in my home economics class, I carefully laid out five place settings.

Abruptly, Mrs. Poole yanked one place setting from the table. "There are only four of us," she said, annoyed. "You can sit in the kitchen at the end of the counter while we have dinner. I'll ring the bell when we need you and again when we're finished. Then you can clean up the dining room, wash the dishes, and help yourself to what's left."

I felt crushed. As I sprang up with each tinkle of the bell, I was overwhelmed with feelings of insignificance. Like a vacuum cleaner, I was useful and necessary but not to be seen unless required for a chore. My eyes welled up as I picked at cold, unappetizing leftovers and scrubbed greasy pots. Yet I kept going; I didn't want Papa to rush back to work too soon.

I thought about him while I labored over my chores, looking forward to my time at home. On my days off, I dropped by the house to check on him. I was pleased that by the second week he no longer grimaced when he moved his lower extremities. With less pain, he started to exercise his ankles and arms to maintain his strength.

I dragged myself back to my employer's residence even though I would have rather stayed at home. Mrs. Poole spoke to me only when there was a task. I received even fewer words from Mr. Poole, a tall, slender man with owl-shaped eyes over a pinched, prominent nose on a narrow face. One morning before school while I was dusting the hardwood stairs to the upper floor, he came down. "Good morning," I said as I squeezed close to the railing to allow adequate room for him to pass. He looked straight ahead and grunted as he continued down the stairs. That was the sole extent of my communication with him during my stay.

After six weeks Papa's pelvis had healed, and although he walked with a slight limp and was still a bit wobbly, he returned to his dishwashing job. By spring, he was strong and healthy, and he decided to go to Portland to find a hotel business. I discovered that he had gone before from Minidoka when we had first received the notice to vacate, but his search for work at that time was unsuccessful. This time many of his associates and friends in the Portland hotel business encouraged him to try again in his hometown. He was hopeful. I continued going through the motions at Mrs. Poole's, waiting for Papa's return.

Four weeks later, he finally came back with good news: He had found what he wanted. I was ecstatic. I could hardly wait to tell Mrs. Poole. I couldn't stop smiling as I practiced how and what I was going to say. The best place and time would be in the kitchen that evening while I was receiving instructions for dinner.

Mrs. Poole had barely stepped into the kitchen when I rushed up to her and almost knocked her down. "I won't be working for you anymore," I blurted out forcefully, forgetting my carefully rehearsed words and demeanor. "I'm going to Portland," I added more calmly.

"Oh, I'm sorry to see you leave," she said in a sincere tone that I didn't expect. But her regret felt hollow and it didn't matter now. "When is your last day?" she asked.

I had planned to stay another week if she needed me, but I said, "This Friday." For once, I had the bargaining chip. Almost dancing, I set the dining table with four placemats.

I was moving back to Portland. I was going home.

THE BACK ROOM

A scream pierced through the landlord's door and down the hallway to our room. It was late fall of 1945. Kiyoko and I looked at each other, then rushed into the hall. We couldn't make out distinct words but could hear a man's muffled voice trying to calm a screaming, sobbing woman. Suddenly, a distant door slammed. A thick, heavy silence hung in the air. We hurried back to our room. Looking back on the incident now, I'm glad Kiyoko was still living at home then, before she married George Hata.

Later that day, as Kiyoko fetched water from the bathtub across the hall for our evening meal, because we had no running water in our room, the old man from the back of the house stepped into our doorway. The graying hair on his head, mustache, beard, and eyebrows bushed out, untrimmed and unwashed. He wore dirty coveralls over dingy underwear. Without a shirt, he exposed the unkempt hair that seemed to sprout up all over his body: on his chest, his back, and down his arms to the knuckles of his fingers. His appearance alone made me want to run from the room, but his sour, rancid body odor repulsed me most.

He hesitated. "You might hear noises coming from my room, but don't worry, it's nothing," he said with a soft German accent. He turned to leave but then changed his mind and entered our kitchen.

Stop! You stink! Don't come in! I wanted to shout. But at fourteen years old, I was too deeply embedded with the Japanese cultural value of acquiescence. Moreover, my previous three-and-half-year displacement in a concentration camp under the rule of authority and my current respect for the fact that this man was our landlord kept my feet glued to the floor and my mouth sealed.

"You know, I'm a doctor," he said.

You? A doctor? You're so filthy, how can you be a doctor? I thought to myself.

"I was trained as an osteopath in Germany. I'm a surgeon. They won't let me have a license here in the United States, so I can't practice as a physician."

Kiyoko and I stood transfixed. He stepped closer.

"I help girls in trouble," he confided quietly. "They come to me and I fix them up. I still have my doctor's bag. All I do is dilate them a little bit, then scrape them out with a curette. It's quite simple and painless. And it's over in a few minutes. Sometimes the girls get scared and cry. But it's really nothing."

We weren't sure how to comment; we just stared at him with blank faces. He said this so matter-of-fact, but something felt creepy. *What's a curette?* I wanted to ask. *And who were the girls? Did he really help them?* With my questions unanswered, he left, his stench lingering in the air.

"P.U., does he ever stink!" I said, pinching my nose. "How can he be a doctor? He's so smelly! I thought doctors were supposed to be clean. And what was he talking about? What's a curette?"

"Well, I'm not really sure, but it has something to do with getting rid of a pregnancy," Kiyoko said. Now twenty-six years old—twelve years older than I—Kiyoko was often the source of my information.

After the old man left, I couldn't stop thinking about the parade of young girls desperately and unwittingly seeking the old man's shady services. When the supper dishes were cleared, my thoughts returned to the sobbing woman. "How do you suppose she ended up back there?" I asked Kiyoko.

"I don't know. It's illegal, so it's all hush-hush," Kiyoko said. "Often doctors who don't want to risk getting caught and jailed for doing the abortion themselves will give only a telephone number on a scrap of paper to the patient in need. The telephone number leads to a middleman who is paid lots of money by the patient to get another telephone number and address of a person willing to do the procedure. It's all 'underground' and no one knows much about these people and whether the person doing the abortion is trained and clean. The woman is usually so desperate that she accepts any arrangement and says nothing because she doesn't want anyone to know that she is pregnant."

"Didn't something like that happen to Charlene's mother several years ago?" I asked. "All I remember is that Charlene was my age at the time, about seven or eight, and her parents were tenants at our apartment house. Then the next thing I heard was that Charlene lost her mother and that her father was having a wealthy couple adopt her. I was jealous of Charlene because she always wore expensive new clothes. I didn't understand why she was crying all the time. I guess I didn't understand what was happening."

"Well, you were pretty young then," Kiyoko said. "Mrs. Swanson didn't want to be pregnant and didn't want anyone to know, so she used a clothes hanger to abort herself."

"A clothes hanger?" I said, astonished. "You mean a wire clothes hanger? That's terrible. Why would she use a clothes hanger?" *That must have hurt something awful,* I thought to myself. "Why would anyone do something like that?"

"Mrs. Swanson must not have wanted another child and felt trapped, with nowhere to turn for help," Kiyoko answered. "She was found dead in a pool of blood. It was pretty awful for the family. I felt so sorry for Mr. Swanson and Charlene."

"Oh my god, that's horrible. Poor Charlene," I said, full of guilt and remorse that I had not known she'd gone through so much. "The beautiful clothes could never make up for the loss of her mother."

After the encounter with the landlord, I noticed that his door was closed from time to time, which was strange because he often left it open to provide ventilation, but I thought less and less about the back room as a flurry of family activities took my attention. In November, there was the wedding of Kiyoko and George Hata. Then, Papa slipped on the icy street and fractured his pelvis, immobilizing him for six weeks. To assist with expenses, I spent the remainder of my time in Salt Lake City working as a "schoolgirl" and was home only on my days off. When Papa's fracture was healed, he went to Portland while the rest of us stayed behind until he found a hotel. In all, Papa, Tom, and I lived in Salt Lake City for about one year. With George gainfully employed at the produce market, he and Kiyoko chose to remain in Salt Lake City.

I had forgotten about the incident until Kiyoko sent me a newspaper clipping about seven years later. Boldly splashed with the banner headline "Abortionist Deported to Germany," the front-page article recounted the trial of our former landlord. A sixteen-year-old girl had died of a fulminating infection following an abortion in his home. He was charged and convicted of manslaughter. Rather than sending him to a U.S. prison, the judge deported him to Germany, the country from which he had fled persecution as a Jew. At more than seventy years of age, he was now being forced to leave his adopted home and return to the land of the Holocaust.

As I picked up a pen and began my letter to Kiyoko, I wondered how many more women had slipped through the alleyway entrance for the old man's services. I wondered if any had suffered complications and how they had fared. I wondered if they'd felt frightened and had reacted as I had to his poor hygiene and squalid living conditions. "Good riddance," I wrote back to Kiyoko. "He won't be able to use filthy instruments in his dark back room ever again."

THE VANPORT FLOOD

When I answered the knock on our door, I was surprised to see a petite Japanese woman who looked like someone's grandmother. Her ancient, bronze face was framed by thin, graying hair pulled back in an unruly bun. A couple of strands drifted across her face. Over loose leggings that ballooned around her bowed legs, she wore a long, dark cotton dress.

She looked up at me. *"Taoru,"* she said, without any introduction or explanation, speaking in Japanese as she always would. She was asking for a bath towel, but it took a minute for me to realize that she was a new tenant in the hotel my father was managing in Portland; permanent renters provided their own bath towels. I was wondering what I should say as Papa pulled out one from our personal supply and gave it to her, but before I could form any words, she took the towel without comment, turned, and slowly ambled down the hall. *My gosh, she never said thank you,* I thought. *Who is this woman?*

About five minutes later, she returned and with a deep sigh asked for a cloth to cover a doorless cabinet. Papa found a faded drape and gave it to her. *"Irumono agenasai.* Give her anything she needs," Papa said to me. She came back several more times that day for a dishpan, a broom, and other sundries.

I was mystified by this Issei woman who asked for things as if entitled and never thanked Papa. Some of her other behaviors didn't fit my view of a Japanese woman either. On one trip to our door that first day, she had her index finger deep in her nostril digging for a nugget. I was so distracted, I had to ask her several times what item she had requested.

Pat, her neighbor living in the same hallway, found her difficult to understand as well. "The old lady is throwing her dirty dishwater on the floor in the sink room," she reported breathlessly. "Someone is going to slip and fall."

"Oh my god!" I shouted. "The floor doesn't have a drain. The water will leak through to the store downstairs. The shopkeeper will sue us if we ruin his merchandise." I hurriedly mopped up the water. Then I tried to explain the rules to our new tenant—"You need to throw the dirty water in the utility sink"—but she gave me a blank look. I left it up to Papa to talk with her, but he hated confrontation and would probably delay speaking to her until an emergency arose.

"Papa," I asked at dinner that evening. "Who is the new Japanese tenant and where did she come from?"

"Banopoto (Vanport)," he said simply.

"Her name is Mrs. Mori," added my sister Shige.

"Didn't you see the newspaper?" my brother Tom asked me. "Vanport flooded yesterday, and over eighteen thousand people lost their homes."

"Vanport flooded?" I asked between bites of chicken, surprised. "Vanport, the housing project? Weren't there a lot of Japanese people living there?"

"The Oregonian says there were nine hundred Japanese housed there," Tom responded.

"Oh yeah," I said, putting down my chopsticks. "When Minidoka closed, a lot of people went directly from camp to Vanport. Because they lost their homes in Portland when they were uprooted, they didn't have a place to live when they returned. Luckily, Vanport was being vacated by workers who were no longer needed for the war effort. I wonder if that's why Mrs. Mori ended up there. And now she's here, because she must have lost her home again. She's only been with us one day, and I sure can't figure her out."

"Nine hundred Japanese! I didn't know so many people were housed there. That's a lot of people trying to find a place to stay. I wonder where everyone will live…Did the paper say everyone was all right?"

"The paper said at least fifteen people drowned and many more are missing," Tom said. "It didn't mention any names, but Ruth, our next-door neighbor, came over earlier to tell us that Mrs. Oyama, the wife of the editor of the *Oregon Nippo,* and Mr. Mizuno, a photographer for the Japanese community, were found in the flood waters. Mr. Mizuno's body had drifted about a mile from his home."

"Oh, that's awful," I said, sipping my tea absently. "How frightening for them. I wonder how Mrs. Mori managed with the rising water. She's so small and old, it wouldn't take much to sweep her away." *It must have been scary for her. She went through a lot,* I thought to myself. *No wonder she said only what she had to and moved so slowly. She must have been exhausted and was maybe still in shock.*

After our meal, I read all the newspaper articles accompanied with vivid images of people being rescued. I wondered if Mrs. Mori even knew the swollen Columbia River had breached a railroad berm that was inadequate to hold back the cresting waters. The forceful cascade quickly filled the flood plain where the largest temporary wartime housing project was built. Within two hours, the swift, hurling water loosened and crushed the flimsy structures, and Vanport, the second largest city in Oregon and made up entirely of public housing, was reduced to waterlogged rubble. I felt concerned as I thought of Mrs. Mori knee-deep in water, frantically wading through pieces of her life.

For the next few days, we continued to provide Mrs. Mori with necessities and assistance when she requested our help. One day Mrs. Mori asked Shige, "Can you write my name and address on a sheet of paper so if I get lost someone can help me come back home?" Shige learned that Mrs. Mori couldn't read or write English *or* Japanese. "That's a smart idea," I said, impressed with the old woman's ingenuity. "I don't think I would have thought to do that."

When she had settled into her apartment, Mrs. Mori tried to repay us with food she had prepared. After observing her personal hygiene and watching her chop and mix the food on the floor, her offerings were difficult to enjoy. We thanked her profusely, but when the door closed, I felt guilty as we wrapped the morsels in newspaper and threw them away.

She seemed eager to help in any way she could. On one occasion, Shige burned her arm on the lip of the cast iron skillet, and as she ran to the sink room to run cool water over the painful, seared skin, Mrs. Mori said, "Put cucumber juice on it—it will heal fast without a scar." I pretended I didn't hear her and busily rummaged in our first aid shoebox for burn ointment. I couldn't find any, so I volunteered to go to Plummer Drugstore and ask the pharmacist for a suitable salve.

Within minutes, Mrs. Mori came back to our kitchen with a brownish rag soaking in a small glass bowl with greenish liquid. Before we knew what was happening, she was holding Shige's arm with a firm grip, and with her free hand she was squeezing the rag of excess fluid and then applying the poultice to the fiery-red skin. "Get something to wrap the arm," she commanded, looking directly at me. I hesitated for a second. I wondered if the dirty rag would cause an infection. But with her authoritative voice ringing in my ears and her unflinching stare boring through me, I hurriedly brought back the bandage.

Even after Shige said the severe pain had eased, I still went to the drugstore. I wasn't sure about the cucumber juice, so I bought the burn ointment. The next day, I unwrapped the dressing. "Look, Shige," I said, amazed. "The redness is gone; it's healing already."

"Yeah, it doesn't hurt at all," Shige answered. "Mrs. Mori seems to know a lot about home remedies."

"She was right," I said. "I guess she knew what she was doing. She may not have much education, but she knows practical things." My realization led to my further speculation: *I wonder how she learned to treat burns. I wonder if she knows how to cure other common health problems.* I was curious. I wanted to know more about her and her background but was hesitant to ask because of her gruff manner. As Mrs. Mori had predicted, Shige's wound healed with no blemish in about two weeks.

Although she didn't shed her messy habits, like shaking her rugs and sweeping her dust into the hall, the other tenants and our family became accustomed to her presence. As she became comfortable with us, she began to share pieces of her story, which gradually fit together like a puzzle.

Before the war, she and her husband, a childless couple, lived near Hood River on a small plot of leased land. As tenant farmers, they worked hard but barely subsisted. Just before Pearl Harbor, her husband died.

One day, I asked what happened when she went to Minidoka. "When I had to go to camp, with no one to help me, I didn't know what to do," she said. "So, I left all my belongings in my cabin. When I came back, a new owner had the farm, and my house and all my things were gone." I listened intently and thought, *How devastating that must have been to find everything she once owned and valued thrown away as if it were trash.* "With nowhere else to live, I moved to Vanport," she continued. "I was told there were vacancies because the wartime shipyard workers had moved out, and many Japanese were living there now."

Over the next three years at Vanport, she gradually accumulated used furniture, cooking utensils, and other necessities. Then, in one disastrous hour on Memorial Day, 1948, all her possessions were washed away. "I didn't hear the siren or any commotion outside," she said. "Before I could do anything, my apartment filled with water. I thought I was going to drown. Suddenly, a man came in the window and pushed me out to another man, who carried me through the swirling waist-deep water. I had only the clothes I was wearing. I lost everything. I had saved two thousand dollars and it

A former resident, Mrs. Wakita, is carried out of floodwaters in Vanport, Oregon, on May 30, 1948. Photo by Mel Junghans, *The Oregon Journal*, 1948. Reprinted in *The Oregonian*, May 24, 1998. Courtesy of *The Oregonian*.

was gone too. I had sewn the paper bills into the mattress, where I thought they were safe. The mattress floated away when the building splintered into pieces."

Since even before the war, Mrs. Mori had frugally saved pennies, nickels, and dimes; she had always hoped to visit her elderly sister in Japan. She had already postponed a planned trip once, when Pearl Harbor was bombed. When Vanport flooded it took not only all of her possessions but also her dream to see Japan again. *How sad,* I thought. *Every time she becomes settled and makes plans, her world collapses, through no fault of her own.* Mrs. Mori simply shrugged her heavily burdened shoulders and sighed. Her eyes showed only resignation, no tears.

In a scant seven years, Mrs. Mori had lost everything she owned not once but twice. *What a survivor; what a warrior she is,* I thought. I began to appreciate the grit, steel will, and street smarts that propelled her through each crushing hardship. She, like other Issei women, showed a toughness and resilience I've come to admire. The immense challenges she faced left little room for her to keep up a façade of politeness, and even less patience to put up with the antics of an untested, naïve adolescent. How annoying it must have been when I interfered with her necessary housekeeping chores and ignored her wisdom and proven skill in healing burns. Only the core essentials mattered; there was no space for nonsense.

The cycle of her hard life became clear: Mrs. Mori had been thrown into yet another strange, unfamiliar environment, in this case our hotel. Now aged and penniless, she was once again mustering her inner strengths, putting her life together one piece at a time.

RETURN TO JEFFERSON STREET

With mounting excitement I walked along Fifth Avenue, heading toward Jefferson Street in Portland. Over eight years had passed since 1942, the year I had been taken from here—my old neighborhood—and shipped off to the Portland Assembly Center. We stayed there for about three months before being moved farther inland to the Minidoka concentration camp. Now, I'd finally made it home.

"City Hall," I almost shouted as I sighted the square portico attached to the rear of the block-long red-brick structure. *How many times had I passed this building as I hurried home from Japanese school,* I wondered.

My gaze shifted left to the corner across the street. My heart quickened when Doc Watson's drugstore came into view. It seemed smaller somehow and run-down, the paint peeling and the ragged awning carelessly rolled over the front entrance. *Mr. Watson was always neat; he would never let his place get so shabby,* I thought. I wonder if someone else had taken over the pharmacy. I hoped they hadn't changed anything, especially the soda fountain. On hot days in camp, I would yearn to order a cool, frothy root beer float at the counter.

As I had done so many times as a child, I pushed open the tall door and stepped over the well-worn threshold onto the wooden floor deeply grooved by countless customers. A few feet from the entry, a dusty oak display case divided traffic to the right and left aisles.

I headed to the right, hoping the soda fountain with the red leather and chrome stools was there. Only three stools remained. *I could have sworn there were more.* Years before the war, I had stood on tiptoes to reach the counter, but now I was tall enough to see my reflection in the mirror behind the dessert glasses and milk shake makers. .

Next to the soda fountain toward the back of the store, a cluttered counter still advertised Carter's Little Liver Pills, Ex-Lax, and Sloan's Liniment, along with film, gum, and cigarettes. On the back wall, the display of trusses, corsets, canes, and crutches stood exactly the same as it had years ago. In Minidoka, the camp stores were never kept so well-stocked. When we were sick, we would head to the canteen, which carried essentials like soap, shampoo, and sanitary supplies but not, to my disappointment, Germol throat gargle and Mentholatum, both effective treatments for colds.

As I stood there remembering the times we had sought Mr. Watson's cure-alls and homespun advice for bad coughs, stomach flus, and other maladies, he appeared from the back, grinning widely. He seemed older, more stooped, but the snowy ruff around his bald pate and his rimless glasses were unchanged. He wore the same crisp white coat that reminded me of why we used to call him "Doc."

"Hello there," he said. "How are you?"

"Fine," I replied, not knowing what else to say. After a pause, I continued, "Your place seems smaller than before. Did you always have just three stools at the soda fountain?"

"Oh yes, nothing has changed. Take a look around," he said as he stepped from behind the counter to accompany me around the store. "You've grown up to be quite a young lady," he said.

"I'm almost five feet," I responded quickly. "Guess I grew a few inches while I was gone." I felt awkward to have his attention on me and wanted to change the subject. "Oh, you don't have my favorite dot candy anymore!" I said. As we proceeded down the aisle past the candy counter, I noted that more than half the shelves were bare.

"No, with the shortage of sugar, we had to cut back on many different ones," he said. *Maybe that's why we didn't have much candy in the camp canteen,* I thought. "We still have Tootsie Rolls and Licorice Twists, though," he said.

The front magazine rack was now almost empty. I made a confession: "Did you know that my brothers George and Tom would stand at the rack and read all the new comics every month, then buy only one comic book for ten cents?" Doc smiled as if he already knew.

We had reached the front door, and I couldn't think of anything more to say. "Well, goodbye, Mr. Watson."

"Goodbye, young lady," he replied. "Nice to see you again."

I pushed the door open, and as I reemerged into the blinding sunlight, I realized that we had never talked about the reason for my long absence. Doc Watson, always a gentleman, probably didn't want to broach the prickly subject of our forced removal into concentration camps, and I, an awkward teenager, wouldn't be sure how to respond if he did ask about my experience. I was largely glad he hadn't asked, but a small part of me wished he had.

I hurried up Jefferson Street, past the plain, beige apartment building where Millie and Johnny lived. I was eager to visit my chum Joyce Chan and her parents, who rented a modest frame house next door.

Where is the screen door? I wondered. I retraced my steps three times before I realized that their small house had vanished. Only two cement steps marked the place where they had lived. *Oh my god. They're gone. Why was their house torn down? Where did they go?* I asked myself, filled with disappointment. *I wonder if I'll ever see Joyce again.*

Still thinking about my friend, I finally caught sight of my old home. *It's still here.* My pulse raced as I continued up the hill on Jefferson Street. My eyes ran along the side basement windows of the apartments where Joe Mujoe, short-leg Johnny, and Daisy Hyland lived. *They'll be surprised to see me. I'll visit them after I check out the lobby,* I told myself. The last window, half the size of the others, seemed much too small to funnel the truckloads of sawdust that fueled the voracious furnace.

Close to the corner of Sixth Avenue and Jefferson Street, I spotted the ivy climbing up the walls of the University Club, across the street. It had barely reached the first-floor windows when I left, but now it covered half the side of the four-story building. The front door, almost hidden in vegetation, remained remote as ever.

Next door, the brick Ambassador Apartments building stood tall and respectable with its lions on pillars guarding the manicured courtyard entry. It looked the same.

Somewhat reassured that the war had not drastically changed my stomping grounds, I continued around to the front of the Angeles Apartments on Sixth Avenue. I caught my breath. Tape held together cracked windows, lace curtains hung in shreds, and layers of grime coated the three-story building my father had managed. *This is awful. Papa would never have let this happen. He would have kept the building clean and painted, with the broken window replaced and the curtains in good repair.* I felt let down, then angry. *That woman who bought the business didn't do anything. She let everything become run-down.*

I approached the first two entry doors that served half the building; they were padlocked. Troubled, I proceeded to the lobby entrance on the other side. At least the heavy oak door with the beveled-glass window was still there. Even with the shirred curtains gone and some letters missing from "Angeles Apartments," the aged door seemed like an old friend. I ran my fingers over the golden patina, then pressed the latch. It refused to move. *What's going on? Why are all the doors locked?*

I peered through the bare window into the lobby. Straight ahead, a large rectangular outline marked the place where the gilded mirror once hung. Smudges and nicks on the other walls hinted at the ebony bench, oak library table, and tall, double-rack hat stand that had once filled the room. Now, only an unfamiliar kitchen chair with a broken rung occupied a corner. For a moment, I saw Papa on hands and knees before the war, hammering a dowel into the legs of a wobbly chair to stabilize it. *Where's all the furniture? Where did it go?* A sinking sensation hit my stomach. *That woman took it!*

Finally, it dawned on me. *The place was bare. No furniture. No people. Nothing.* The hair on the back of my neck rose. It felt as if a close friend or relative had died, and something beloved had been taken away, leaving only the empty coffin.

What happened to everyone? Where did they go? Why did they move out? I wondered spitefully if the landlady had done such a rotten job that the place had been condemned.

Unanswered questions whirled in my mind as I halfheartedly completed my tour at the rear of the structure. How many times the feet of my brothers and myself had rattled across the weathered porch and down the back stairs on our way to Doc Watson's drugstore, Joyce Chan's house, or to play follow the leader across the billboard catwalk two stories above the ground. The narrow entry to the U-shaped courtyard brought back memories of my staged productions, for which I used a sheet as a curtain and charged admission to naïve younger children. Despite my sadness, I couldn't resist a chuckle.

As I took one last look around the Angeles Apartments, I felt puzzled and resentful. I had returned to the old neighborhood full of anticipation, expecting to see my friends and visit the home of my childhood. Instead,

A demolition permit for the Angeles Apartments, Portland, Oregon, September 1952. Courtesy of the Building Records Resource Center, Portland, OR.

the Angeles was abandoned, Joyce's home was leveled, and except for Doc Watson, no one was there.

Over the next few years, a strange mixture of dread and fascination churned inside me as I passed near the area. At times, I walked blocks out of my way to avoid witnessing the destruction of all that was once so familiar. Other times, I was morbidly curious to learn what was happening in the present.

Like an old soldier, the Angeles Apartments stood erect for another year while buildings all around it were demolished. Then, one day in the autumn of 1952, it was a pile of rubble. About two years after my visit, Doc's lease expired and he vacated the building. I couldn't watch the wrecking ball crush the old drugstore. One at a time, the remaining structures on the block collapsed under the relentless destroyer until the landscape resembled a bombed-out war zone.

Although I don't know the exact year the block was finally leveled, I do know it was before I left Portland in 1962. I expected to see new buildings spring up immediately, but it took more than twenty-five years before steel girders outlined new structures. "Guess they'll build only office buildings because they tore down all the houses and apartment buildings," I said to Tom as we passed the barren landscape. "I don't think they want people living here."

When the twenty-nine-story skyscraper, named Pacwest Center and occupying the entire block, was finally erected in 1988, I was proven wrong. Floor upon floor of sleek steel-and-glass condominiums were stacked above first-floor shops and offices that had replaced the small houses, the two- to three-story housing units, and the Angeles Apartments.

Across the street, the Ambassador Apartments, retaining its groomed shrubs, was converted to upscale condominiums, and the University Club received Historic Landmark status. These two neighbors will never see the wrecking ball; younger generations will enjoy their history and charm for years to come. But the place that had been my beloved home before our forced removal…it is gone. Not a trace remains. Not the soda fountain counter where I sipped root beer floats and watched Doc Watson dispense his homespun remedies. Not the footsteps my brothers and I made running up and down the back stairway. Not the table and chairs Papa repaired with hammer and nails. The three-story building that was once my refuge and playground exists only in memories.

BREATH

She was dying. She was lying comfortably in her own bed at home surrounded by her family. Over the past month her legs had weakened and

The University Club of Portland, listed on the National Register of Historic Places, remains in the neighborhood. Photo taken in Portland, Oregon, 2009.

no longer supported her, and eating solids had become an act we measured in bites. She talked less and seemed to be withdrawing into a sleep where she breathed comfortably. At almost ninety-nine years old, my best friend Kim's mother-in-law was worn out and ready to leave. The family and I had hoped to celebrate her one hundredth birthday, but that wish felt selfish in light of her suffering.

In early August 1988, I wanted both to let her go and to make her stay. If she could hang on, live long enough, she would be eligible for the redress and reparations promised to us by the government. The legislation clearly stated that only the formerly incarcerated individuals alive on the date when the bill became law would receive the twenty thousand dollars and an official apology from the president. More than forty-six years had passed since the unjust confinement had occurred, and about half of the affected Issei, including this dying woman's husband, were gone. Every day we were losing more of our aging parents' generation. She was among the ones who sacrificed and suffered the most and should receive compensation, but too many of the Issei would die before they could collect their rightful restitution. For Grandma Takeda it was a race against the snail-paced congressional process to get President Reagan's signature on the bill. The legislation had passed both houses of Congress and was now wending its way to the president's desk.

We listened intently to the television news and read the paper every day with disappointment. August 5, 1988, and still no news that the bill had been signed. She was slipping away. She no longer took food, and she drank only small quantities of water served through a straw to moisten her parched lips. Mostly she slept, her breathing soft and regular.

"Grandma, it's Hannah, it's me," her favorite granddaughter greeted her, leaning close to her best ear. "*Mah, mah,* Hanna-chan," Grandma Takeda would always respond, smiling broadly whenever Hannah visited. But today her eyes opened to our faces unfocused, the world in a haze. Soon they closed. Her vision, like her energy for words, was nearly gone.

Grandma, hang in there, I thought to myself, my guilt rising up again, my mixed feelings blurring what outcome would be best. To say out loud that I hoped she would live long enough to receive her compensation seemed inappropriate, too self-serving. Yet Grandma, with her husband and four of her five children, had been forcefully uprooted and placed in Minidoka concentration camp during the war, and in the process, they had lost their restaurant business and home. Kim related to me that just as they were leaving for camp, Grandma's oldest son, Abe, who would later marry Kim, enlisted in the army and served with the 442nd infantry regiment. "When Grandma heard of the battalion's fierce battles in Italy and France, her *ojuzu* (Buddhist prayer beads) became a constant companion," Kim reflected. Abe returned alive but scarred with shrapnel wounds that earned him two Purple Hearts and a Bronze Star. Grandma Takeda received no government payment for sending her son to battle, but she most assuredly deserved the reparation for the loss and suffering caused by her family's three and a half years of forced exile.

The days dragged on. *What was keeping the bill from being signed?* I wondered. August 8 came around. *A perfect day to sign the legislation,* I thought. Everyone would remember 8/8/88, but again, no word from Washington. Grandma was now unconscious. Her breaths came at longer intervals.

August 9. Rumors circulated that the signing ceremony was imminent, but by the end of the day, it hadn't occurred. I paced the room. Grandma's breathing became irregular. Sometimes it stopped, and those of us in attendance thought that the end had come. Then, with a deep inhalation, she would begin to breathe again. It was as if she knew she had unfinished business to complete. She was holding on—but barely.

August 10. The telephone rang. Kim heard the news on the radio. The bill was signed. I felt relieved. The legislation was law at last. Grandma's breathing was more like sighing now. Her face was peaceful.

The following morning, on August 11, 1988, Grandma took her last breath.

President Ronald Reagan signs the Redress Act on August 10, 1988. Courtesy of the National Archives, Washington, D.C.

Manabe family, c. 1940. Back row: Mama, Papa, Fumi. Front row: Grace Keiko, Sam Kiyoshi, May Yoshiko.

In 1926, Fumi Manabe was born to Salvation Army Captains Takeji and Chitose Manabe in Oakland, California. The family moved to Berkeley and soon after became members of the Christian Layman Church. Fumi entered kindergarten speaking little English.

From April 1942 to December 1944, Fumi and her family were incarcerated at the Tanforan Racetrack Assembly Center, just south of San Francisco, and then at the Central Utah Relocation Center, known as Topaz. During Christmas of 1944, Fumi and her younger sister, Grace, took student leaves from Topaz to attend two different schools in St. Louis, Missouri. Not until 1946 did Fumi rejoin her family in Berkeley.

In 1947, Fumi married Tad Hayashi, whom she had met at Tanforan after he had fulfilled his tour of duty in Japan with the United States' intelligence unit under General MacArthur. Together they raised three children in Berkeley and were active with various community groups. Fumi has enjoyed her retirement years visiting with family and friends as well as participating in quilting, writing, and other activities at the Japanese American Services of the East Bay Senior Center.

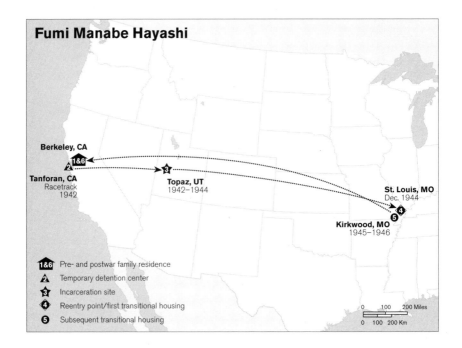

Fumi Manabe Hayashi

Berkeley, CA

Tanforan, CA
Racetrack
1942

Topaz, UT
1942–1944

St. Louis, MO
Dec. 1944

Kirkwood, MO
1945–1946

1&6	Pre- and postwar family residence
A	Temporary detention center
3	Incarceration site
4	Reentry point/first transitional housing
5	Subsequent transitional housing

0 100 200 Miles
0 100 200 Km

LEAVING TOPAZ

In June 1944 I graduated from Topaz High School, an institution that was part of the Central Utah Relocation Center located in the Great Basin Desert. We called our Relocation Center "Topaz, the Jewel of the Desert." The days were dry and windy, and the ground had little vegetation, the weather ranging from very hot to very cold. Our school consisted of picnic tables and benches. We had no labs, no reference books, and only a few textbooks. Fortunately we students could participate in any activity we chose. We could run for student government, play any sport, or join social clubs. We published our own newspapers and yearbooks, and we staged plays. Later, I found out that a group of the older kids had spent time scheduling sports events and organizing games for us younger students.

At Berkeley High School, my former school, members of sororities and fraternities ran the student body; students who lived in the wealthy, exclusive "hills" areas voted each other into committees and offices. In Topaz, however, we were all members of Japanese immigrant families who had been denied the privileges of citizenship, home ownership, and most job opportunities. Before our incarceration, most of us lived in small areas confined by real estate covenants or on truck farms. Paradoxically, in Topaz we were "free and equal" despite our enforced confinement.

Racial discrimination was everywhere outside of camp. For instance, in the 1940s Berkeley High allowed only one black player at a time on its basketball team. One student was so good that he later played in the NBA, but because he would have been the second black player on the Berkeley High Varsity team, he wasn't allowed to play for them. He did, however, play with two Nisei from Berkeley High on an intramural three-man team; they won all of their games. In Topaz, our basketball team members were shorter than members of the neighboring high school teams, but our Topaz team played harder and won most of its games.

After almost three years of imprisonment, life in Topaz and at Topaz High settled into a steady, predictable, and boring routine. Many students would just "hang out" instead of focusing on school. Often we would not complete our homework because we found it difficult to study in our one-room homes, but mostly we just did not care enough to do our best. We would get up in the morning, straighten the bed, get dressed, go to the latrine, do our stuff, go to the mess hall. We were never hungry, but we had long ago learned not to expect anything special at mealtime.

Christmas dinner shared at the Block 22 Mess Hall at Topaz, 1944. The Yuto family is seated in front, with the Hayashi family, near the post, at the table behind.

Tad, my "steady," would come by my barrack "apartment" and walk me to school. We would pass by guards with rifles behind barbed wire fences, but after a while I didn't even notice the guards anymore. I can't remember the face of a single guard, and I never talked with one. The guard towers were small—perhaps a five-foot-square platform—roofed, but open to the weather. The guards could walk around and around in that small tower, but they had to watch us. I know they couldn't talk to each other; they were posted too far apart. We believed that our guards were poorly educated recruits who didn't qualify for more sophisticated duty elsewhere. They must have been terribly bored, trying to break the monotony by pacing in their cramped spaces.

One day Mr. Wakasa was shot and killed while he was walking his dog within the perimeter of the camp. There had been at least ten shootings at us prisoners prior to this killing. Mr. Wakasa had been a very quiet bachelor with no known family to speak of. Had he left behind angry parents, a weeping widow, or a stunned family, the outcry after his death would have been far, far worse. Before the incident, we had thought the guards were less threatening, as there had been shootings but no actual killings. We didn't feel like the guards or fences were such a big deal—both were just always there. Previously, many of us had enjoyed collecting arrowheads, trilobites, rocks, and other fossils near the edge of the camp, but the killing of Mr. Wakasa made us more aware of our vulnerability.

Many years after we left Topaz, my friend Sumi, a junior high student while in camp, told me, "Mr. Wakasa was shot near my block." Her mother warned her, "Don't go out on that road. A man has been shot." Sumi told me, "Of course, I had to go out and see for myself," and when she did, she saw a man lying dead on the ground.

Not long after this shooting, a group of boys from my class snuck out of camp to look for Lake Sevier, which we had heard was nearby. They crawled under the barbed wire, only coming back late at night to find their families and friends huddled next to the shadows of the barracks, waiting and praying for their safe return. Sumi's brother was one of the boys out in the desert. Sumi, her mother, and most of the residents of that block hid quietly, not wanting to attract the attention of the sentry on duty. "Be very quiet and don't let the guards see or hear you," her mother warned. "We don't want them to find out that the boys left camp." When the boys finally returned, they said it was, "no big deal," but I think they enjoyed the attention and notoriety of their exciting and risky trip.

But such adventures were rare. Mostly we just went to school. Our Topaz High classes were very simple. We studied English and history, and our science classes were lectures without books or labs. My fun class at Topaz High was cooking. I used a huge wood-burning stove and learned practical things, like if you could hold your arm in the oven for a count of three before moving it away, the temperature was close to 350 degrees and hot enough for most roasting and baking.

Sometimes we had parties at school, but they were never elaborate. One special lunch consisted of potato salad, and our "party drink" was diluted grape jelly with a touch of lemon, if we could find one.

Many students, however, were demoralized. "Waste time." "Why study?" "Waste time." We heard the cry "waste time" over and over again. Our schooling was often disrupted, since many of the teachers, who were also camp residents, had to leave the school when they were relocated. To fill in the gaps, several high school students (including me) taught in the elementary and junior high schools, and it wasn't easy. When I taught a music class at the junior high, the students would not pay any attention to me. I had studied piano for ten years and had sung in various choirs, but I couldn't control or teach these students. I only knew that the former teacher had left Topaz and that the students needed someone to oversee their required classwork and to give them credit and grades. I was not paid for my efforts, and no school administrator ever tried to help me with lesson plans or give me suggestions on how to teach this group of students. We all—students and teacher— suffered from this haphazard arrangement.

Back in Berkeley in 1931, I had enrolled in kindergarten speaking very little English, and school was very difficult for me. My mother was told, "Your daughter will never qualify for high school graduation," and yet here I was, in 1944, in a makeshift school in the Great Basin desert, finally graduating from high school. My parents still worried about my future, though. What value would a diploma from Topaz High have? Would I ever qualify for a job? They wanted me to leave camp and attend an accredited school outside.

In 1944, we still did not know what plans the government had for us. How long would we be kept under guard? Would our Issei parents ever be allowed to return to California? We certainly never considered going to Japan. Large universities with military students would not accept Japanese American applicants, and most large industries would not hire Nisei.

I wanted to stay in Topaz because I had become very comfortable there. The "outside" seemed scary. We wouldn't have family or friends there, and who knew how we would be accepted. In contrast, I had lots of friends in Topaz. I went to parties on weekends, I enjoyed church and camp activities, and I had been granted visits to Salt Lake City and Provo, in northern Utah, and to Wichita, Kansas.

I had more and closer friends in Topaz than I ever had in Berkeley. Everybody was nice to me. No one scolded, yelled at, or hurt any of us. We could go to the latrine during the night or come home after dark, and we did not worry about personal attacks. But I also believed that we could not continue to stay locked up forever and that we would eventually have to make our way in the outside world. We would no longer have to live our lives out of Sears catalogs; if we wanted to buy shoes we could go to the store and try them on first. We would also have to find real jobs to make the money to buy them.

I cried as I left Topaz. Topaz had become our home.

THE BANK BOOK

Before World War II, we had several distinct banking systems at our home. My dad had a regular Bank of America checking account, and I can recall him sitting at his desk writing checks—checking and rechecking his balances on little pieces of paper. He would sometimes sigh and shake his head a little, but he never denied us anything that we might need for school. Class trips, special projects, piano lessons—he funded them all.

Mama had a *he so kuri* account. Just as many women today create private "nest egg" savings, Mama also carefully hoarded and saved money from her household accounts. After I became an adult, she told me stories about this special account: "In Japan," Mama told me, "women stashed money in belts tied around their midsections—*he so* (belly button) *kuri* (around)." To Mama, the *he so kuri* account was secret and very special, and only she decided how the funds would be spent.

When we were younger, she told us many stories of her own childhood, usually after dinner while we did the dishes. One of us would clear the table, Mama usually washed, another would dry, and the last person would sort everything and put it away. Mama had grown up during a depression in Japan, and I often wondered if she regretted leaving her own mother behind to seek better opportunities in America. "No," Mama told us, "I wanted to come to America." Here, her *he so kuri* was an investment in her hopes and dreams for us. She had created a good life here, and as children we never really understood the hunger mother had experienced when she was young. Knowing I hated eggs and refused to eat them, Mama said, "Once I was really hungry and wanted an egg for lunch. I begged and begged my sister to fix an egg for me." Finally, Mama's *nesan* (oldest sister) shaped some starch and added a yellow center. "She had made an egg for me." Mama continued, "I never again complained about the food that was served to me."

Because we were short on money in Berkeley, we often moved from one rental house to another, sometimes to a larger house or better location but most often to something more reasonably priced. Wanting very much to buy a house of our own, Mama kept her ears and eyes open, and then, in the mid-1930s, she heard that neighbors on our block wanted to sell their house, 1616 Russell Street. "I found a very good house for us to buy and it's very close," Mama said excitedly. "Let's go see it now."

At the time, the house was a wonderful buy—an older, large home sitting on a double lot. The brown redwood-shingle house, wearing its many years proudly, seemed to be waiting just for us. The upstairs floor contained three bedrooms and a small bathroom. A dining room, living room, and very large kitchen filled the downstairs. A large washroom and bathroom completed the lower floor, which had an attached garage with a very large room over it.

When 1616 Russell finally became available to us, only Japanese who were born in the United States and were of legal age could buy property. Papa and Mama and all other Japanese immigrants were being denied U.S. citizenship and thereby home ownership. Only years later, in 1947, would the Supreme Court overrule California's Alien Land Laws, and the Issei would not become eligible for U.S. citizenship for another handful of years, in 1952. Nonetheless, we wanted 1616 Russell. Mama and Papa worked out a plan with the next-door neighbor's children, who were American-born citizens and had reached the legal age of twenty-one. They "bought" the house for us, but Papa made all of the payments; when I reached twenty-one years of age, the house would be deeded to me. Mama's *he so kuri* account provided the down payment. We purchased 1616 in the late 1930s.

Once we moved in, the room above the garage made a perfect study for Papa, who owned many books and seemed to enjoy the ritual of reading aloud to himself. This habit had started when he was very young and attended a small country school in a remote area of Shikoku, Japan. "I can hear your father singing," my friends often said when we heard him preparing the sermons and religious commentaries he gave at church. He only did this when he was reading Japanese; when he read English, he did it quietly to himself.

As we all settled in to our new house, I looked forward to bank days at school, when we would learn about saving for the future. Mama always made sure that we had our dimes and quarters ready to take to school on Tuesdays. We students would bring our coins, and the teachers would help us fill out forms and bank our money. Bank days allowed us to create our own special savings; I felt proud to hand over my money and have it entered into my very own bank account and bank book. These three banking systems—Mama's, Papa's, and mine—worked just fine.

After World War II broke out, my parents, both Issei, faced many rules and restrictions. They had to be at home by eight o'clock every day; they could not travel outside of a five-mile perimeter; they could not have cameras or radios; their bank accounts were frozen. Yet my little school bank day account was an *all-American* account, owned by an American citizen—me— and it was available for use by the whole family. I felt even prouder. We took my little brown passbook with us to Tanforan, and later to the Topaz concentration camp in Utah.

When my sister Grace and I left Topaz for school in St. Louis, my mother gave me the book. I knew that I could spend that money, but I kept it for any emergency that might arise. We had lived under a dark cloud of uncertainty since Pearl Harbor, so who knew when or what kind of new ruling would be issued against us, even after we left camp?

In St. Louis, we didn't feel like a part of any group, nor did we feel like true members of our neighborhood. We didn't know who or what we were. Whereas in Berkeley I knew all my neighbors, in St. Louis I didn't know a single neighbor or shopkeeper. Tad, my friend from Tanforan, who was attending the U.S. government's military intelligence school in Minneapolis, came to visit me twice in St. Louis, but he never really entered the house where I worked as a maid. He took me out and then returned with me, but he never stepped beyond the front door. None of my schoolmates ever called on me while I lived in St. Louis. Although one schoolmate saw me off when I left for Berkeley in 1946, I never felt I was a part of St. Louis.

Being separated from our family added to the feelings of isolation my sister and I experienced. We had "resettled" in St. Louis, where we were no longer eligible for any help from the WRA, and we were out of regular contact with the rest of our family. "I hired myself out to a farmer in Idaho to earn money for the family," my father told me years later. "The owner of the farm never let me leave or use a phone," he emphasized, so we understood why he couldn't communicate with us or others during that time.

Finally, one year Papa borrowed five hundred dollars from a bachelor friend. The debt loomed large, since his monthly salary in Topaz was only sixteen dollars, but Papa told me, "I needed to have enough for train tickets for your sister, you, and me." To my surprise and delight, one day my father showed up in St. Louis and told us he had saved enough to take Grace home to California with him. My mother, my other younger sister, and my brother had already returned to Berkeley from Topaz, but I still had school to complete in St. Louis and so stayed on for a few more months. In 1946, I was relieved to join the rest of my family in Berkeley.

After the war, I knew that my bank account held less than two hundred dollars, but it was still my ace in the hole. Even in St. Louis I had been haunted by constant feelings of uncertainty and the threat of more restrictions or further confinement. Then, the war was over. Topaz closed. All of us who had been imprisoned were now released. No more guards, no more fences, no more rules. We had been forced into prison camps in May of 1942, and in mid-1945 we were "set free" to restart our lives with a twenty-five-dollar stipend from the government. I was glad to have my bank account.

Everyone in our family had made it back. At last, we were all back together in our home, 1616 Russell Street. Mama managed our household accounts, Papa worked long hours at gardening jobs and at our church. We worked hard to rebuild our lives. While I was grateful for the comfort my grade school bank book had given me over the years, I was also thankful that I no longer needed it to be my talisman.

1616 RUSSELL STREET

Our home on Russell Street in Berkeley was an old but large and friendly house sitting on a double lot. A two-story home with a high roofline, it towered over the neighboring bungalows. Mr. Groespeck, a Christian worker from a nearby church, looked after our house during the time we were locked up at Topaz. He found a family to rent the house, collected the rent each month, paid the mortgage, and saved our home for our return. We did not know Mr. Groespeck well, but I later heard from a neighbor that he died in the Philippines while working there.

After our return from camp, our house wasn't in perfect condition, and our Berkeley neighbors told us what had happened while we were gone: "The original renters sub-rented your house to many workers who had come out of the South for jobs at the Richmond Kaiser Shipyards. Several families squeezed into the house at one time. Many people drifted in and out of 1616." As a result, the house suffered much damage. Papa had built a storage area in the basement for some of his tools, and that area had been trashed. The garden was trampled and overgrown. Paint and wallpaper were peeling.

Despite our upset over the damage, though, we felt truly fortunate. We had a house waiting for us; most of those released from the camps had no shelter. Some families lived in churches and slept on the floor. Even while still in camp we had wondered, *Who would rent to us Japanese? And how could we find jobs?* Three and a half years of living on a sixteen-dollars-per-month salary meant that most of us returned to California in debt and with little or no savings. When we were first ordered to leave Berkeley for camp, we had to get rid of most of our possessions, taking only what we could carry. Upon our release, we had little more than that with which to start our new lives.

My father, however, would do any kind of work to help make life better for us after the war. He worked as a gardener, sold plant cuttings, fixed plumbing, and still prepared sermons for Sunday services. As we and other families tried to resettle, many of us junior high and senior high students also helped our families by earning our room and board through cleaning houses, babysitting, gardening, or working as "schoolboys" or "schoolgirls" (domestic servants). While attending classes in St. Louis I had been a schoolgirl to earn my room and board. I felt like an unwanted second-class member of that family; I never ate with them but in the kitchen by myself.

Back in Berkeley after the war, we did what we could to help those in our community. Our former next-door neighbors, the ones who had helped us purchase 1616, lived in the room over our garage until they were able to find a place of their own, and we were happy to be able to return the kindness they had shown us earlier. One member of our church stayed in our living room. A proper gentleman who was always dressed in a shirt, tie, and jacket, he had never so much as boiled water or served himself tea, and he always came to the breakfast table dressed properly, sitting there until he was served. Although he was a great pain, he had no place else to go—he had been a literary writer and could not find work. Eleven to thirteen people at a time shared our one bathroom at 1616, but after having lived in Topaz, where some fifty folks shared a single bathtub, we managed just fine.

Many families were fortunate to qualify for rentals in housing projects built for dependents of those serving in the Armed Forces. My friend Tad's family moved into the Cordonices Housing Project; three of their sons were currently servicemen. Tad was under General MacArthur in Japan, Paul was with Counterintelligence in Hokkaido, and James was serving in the army stateside.

The war had scattered everyone I knew, and back in Topaz I had spent many hours trying to imagine what my former Berkeley classmates and neighborhood friends were doing. Where were they all? Had they gone away to college somewhere? I recalled that most of the girls in Berkeley wore white shirts, pastel sweaters, and saddle shoes, and I knew they were not wearing the pants and mackinaws, left over from World War I, that we were wearing in Topaz. Yet when I finally returned to Berkeley, I did not seek out any of my old friends. I could not imagine facing them again and trying to fit back into their world.

When I look back at Spring 1942, at leaving 1616 and Berkeley High, I wonder *Did anyone miss us?* At school, no one had said goodbye or even "See you later." We turned in our textbooks and even our homework. But did we think that we would be gone for a few weeks, possibly a few months? Some thought we might go to farms to help produce food for the war effort. But for how long? Where? Why? Eight thousand people locked up within one square mile? No way. Guards? Rifles? Who could imagine such a thing? I was determined to leave Berkeley High with my head held high. I would not let anyone see my tears or note my confusion and sorrow at being suspected of disloyalty or treason. Now when I think about those days, tears fill my eyes.

The Berkeley policemen who fingerprinted and registered us were kind and helpful. Ladies at a local church who drove us to the point of embarkation for Tanforan served us coffee and rolls. Soldiers stood tall and still as they guarded us, their rifles ready. Or maybe they were guarding the church. Our neighbor friends had come to our house and had stood in a semicircle around us as we left 1616. We exchanged sad looks but no words.

In 1946, we were all finally back in Berkeley again. 1616 welcomed us all home, and now it was full of activity. By the end of that year, Tad had returned from the occupation of Japan, I had finished my training in St. Louis, and my younger siblings were enrolled in their Berkeley schools. (Eventually, my sister Grace, who had gone to St. Louis with me, would graduate from the University of California, San Francisco, as a public health nurse, and my other sister, May, would earn her master's degree and become a math and science teacher. My brother Sam, the youngest, later worked as a research engineer.) Meanwhile, 1616 still stood majestically, although its brown shingles were tired and worn. Some windows were stuck shut and the roof leaked. It had sheltered many families, and now it was our turn again in 1946. The Berkeley fog was cold, and we tried to stay warm even within our house, yet we were overjoyed to be in our own home again, living in our beloved city among friends who were familiar to us.

Papa and Mama still worried about their families in Japan, though. Our relatives in Tokyo and Kobe suffered through incendiary bombings, food shortages, and lack of hope, and we tried to help out in any way we could. Papa and Mama bought clothes at secondhand stores, cleaned and repaired them, and sent boxes of clothing and dried food to Japan. It was a nightly ritual to pack these boxes. We mailed dried soups, candy bars, saccharine tablets, fruit, and fish.

Mama and Papa worked extra hours to not only support us and help our relatives but also to restore our church. It had suffered during our absence and needed extensive repairs. Our church was old, the Sunday school rooms dark and dingy. It needed our care. The community came together and built a chapel from the bottom up, painting it and putting in stained-glass windows.

When we finished, I stood and looked at our accomplishment. Those years were very busy, but we bustled with happiness and satisfaction.

In 1947, Tad and I were married in the front parlor of my family's home, and we left 1616 to start our new life together. The resettlement of the Berkeley Takeji Manabe family was off to a glorious start.

Fumi and Tad Hayashi on the steps of 1616 Russell Street. Berkeley, California, c. 1946.

TRILOBITE

I met Sherman Thomson while he was a graduate student at the University of California in Berkeley. After he was awarded his Ph.D. in plant pathology, he returned to his home in Utah, and on one of his trips as an agricultural extensionist to the south-central part of the state, he came upon what remained of the Central Utah Relocation Center, a place that we—imprisoned in the camp—chose to call "Topaz, the Jewel of the Desert." During the late 1970s, Thomson returned to Topaz with his older children to show them the site. While there, the family picked up a rusty toy knife, a broken jack, and a nicked marble. They mailed these to me.

I wanted to display these items with some rocks that I had found on recent trips to my former desert home, but I couldn't figure out quite how to arrange them. Place them in a dish or frame them? More than twenty five years later, I finally came up with a great idea for an arrangement: I placed the items inside a bowl along with two blue glass balls that had been part of a Japanese fishing net, which to me represented my parents' long journey across the vast Pacific to the United States. They had come seeking peace and fulfillment in their new homeland. The rusty toys from Topaz symbolized the time of our imprisonment in Utah, and to those I also added a few small succulent plants. I watered the plants carefully, one or two teaspoons per week. I was pleased with my handiwork.

As I looked at my arrangement, I remembered how rock collecting had been a favorite hobby of many in Topaz. Some had a strong need to leave the one square mile of housing enclosed in barbed wire and to walk about freely, even in the inhospitable desert, and it was possible to apply for and receive a single day's leave from the guarded, fenced area. Local rock hounds found interesting rocks and even some evidence of other people who had lived in this very same area, perhaps as long as fourteen thousand years ago. Collectors searched among the shale and found trilobite fossils that were some one hundred thousand years old. Trilobites can be found all over the world, but a good concentration of these fossils was unearthed at Antelope Springs, an area near our former camp. Some camp prisoners polished and made beautiful objects using trilobites, and their artistic works were displayed at our festivals in Topaz.

In the spring of 1993, over three hundred former Topaz residents returned to Utah to visit our wartime home. I met Joe, another former inmate who had lived in the block next to me but whom I didn't remember. As we searched for the outlines of our old barracks, Joe said, "I really enjoyed hiking out in that desert. An experienced Issei hiker taught me to always bring a jug of water, a long pole, and a flag with us. We would hike as far as we could go and still see Topaz. We would dig a hole, bury the water, plant the flag, and hike until we could barely see our flag. Then we knew we had to turn around and return to camp. We found beautiful rocks and fossils. On one hike, we found an Indian grinding stone and pestle. It was too heavy to carry back to camp. We carefully noted where we had left the grading stone."

While riding around the site during the 1993 reunion, Joe was confident that he would be able to find his treasure again. But the landmarks of the camp had weathered or disappeared, and sadly, Joe realized that he could never orient himself well enough to find his grinding stone again.

Unlike Joe, I was never one for hiking and I considered walking around for miles in the hot sun to be a type of punishment, but I still would have liked to have found an arrowhead or a fossil or a bright, shiny topaz. I did find an interesting bone during a short walk in the desert once, and I took good care of it. It "relocated" to St. Louis with me, and after bringing it home to Berkeley, I took it to the University of California for an analysis. I found out that my treasure was not even a bone, as I had thought, but just some kind of a sandy rock formation. But I still haven't thrown my "treasure" away.

One of my other beloved artifacts was a trilobite fossil given to me by Jane Beckwith, president of the Topaz Museum. It was one and a half inches wide by two inches long and two inches thick, still encased in rock. I added it to my arrangement of camp memorabilia.

When Jane was a youngster growing up in Delta, Utah, her father often took her and her sisters to look for fossils. In the early 1980s, Jane, then an English teacher at Delta High School, encouraged her students to research whatever they could find about Topaz, which was nearby. They soon learned that very little written information existed in their local libraries. To remedy the situation, Jane and her students began extensive interviews of those who had had any dealings with Topaz and found out that the old barracks had been renovated—primarily into homes. They heard many stories—some amusing, some sad, and many angry. There were townsfolk who were compassionate and others who disliked and distrusted us Japanese.

Jane entered her class's finished project in a national history contest, and Delta High School won a special prize for it. To help raise funds so the students could go to Washington, D.C., to see the capitol and receive their prize, the newspaper of the Japanese American Citizens League printed a short article on the project and requested donations. I saw the article and sent Jane some money. In 1983, she took her class to Washington.

Just before leaving for another visit to Topaz on June 29, 2007, I took a good long look at my arrangement of artifacts. I was looking at the trilobites and thinking of Jane, who had given them to me, when I suddenly noticed mud. *It can't be,* I thought. *Surely no one would put mud on my display.* At that moment, I was waiting to be picked up for a ride to the airport, where I would travel to Salt Lake City, and then on to Delta and finally Topaz, and I knew now was not the time to start a new project; I should wait and take care of everything on my return. My curiosity got the better of me, however, and I took a dampened Q-tip and swiped my trilobite. There it was: a whole Q-tip full of mud.

But the muddy trilobite fossil would have to wait. I met my friends and we flew to Salt Lake City. We took a leisurely tour of the city and Temple Square. The surroundings were beautiful and very clean, but the weather was hot at over 100 degrees. We dodged from one air-conditioned building to another. We greatly admired the Mormons, who had hauled huge slabs of granite from the mountains to build their temple; their culture, like ours, was marked by faith, hard work, and perseverance. After we attended a concert on the temple grounds, listening to music from the organ built by the Mormons, we drove to Topaz, to our old memories.

At the Salt Lake City airport. Fumi stands to the left of Jane Beckwith, who is speaking with Mrs. Hisayo Mori, wife of Nisei writer Toshio Mori.

Long ago, when I would tell my children about being confined in Topaz, I always ended my stories with an emphatic, "I'll be damned if I'll ever go back there again." My daughter pointed out, "But Mom, you've been back four times already." Although I still feel very uneasy when I'm at the actual campsite, I have enjoyed the town of Delta and have deep admiration for the Topaz Museum board and its president, Jane Beckwith. The town has always been hospitable when we have visited, and that time, in 2007, I was privileged to meet a Delta gentleman who as a young boy had helped start a Boy Scout troop in Topaz during the war. He'd spent several overnights in camp with his newfound friends, the Japanese American inmates. The Boy Scouts of America awarded him with special recognition for his efforts and spirit.

Jane's grandfather, Frank A. Beckwith, had enjoyed hiking and collecting in the desert surrounding Topaz, and from 1943 to 1945, while we were in Topaz, he wrote articles for the *Topaz Times* about his walks and finds. He found a species of trilobite that had never before been described or cataloged, and his discovery—which was named after him, *Beckwithia typa*—is now housed in the Smithsonian's National Museum of Natural History, in Washington, D.C. Jane arranged to have his trilobite on display for her students to see during their stay in Washington.

Jane has collected and saved many artifacts from Topaz, including some of the buildings. She has helped to preserve one half of a recreation hall, and she and her board have raised funds and purchased almost all of our former camp area. After much work, in the spring of 2007 the Topaz campsite received National Landmark designation. The governor of Utah and many dignitaries came to Topaz to commemorate our past, dedicate a plaque, and express the public's debt to and appreciation for Jane Beckwith's long, hard efforts. Indeed, Jane has inspired us and helped to preserve the legacy of our wrongful incarceration.

After the long weekend in Utah, I returned to Berkeley. I placed a large towel on my dining room table and took apart my arrangement. It seemed that my watering of the succulents had caused the rock of the trilobite fossil to disintegrate. Parts of the shale had come apart; the rock had become mud again. My large specimen from Jane broke in half, and at first I was devastated. Then, as I took the pieces of rock apart, I found more trilobites inside. One was an inch in length, and some were less than a quarter-inch long.

Here I am, I thought. *Safe and comfortable in my own Berkeley home, with the artifacts of my camp experience. I am over eight decades old. I have acquired more aches and pains these past few years, but I remain healthy and happy. I* think back and I realize that Topaz is still a large part of my life. As I sat in my dining room that day, I found that I was once again hunting for fossils, only not in the Utah desert, and this time using quilting needles for picks and magnifying glasses to help me see. And I was unearthing fossils from my past, long-buried trilobites, eight of them so far.

Threads of Remembrance, a quilt made for *Strength and Diversity: Japanese American Women, 1885–1990*, exhibited at the Oakland Museum of California and sponsored by the National Japanese American Historical Society, 1990. Photo by Sharon Risedorph. Courtesy of the National Japanese American Historical Society.

NAOKO YOSHIMURA ITO

Naoko Yoshimura Ito was born in 1926 and raised in San Francisco's Japantown, where her father owned the Hokubei Hotel. Her family was one of the last to be forcibly removed from San Francisco. From 1942 to 1945, they were incarcerated at the Heart Mountain Relocation Center, in Wyoming, where she graduated from Heart Mountain High School.

After the war, Naoko's family returned to the Hokubei Hotel. She later married Takeshi "Peter" Ito, and together they raised three children in Berkeley, California. In addition to being a mother, Naoko has worked as secretary for the Berkeley Unified School District.

Today, Naoko enjoys traveling and cooking, and she remains passionate about quilting. A founding member and a past president of the East Bay Heritage Quilters, she coordinated the first United States/Japan Quilt Symposium in Tokyo and Kyoto, Japan, in 1983; she remained coordinator of the event for four subsequent years. Her quilt work has been included in books and shows, and one of her quilts, "Letting Go," depicts her camp experience and was featured in a civil rights poster produced by the Southern Poverty Law Center.

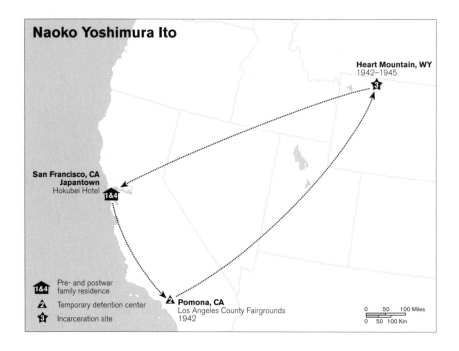

Naoko Yoshimura Ito

Heart Mountain, WY
1942–1945

San Francisco, CA
Japantown
Hokubei Hotel

Pre- and postwar
family residence

Temporary detention center

Incarceration site

Pomona, CA
Los Angeles County Fairgrounds
1942

0   50   100 Miles
0 50 100 Km

STITCHING

Author's note: In writing "Stitching," I am indebted to my brother, Akira Yoshimura, who told me this story, and to the memory of my mother and her resourcefulness. The piece is told from Akira's point of view.

I took up judo in camp but did not have a *gi* (judo uniform). Our family could not buy one during wartime because they were made in Japan and the stores in camp did not stock them. I really wanted a *gi*. Everyone else had one that they had bought before the war, when the uniforms could still be imported from Japan.

Mama came up with a solution. She cleverly gathered rice sacks, bleached them, and made me a *gi*, stitching it with recycled string. Mama had to sew rows and rows of stitching to reinforce the fabric, ensuring that it would not rip when an opponent grabbed it. It must have taken Mama hours and hours to push the needle threaded with thick string through the stiff, coarse rice sacking. She did not have a thimble, so I can imagine her fingers throbbing. I was ashamed that my uniform was homemade, with uneven stitching, but today I realize that Mama really loved me to be so thoughtful and resourceful, creating a judo uniform from rice sacks and string.

THREADS OF REMEMBRANCE

One day, Daisy Satoda, who was on the committee for an exhibit entitled *Strength and Diversity: Japanese American Women, 1885–1990,* looked at me with hopeful eyes and asked, "Can you coordinate making a quilt for this exhibit?" Anticipating my positive response, she explained that the exhibit was being sponsored by the National Japanese American Historical Society and would be held at the Oakland Museum of California from February 17 to May 13, 1990. Honored that she had asked me, I answered, "Yes, I'll do it!" and went to work.

I pored through the roster of my guild, the East Bay Heritage Quilters, and from the 750 members picked out all the quilters with Japanese surnames: Bess Kawachi Chin, Margene Fudenna, Dolores Hamaji, Ruth Hayashi, Jan Inouye, Julie Kataoka, Karen Matsumoto, Phyllis Mizuhara, Hazel Nakabayashi, Iku Noma, Alys Sakaji, Kay Sakanashi, Setsu Shimizu, Tami Tanabe, Yuri Uchiyama, and myself. Our group consisted of thirteen Nisei and three Sansei. We did not all know each other, but we all became enthusiastic participants and later would come to call ourselves "Threads."

Since some of us did not know the others, I thought a quilt show in Marin County would be the ideal place for us all to meet. After seeing the show, we had a picnic together and discussed the answers to this question:

Members of the Threads group at Ruth Hayashi's house for a short segment on Channel 5. Back row: Yuri Uchiyama, Dolores Hamaji, Phyllis Mizuhara, Ruth Hayashi. Front row: Margene Fudenna, Bess Kawachi Chin, Karen Matsumoto, Alys Sakaji, Naoko Ito, Setsu Shimizu, and Jan Inouye. Not pictured: Hazel Nakabayashi, Kay Sakanashi, Julie Kataoka, Tami Tanabe, and Iku Noma. Courtesy of Phyllis Mizuhara.

What kind of quilt do we want to create? Some of the participants were leery, feeling in typical Nisei fashion that their work might not be good enough for a major exhibit. At first, a kimono quilt was suggested, but we decided that was "corny." We wanted to make a quilt reflecting the experiences of our parents and ourselves.

We visited the National Japanese American Historical Society to look at old photographs and, after much discussion, selected the images we wanted to include in our quilt, which we named *Threads of Remembrance* (see p. 74). First, we thought it was important to portray the experience of "picture brides" who took a big risk in coming to America, an unknown place, for arranged marriages to men they barely knew. Second, we wanted to show the experience of farmers' wives who took care of their families, stoked the flames for the Japanese baths, and worked in the fields with the men they also cooked for. When we were sent to camp, it was the time for harvest, so many of the Issei and Nisei lost all their work for the year—the crops left behind at peak harvesting season. Third, we wanted to portray the children who were sent to camp and the mothers who could not protect them even though the children were United States citizens. Finally, we decided to include a "Gold Star Mother" holding the American flag that was given to the family of a soldier who died in World War II.

Jan Inouye designed a three-panel quilt like the Japanese *noren,* a divided curtain. The quilt depicts a crosssection of Issei, Nisei, and Sansei women, beginning with the earliest immigrants who landed in 1885 and continuing through to the present generation. We started the quilt in May 1989, and we were all quite excited about the project.

We, as quilt makers, became engrossed in telling the story of the women depicted in the quilt itself. We made the fans in the first panel from beautiful Japanese printed fabrics, which represented what the Issei brought from Japan. We appliquéd images of a picture bride, a farmer, a mother carrying a child, a child alone, and a Gold Star Mother. Setsu Shimizu chose to do the appliqué of the picture bride. Tami Tanabe, whose father was a farmer, appliquéd the farmwife and incorporated her own daughter's hair into the farmwife's bonnet; "I remember how hard my mother had worked, tending the children and cooking for the other farmworkers," Tami recalled. Bess Kawachi Chin sewed the mother carrying a child. Karen Matsumoto put her own mother's camp family identification number on the identification tag of the child on the quilt who was on her way to camp. Yuri Uchiyama wanted to sew the Gold Star Mother, since she had known many mothers in camp who had lost their sons during the war. In fact, one of my high

The Threads group works on a quilt in 1990 at the home of Setsu Shimizu. The group continued to meet annually for over ten years. Top: Setsu Shimizu, Kay Sakanashi, Phyllis Mizuhara, and Naoko Ito. Bottom: Phyllis Mizuhara, Alys Sakaji, Tami Tanabe, and Dolores Hamaji. Both photos courtesy of Phyllis Mizuhara.

school friends volunteered for the army from camp and died in Europe while fighting for his country.

The middle panel of the quilt represents the concentration camp experience. To make sure that all of the camps were represented, we created ten barracks and embroidered their names on the rooftops. They are: Granada (Amache), Colorado; Gila, Arizona; Jerome, Arkansas; Heart Mountain, Wyoming; Manzanar, California; Minidoka, Idaho; Poston, Arizona; Rohwer, Arkansas; Topaz, Utah; and Tule Lake, California. We appliquéd the barracks on gray pebbled fabric to represent the sandy earth that swirled around the camps. Using red thread and in the *sashiko* style (a traditional Japanese quilting/embroidery technique), we stitched the watchtower in the background as "a shadowy reminder that all of the camps were, after all, prisons" (*Nichi Bei Times,* San Francisco, February 15, 1990). The watchtower's guards (stationed to protect us, according to the government) are pointing their guns toward us—even though we are the ones imprisoned without just cause—and not away from us, outside the camp, for our safety. We knotted narrow strips of fabric to make the barbed wire that is laid throughout the quilt.

In the third panel, we created the Manzanar peace monument plus a Gold Star Mother holding an American flag. Many Gold Star Mothers lived in the camps even as their sons were killed defending the country that was incarcerating their families; they suffered to demonstrate their loyalty to America. The appliquéd women in the foreground, looking back in history, "are a multicultural chorus of Japanese American women: Issei, Nisei, Sansei, and Yonsei. They are silently observing their remarkable, but overlooked, contribution to the growth of America" (*Nichi Bei Times,* San Francisco, February 15, 1990).

After the quilt top was finished, we added batting and a fabric backing. Then we took it to various Issei and Nisei communities. The quilt traveled with the exhibit to many venues: Hawaii, Oregon, New York, Georgia, Kansas, and Canada. We had attendees at the community events sign a book so that our exhibit would be documented. The quilt received lots of newspaper coverage, as well as two stories on Channel 5/CBS with reporter Mike Hegedes, who wanted those beyond our community to learn about our imprisonment experience. We even took the quilt to Japan and got its photo and story published in the *Asahi Shinbun,* a Tokyo newspaper.

The widespread impact of this quilt is further evident in the personal responses it received. On our visit to the Japanese American National Museum in Los Angeles, we wanted as many of those once incarcerated as possible to take a symbolic stitch in the quilt. Issei women approached the quilt and looked for the barrack representing their camp. As they stroked the quilt, some of them with tears in their eyes, they urged, "Don't forget this incident ever."

Author's note: All the dates and information regarding this quilt are from the unofficial historian of the Threads group, Phyllis Mizuhara, who kept a scrapbook documenting all the events. The quilt is stored at the National Japanese American Historical Society in San Francisco.

Flo and Harry in 1946.

FLORENCE MIHO NAKAMURA

Florence Miho Nakamura was born in the South Park neighborhood of San Francisco on July 12, 1929. She was the youngest of Shime and Shizuko Miho's three daughters.

Florence lived in San Francisco up until her imprisonment, first at Tanforan Assembly Center, in San Bruno, California, and later at the Central Utah Relocation Center, in Topaz, Utah. She was eleven years old when she was taken to camp and sixteen years old by the time she returned to San Francisco. Florence and her husband of more than fifty years, Harry, resided in San Francisco together until Florence's passing in 2007.

Florence is survived by two grown children, Sharen and Scott. Florence called her five grandchildren the "joys of her life."

KRISTEN LANGEWISCH MARCHETTI

Kristen Langewisch Marchetti was born in Burlingame, California, on September 17, 1982. She is the eldest of Florence Miho Nakamura's five grandchildren. Kristen grew up San Ramon, then moved to Santa Barbara in 2001 to attend the University of California, where she earned a degree in communication and minored in art history. Kristen currently lives in Thousand Oaks with her husband, Trenner Marchetti.

Growing up in the Bay Area, Kristen developed a strong relationship with Florence, who lived just a short distance away in San Francisco. When Florence enrolled in the Internment Autobiography Writing Workshop and began to open up about her experiences, she and Kristen worked together to chronicle the story of her life before, during, and after the incarceration. Kristen thanks Brian Komei Dempster and her relative Ellen Sawamura for involving her in the project and giving her the opportunity to share some of that work in this book.

Editor's note: Our group was deeply saddened by the passing of Florence Miho Nakamura in November of 2007, shortly after we began our resettlement writing project. In June of that year, I visited Flo and showed her an old story of hers, which she had originally written for our Internment Autobiography Writing class in 1999, and both she and I were eager to have her involved with our group again. I—along with the group—was dismayed by her sudden passing in November. As our tight-knit circle grappled with this loss, we reflected upon the best way to properly honor Flo.

I got in touch with Flo's granddaughter Kristen Langewisch Marchetti, who graciously provided me with writings that she had transcribed from Flo's notebook. In addition, Kristen sent me other notes from an in-progress family history project and a powerful essay she had written for her college writing class based on interviews about Flo's incarceration and postwar experience. With her family's permission and blessing, I liberally restructured and shuffled the order of Flo's passages and cut away or merged material in order to create a focused and coherent narrative. Kristen provided further editorial help with Flo's works; moreover, Kristen effectively revised her own writings into a reflection (in italics) that follows Flo's stories (in regular text). Accompanying these pieces are relevant photographs generously provided to us by Flo's son, Scott. The following section honors Flo's memory and her granddaughter Kristen's caring documentation of her grandmother's story, and it gives voice to Flo's resettlement experience from multiple perspectives.

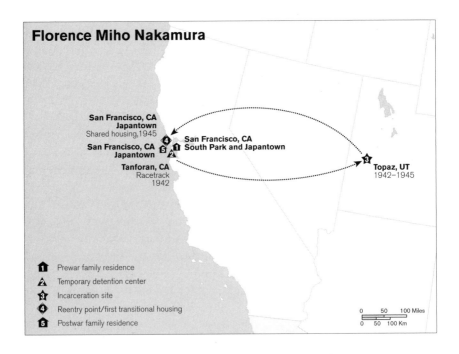

Florence Miho Nakamura

San Francisco, CA
Japantown
Shared housing,1945

San Francisco, CA
Japantown

San Francisco, CA
South Park and Japantown

Tanforan, CA
Racetrack
1942

Topaz, UT
1942–1945

1   Prewar family residence
2   Temporary detention center
3   Incarceration site
4   Reentry point/first transitional housing
5   Postwar family residence

0   50   100 Miles
0   50   100 Km

DUST STORMS

Dust storms became a regular occurrence in Topaz, which was located in the middle of the desert in southwestern Utah. They would come up suddenly, blowing dirt across the vast expanse of land and into your eyes and mouth, leaving a film of fine sand from head to toe. If I saw one coming from afar, I tried to seek shelter from the storm, but I wasn't always successful if I wasn't already close to some structure. When a storm struck, I would run into our barrack and close the sliding windows, but the fine dust seeped through all the little crevices and it was as though a fine veil covered the one room that was our home at Topaz.

Years later, I would visit my daughter and her family in Rock Springs, Wyoming, and as we drove through the desert to her home, I could not help but be reminded of the dust storms at Topaz.

SCHOOL IN TOPAZ

I felt that school in Topaz was not challenging. We did not have any textbooks and were instructed by apathetic teachers mostly from the "outside." One teacher, an elderly man, was more interested in telling of his shot-putting prowess than in instructing his students. I took typing and sewing from two Nikkei teachers; these are the only two subjects in which I learned lasting skills.

In camp the high school consisted of twelve bare barracks in the middle of the desert—six barracks on each side, with the latrine and one long building cutting lengthwise through the center. One entire camp block was utilized for this purpose. No meals were served at school, so we had to trudge back to our home blocks for lunch in the scathing heat of summer and the freezing cold of winter.

Our school wardrobe initially consisted of slacks and skirts with sweaters and blouses and saddle shoes. One day, while walking back to our blocks after school, a few of us girls decided to be trendsetters and agreed to wear Levi's jeans the next day instead of slacks or skirts. When I came to class the next day I was the only one wearing Levi's, but from that day forward they became the new "unofficial" school uniform.

VALENTINE'S DAY

The approach of Valentine's Day was not very exciting for me in 1945. My boyfriend, Harry Nakamura, was living and working in Salt Lake City while I was still in Topaz. A dance was being planned at the high school with red colored hearts and cardboard cupids, and I was going to attend with my

Flo and Harry, camp sweethearts, pose for pictures prior to a date after their return to San Francisco, 1945.

friends, but I would have been more eager to attend if I had my Harry as my date.

On the day of the big dance, I was delighted and surprised to find Harry waiting for me in camp. He presented me with a huge, red, padded, heart-shaped box of chocolates. Because it was wartime, candy was scarce, but he had stood in a very long line at the Martha Washington candy store to get me this special treat.

I was very happy with the candy but even happier to have my date for the dance. I had a wonderful Valentine's Day that year. This year, fifty-five years later, he gave me a cellophane-covered pack of conversation heart candies he had taken from a basket in our doctor's office.

RETURN TO CALIFORNIA

The war was over and we were leaving Topaz! After three and a half years in camp, we were free to return to California. The government gave us each twenty-five dollars and a one-way ticket back home. I was anxious—but not eager—to return home in time for the start of the school semester in September. I traveled back to San Francisco with my friend Margaret

Kawaguchi Kitagawa; we took the train from Topaz to Oakland and then the ferry from Oakland to San Francisco.

My father met us upon our arrival in San Francisco. He had returned a few weeks earlier and found lodgings for our family on the first floor of an old Victorian house on Bush Street, next door to Kinmon Gakuen, the Japanese school from which we had departed for Tanforan three and a half years earlier. The new house had been split up and rented out to two other families in addition to my own; our family occupied two of the four bedrooms in the home. The kitchen and bathroom on the second floor were used primarily by our family, but we also shared them with some of the other tenants. We were privileged to have rented rooms in a house that had two bathrooms—one on each floor—considering most houses had only one bathroom in those days. Every room but the kitchen and bathrooms was used as a bedroom during this time. I lived here for three years, until 1948, when Harry and I married and moved into our own home on California Street.

I do remember one unusual thing in the kitchen: it had a dumbwaiter—a small cupboard-like box that you could pull up and down to move things between floors. It must have previously been used by maids in the house to transport food. The old Victorian house is still there today, and I imagine it must have been restored inside by now. I thought it was an old, ugly house at the time, but now they are again fashionable.

Flo and Harry were married in 1948.

Back to School

When we left San Francisco in 1942, I was in the eighth grade at Pacific Heights Elementary School, on Jackson Street between Webster and Fillmore. When we returned to San Francisco in 1945, Margaret and I registered for classes at Lowell High School. At Lowell, the school year was divided into two parts, called "high" and "low"; I was a high junior and Margaret a low senior. I was very self-conscious, and it was intimidating to be back in a "real" high school. I was the only Japanese American in my classes, so no one spoke to me. No one was mean, but nor were they kind. I was invisible to them. I do, however, remember that on the first day of school one girl, Norma Moser, came to me and said, "Hello."

One day in homeroom, I overheard some girls talking. One was describing a visit she and her family had taken to a property they owned, and she said, "You know how it smells after Japanese people live in a place." Her friend nudged her and, after looking toward me, they fell silent. I felt terrible. I was one of those Japanese people whose house smelled. Although I hadn't done anything to feel this way, I felt victimized and ashamed.

On another occasion, I had returned to school after a bout with a nervous stomach, and I handed my written excuse to Mr. Libby, my homeroom teacher. After he read the note, he asked me, from the front of the classroom,

Flo graduated from Lowell High School in 1947.

"Did you eat too much raw fish?" Orissa, who sat by his side to take roll, turned and reprimanded him for his remark. I was grateful for her sensitivity but was too embarrassed to acknowledge her kindness.

We Niseis stuck together. We felt comfortable with each other after the years of being segregated in camp. Margaret and I were joined by Ashi, Roz, Joanne, and Miyo. Ashi and Roz walked from their homes to meet Margaret and me before class, and then we walked to Fillmore Street for the streetcar to take us to school. We didn't have classes together, but we met for lunch, eating our bologna sandwiches together at our own table.

Although I was a good student before my incarceration, when I returned to "civilization," I had difficulty setting good study habits. After graduating, in January 1947, I decided not to go any further in my education. My father encouraged me to continue, but I had lost interest. My experiences at Topaz and Lowell were very discouraging, and I felt out of place in academia.

REFUSING TO BE FORGOTTEN

Despite the hardships that Japanese Americans encountered during World War II, many survivors found the courage to overcome their sorrow. Rather than concentrating on feelings of pain and embarrassment, Grandma, you chose to look at the positive aspects, like the companionship that you found with others like you and the time you spent with your boyfriend, Harry. You shared your story with your children and grandchildren in the hopes that we will remember what happened to you and other Japanese Americans and how this experience influenced the identity of Japanese Americans today.

In those days leading up to your release from the Topaz concentration camp, I can only imagine the worry and anxiety that you must have felt: What hardships would you face when you returned to San Francisco? Would the city you once called home feel strange or unwelcome? Would people treat you like an outsider and view you as a traitor? In this time of uncertainty, you were sure of one thing: returning would not be easy. The incarceration had deeply affected you; it forced you to see that the world can be unfair and unkind, and you learned that people would judge you based on your race. You were no longer the young girl you were in those days leading up to the bombing of Pearl Harbor. Your imprisonment experience forced you to see the world in a newer, harsher light. You were growing up.

When you started classes again in the fall of 1945, your experiences at Lowell High School deepened your aversion to school rather than encouraging you to further your education. While the courses you took in Topaz served primarily as a way to socialize with friends and pass the time, the limited supplies, textbooks, and instructors prevented you from adequately developing your academic skills. After the war, Lowell High School offered better teachers, tools, and structured classes, but you were ignored and ostracized by your fellow classmates. After graduating from high school in January of 1947, you chose not to continue your education due in part to your vastly different but equally discouraging experiences at camp and at Lowell. I know that you regretted this decision, but I could not imagine that you would have chosen another path. I remember how happy you were when you attended my own college graduation ceremony and they announced that I had graduated with highest honors. It was as though I had filled a hole of regret that you felt in your own life, and through me you could experience the pride and achievement that you had missed out on in academia.

Although you experienced bitter feelings after the incarceration, you explained to me that "it was not guilt. We felt bad because it was Japan that attacked the United States, and we were of the ancestry. We went into a kind of shell because if we didn't talk about it, maybe nobody would remember." You avoided acknowledging your experiences until the 1980s, at which time people within the Japanese American community began to talk about requesting a formal apology. In 1988, President Ronald Reagan signed the Redress Act and, shortly thereafter, President George Bush sent a formal apology and twenty thousand dollars to each surviving former prisoner as reparation for their incarceration. In November of 2000, you and hundreds of other Japanese Americans attended the dedication of the National Japanese American Memorial in Washington D.C., facing your troubled histories together and refusing to let your experiences be forgotten.

Grandma, I have missed you each day since your passing in 2007. I am grateful and so proud that you had the courage to speak out and tell your story. I know that it could not have been easy for you to acknowledge and reflect on this period in your life, but you will continue to live on in the pages of these stories and in my memories of the conversations that we shared about your experiences in Topaz.

Flo with granddaughter Kristen Langewisch at a birthday/Thanks-
giving celebration for her children, Sharen and Scott, November
24, 2005. Courtesy of Scott Nakamura.

RUTH Y. OKIMOTO, Ph.D.

Ruth Yoshiko Okimoto was six years old on May 1, 1942, when U.S. soldiers forcibly removed her family from San Diego to the Santa Anita Assembly Center, where her youngest brother was born. Four months later, her family was taken to the "Poston Relocation Project" on the Colorado River Indian Reservation; they were incarcerated for three years in Poston Camp III. After the war, Ruth's family returned to San Diego on September 11, 1945.

As an adult, Ruth worked as a college administrator, a human resources manager, and a career counselor before enrolling in graduate studies at the California School of Professional Psychology, where she earned her M.A. and Ph.D. She also holds a B.A. from Mills College and has studied art at the California College of Arts and Crafts. Her research on the links between Japanese American inmates and the Colorado River Indian tribes culminated in "Sharing a Desert Home: Life on the Colorado River Indian Reservation," which was published by Heyday in 2001 as a special edition of the quarterly magazine News from Native California.

Today, Ruth lives with her husband, Marvin Lipofsky, in Berkeley, California. She is the mother of three grown children and one stepdaughter, and grandmother to a grandson, a granddaughter, and two step-grandchildren.

Opposite page:
Top: The three Okimoto children sit on the steps of the church, San Diego, 1940. Left to right: Joe, Ruth, Paul. Photo by Tameichi Okimoto.

Center: San Diego Holiness Church and parsonage, 3030 and 3042 Webster Street, 1940. Photo by Tameichi Okimoto.

Bottom: The Okimoto family returns to San Diego in 1946. Left to right: Ruth, Daniel, Joe, Paul. Photo by Tameichi Okimoto.

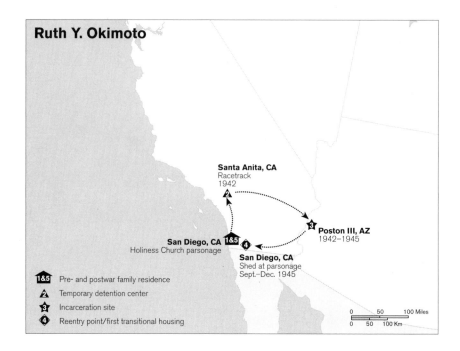

Ruth Y. Okimoto

Santa Anita, CA
Racetrack
1942

Poston III, AZ
1942–1945

San Diego, CA
Holiness Church parsonage

San Diego, CA
Shed at parsonage
Sept.–Dec. 1945

1&5 Pre- and postwar family residence
2 Temporary detention center
3 Incarceration site
4 Reentry point/first transitional housing

0   50   100 Miles
0   50   100 Km

THE DIAMOND RING

"Look at the diamond ring," my father said to me as we both stared through the hazy glass window of a jewelry store. I can still visualize the scene of my father and I gazing in amazement at the diamond ring encased in the black velvet box. With few people on the street, the town felt deserted. Here, in front of the store, we stood for a few moments. I was transfixed. Suddenly, my father said, "Yoshiko, some day I will buy you a diamond like that." As a nine-year-old child, I thought nothing of the price and didn't know the real value of such a ring, but the promise was exciting.

"Yoshiko, it's time to go," my father said, bringing me back to reality. I don't recall if he led me by the hand or if I followed him, and I don't recall how far the train station was from the store. I only know that we returned to the train and boarded it, rejoining my mother and brothers for the trip to San Diego. I don't recall the rest of the journey, but I must have pondered the diamond ring as I looked out the train window at the ocean and hills.

Just days before we stood in front of the store, my parents had packed up our family possessions, acquired during our three-year imprisonment from 1942 to 1945 in the hot desert of Poston, Arizona. Here, we were incarcerated on the Colorado River Indian Reservation. Our train ride back to San Diego, California, had seemed uneventful except for that one scene with the diamond ring, now seared in my mind. The "freedom" train from Parker, Arizona, a town near Poston, took us to Union Station in downtown Los Angeles, where we would switch trains for the last leg of our journey home to San Diego. With little time to spare before our departure from Union Station to San Diego, my father and I went for a walk while my mother and brothers stayed behind, and that was when I saw the ring.

From time to time, when I think of my father's promise, I'm filled with mixed emotions of both sadness and happiness. After World War II, my parents struggled to keep our family fed and clothed; the thought of getting a diamond ring seemed as remote as trying to grab a star in the night sky.

But my parents did give me other symbols of "diamonds." One was the reachable "diamond of education." They insisted that I "study hard for the future," and their gentle encouragement gave me the determination to complete my studies. From them, I learned the value of setting goals and sticking to what I set out to do. I never received from my father the diamond we saw in the jeweler's window, but he and my mother gave me other precious "diamonds" that I cherish today.

The Okimoto family moved from San Diego in 1946 when Rev. Tameichi Okimoto (Ruth's father) was reassigned to serve the San Lorenzo Holiness Church. From left to right, back to front: Rev. Tameichi Okimoto, Kirie (Kumagai) Okimoto, Paul, Ruth, Joe, and Daniel.

Artist's statement: Art became a means for me to probe into my subconscious memories of the incarceration (1942–1945) and the subsequent identity issues I experienced as an adult. It took two decades after leaving Poston Camp III before I was able to visually address the experiences and explore my feelings. Until then, I had no idea that I carried such buried feelings of anger and shame. I'm grateful for the medium of visual expression that allowed me to examine the war years and civil rights era. For me, the issues of race and gender remain live ones; the topics are more complex today but just as vital and important.

Two Faces. Oil on canvas. 18" x 20". 1971.

TWO FACES

This was my first ever oil painting, done in a 1971 class at the California College of Arts and Crafts (today known as the California College of Arts). The face on the right is me as child; the face on the left is me as an adult. The flag covers the child's eyes to represent the camp experience I couldn't see, and the adult mouth shows the pain I couldn't speak.

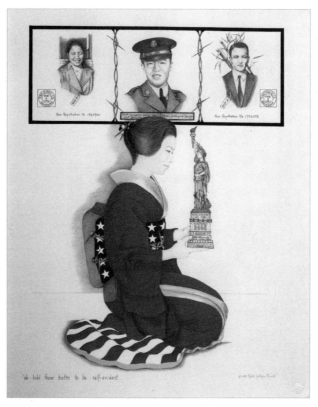

We hold these truths to be self-evident.... Colored pencil and acrylic on paper. 22 1/2" x 29 1/4". 1998.

WE HOLD THESE TRUTHS TO BE SELF-EVIDENT...

Shortly after I received my redress check of twenty thousand dollars, in 1998, I drew this portrait. The kneeling female figure in the foreground is loosely based on me, the barbed wire on the sash and in the hair showing the pain of imprisonment. The woman gazes at the iconic figure of the Statue of Liberty, which is humanized and yet contains dates representing significant, conflicting historical events—in particular the signing of Executive Order 9066, in 1942, and the passing of the Civil Liberties Act of 1988. The top image in the middle is of a man we called Uncle George, who served in the 442nd infantry regiment and represents all those who performed military duty while their families were incarcerated. Separated by barbed wire, the right and left images at the top are from my parents' Alien Registration files and include their identification numbers and the dates they were forced to register with the government: February 3, 1942. These juxtaposed images and dates show the contradictory ways we were treated as Japanese Americans, and my own conflicted feelings.

Entrance to the Tule Lake Stockade. Photo from *Second Kinenhi: Reflections on Tule Lake*, a joint project of John R. and Reiko Katsuyoshi Ross and the Tule Lake Committee (San Francisco: Tule Lake Committee, 2000). Photo by R. H. Ross, Wartime Relocation Authority, National Archives, Washington, D.C. Used with permission from the Tule Lake Committee.

Wayne (far right) stands next to Morgan Yamanaka along with two unnamed friends behind the Tule Lake fence, 1945.

Yoshito Wayne Osaki was born near Courtland, California, in 1923. When Pearl Harbor was bombed, he was a junior at Clarksburg High School. His family was sent to the Tule Lake concentration camp, where they stayed for the duration of World War II. When Wayne returned from camp, he resettled in San Francisco. His camp experiences inspired his concern for civil rights, and he helped rebuild the Japanese American community after the war.

Wayne studied at San Francisco City College for three years and then transferred to study architecture at UC Berkeley, from which he graduated with honors in 1951. He established a private practice in 1958 in San Francisco and designed more than sixty-five churches throughout Northern California. Many of the ethnic churches he designed reflect the cultural heritages of their congregations. He was also involved in the design of several schools. Wayne believes religion and education can help improve society and, as a result, lead to a more harmonious world.

After forty years spent designing various types of buildings, Wayne is now retired. He and his wife, Sally, are the parents of four sons—Glenn, Paul, Dean, and Jon—and the grandparents of three grandchildren—Shannon, Mika, and Lee. In 2009, Wayne and Sally, along with their son, Paul, took their twenty-one-year-old granddaughter, Shannon, for her first visit to Japan. The highlight of their trip was taking Shannon to visit the former Osaki family land in Gotsu, Shimane-ken, which is referred to in Wayne's story "The Tanto."

SALLY NODA OSAKI

Sally Noda Osaki was born and raised in Selma, California. At the age of nine, she was incarcerated at the Gila River Relocation Center in Arizona, where she lived for two years. In 1944, her family relocated to Seabrook Farm in New Jersey, and in early 1945, shortly before the end of the war, they returned to their farm in Selma during a period of intense racial hostility. Sally moved to San Francisco in 1950.

Sally worked for twenty-two years in the legislative, executive, and administrative branches of city government for the City and County of San Francisco. In 1981, she accepted a position as an administrative assistant to Louise Renne, then a member of the Board of Supervisors, and three years later she took a leave of absence from city government to work as the Director of Volunteers for the 1984 Democratic National Convention in San Francisco. When she returned to City Hall, she served as a budget analyst and staff assistant for public health issues for Mayors Dianne Feinstein and Art Agnos. In 1989, she left City Hall to work as the executive assistant to the Director of Health, and she finished her career as a financial analyst at the San Francisco International Airport. She retired in 2003.

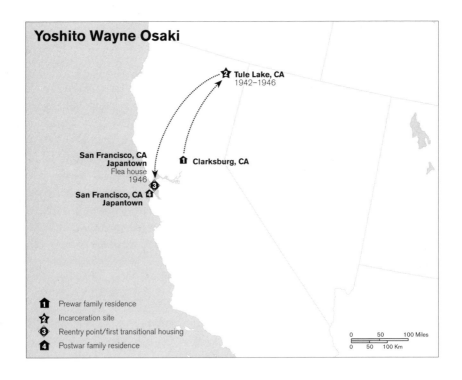

Right: Wayne and Sally were married on
April 12, 1958, at Pine Methodist Church
in San Francisco's Japantown.

Below: Wayne and Sally celebrate their
fiftieth anniversary in 2008.

Editor's note: From 1999 to 2000, while writing stories for From Our Side of the
Fence *in the Internment Autobiography Writing Workshop, Wayne wrote his own
autobiography and family history at the request of his sons. For the Resettlement
Writing Class, Wayne was unable to participate due to health issues. At the urging
of their sons, his wife, Sally, worked with Wayne to write stories about the actual
incidents he experienced. We extend our gratitude to Sally: for her unwavering
commitment to the group; for her care as she patiently gathered important details
from Wayne and prepared the final drafts for his approval; for her diligence as she
shaped and revised his stories; and for her sense of integrity and discretion when
using her imagination to fill in the gaps.*

THE *TANTO*

As the embers from the fire died down, I knew the last item I had to dispose of was the *tanto*. I could not bear the thought of losing it forever. As I hesitated, I recalled the stories my mother had told me about why my father had come to America: "His dream was to make enough money to reclaim the family fortune and lands that his father, a playboy and gambler, had foolishly squandered." This sword—this *tanto*—connected me to my father's dream and his heritage.

I looked into the flames, hoping that my father—the sword's formal owner—would someday pass it down to me. He had kept this *tanto,* a short Japanese sword, for years. It was a foot long with a plain wooden *saya* (scabbard), and it was probably a gift from a friend who had visited Japan. While the sword was not an antique and did not have much value, it linked me to the old samurai family from which my father descended; an Osaki ancestor, Tsuno San Saburo, was killed in battle when Toyotomi Hideyoshi invaded Korea five hundred years ago, and his remains were brought back and buried in the temple cemetery, since he was a samurai priest. As a boy, I used to look at the *tanto* and dream about being a samurai like my ancestor.

And even now, over sixty years later, I can remember the feel of the *tanto* in my hands as smoke rose in the backyard. Indeed, the *tanto* still links me to the centuries of ancestors buried in the Osaki family cemetery in Gotsu, Shimane-ken, along the Japan Sea coast. My relatives have been buried there since the twelfth century, and, in order to honor my father as the eldest son of his generation, some of his ashes, as well as those of my mother, are buried in this cemetery as well—on a hillside clearing in a lush, verdant forest of bamboo and *hinoki* (cedar) trees, near the site where the Osaki family home once stood.

How did I end up here? I remember asking myself back then, holding the sword before the fire. Right after Pearl Harbor, we and other Japanese American families had disposed of anything that the FBI might think was contraband or an indication of loyalty to Japan. They considered suspect any document that held associations with the military or any picture of the Japanese flag or the emperor. We were forced to discard photographs showing our family in Japan wearing school uniforms that looked too military-like. My parents were both Japanese language teachers in the Clarksburg area, just south of Sacramento, so we took extra precautions to get rid of anything that might be mistaken as a sign of patriotism to Japan and disloyalty to America. The FBI actually came to question my parents twice and to look around the school. They checked the classrooms and even went through my parents' desks. "Japanese language teachers all over the state are being arrested," we heard from various friends. These visits, combined with such rumors, made us very anxious. I have always wondered why they did not take my parents away. Perhaps my parents were saved by the American flag and portraits of George Washington and Abraham Lincoln that they displayed at the fronts of their classrooms to teach students the principles of the founders of this country. Whatever the case, we were grateful.

The difficult task of getting rid of anything that might be deemed suspect fell on me, since my older brother was still at UC Berkeley. I watched my parents sorting through our belongings, deciding which should be destroyed. Most had been accumulated over many years, and it pained me to watch my parents filling boxes with books, photographs, and other documents they used to teach the language and, by extension, the culture and moral values of Japan. I knew that some of the items were the only family gifts given to my parents when they left Japan to come to America. My parents were stoic, saying, "*Shikata ga nai,* it can't be helped," but I was angry that irreplaceable mementos from their families were considered suspicious.

Most of the items were paper goods, so I burned them under the *furo,* the wooden Japanese bathhouse. I also burned the Japanese flag and a picture of the emperor. I was left alone to tend the fire and watch my parents' remembrances of their homeland drift away as smoke and ashes in the hot Sacramento Valley air.

As I held the *tanto* for the last time, I knew I couldn't burn it. While flames would consume the wooden *saya,* the steel blade would not melt. I thought about throwing it into Elk Slough, a branch of the Sacramento River that ran along the levee next to our house. Instead, I hid it in a woodpile composed of limbs and branches from the nearby cherry orchard, lifting pieces of wood and burying the *tanto* at the very bottom of the pile, feeling relief and hope. Because I didn't know how long we would be incarcerated, I saw this as my only chance to reclaim the sword for my family upon our return. I knew that this little sword would be considered contraband, so I never told my parents that I had hidden it.

Since we could only take to camp what we could carry, after selling a few items, including our car, we stacked wooden crates of our belongings in the largest classroom of the Japanese school where my parents were teachers. Some of the items, including family scrolls and woodblock prints, held great historical and cultural value for my parents; other items, such as family photos, were irreplaceable and filled with sentimental meaning. We also broke down our furniture and roped the beds together with the mattresses and folded-up bedding. We boxed up Japanese vases wrapped in newspaper, along with some books. In addition, we packed certain items separately. Later, my sister's high school teacher, who was white, would send us these things in camp: a phonograph and records, clothing, a sewing machine, and an electric hot plate. While we went through this process of crating and storing all of our family's possessions, I was struck again by my parents' ability to *gaman* (endure). Although our future was uncertain, both Mother and Father quietly went about these tasks without complaint.

Years later, long after I had stood over the fire, long after I had hidden the *tanto,* long after the war and resettlement, we finally made a trip to Clarksburg. We found that the Japanese school had been broken into, and almost all the items of value we had stored there were now gone. When we searched through the upturned boxes and found photo albums of our family and loose photographs of family and friends in Japan, my mother shed tears of happiness and my father smiled. My mother glowed as she shifted through pictures of her days as a student at Tokyo Women's College and as a teacher at a private girls' high school in Tsu City, Miye-ken Province. My father, usually stoic, beamed with tears in his eyes when he found photographs of his family and his ancestral home. I found a faded photograph of my dog, Teny, whom I'd had to leave behind when we left for the Tule Lake concentration camp. (Later, in 2005, I adopted a part-Shiba rescue dog and named her Teny as well.) Seeing this image of my dog brought a lump to my throat, and I wondered, as I had many times before, if she had found a home with a good family. The things the thieves had deemed worthless were the things we cherished most.

On the steps of the prewar Osaki family home in Clarksburg, California, is father, Isao, with dog Teny on the porch, and mother, Tomi, at lower right.

While my parents went through what remained of our possessions in the school, I hurried next door to our old house, anxious to find the *tanto*. Instead, I felt regret and loss when I saw that the Japanese *furo* had been torn down. There was no trace of the woodpile where I had hidden the *tanto,* just my memories of flames and smoke.

THE STOCKADE IN TULE LAKE

At the time, I could never have known my stint in the stockade would arise out of an innocent act. My mother had loaned some Japanese records to a neighbor who wanted to broadcast popular Japanese songs for the enjoyment of us prisoners, and somehow several ham radios picked up the broadcast outside of the camp. When the camp authorities investigated, they found our family name on the records that were being played. The day the soldiers came to our barrack, I was arrested since I was the only one at home who spoke English. Bewildered, I had no idea why I was going to be thrown into the stockade along with suspected dissidents who had been picked up during the camp protests. The soldiers would not respond to my question, "Why am I being arrested?"

In the stockade, I was disturbed by the sight of the other inmates—five other Niseis and three Kibeis (people born in America but educated in Japan)—who had been beaten and wore bandages to cover their cuts and bruises. I heard the same phrase from many of them: "I have no idea why I am in the stockade." Two of the inmates said, "We got arrested for going to the latrine between the 7:00 p.m.-to-6:00 a.m. curfew; this was imposed on us following our mass protests for better medical care, upgrade of food, milk for children, and better working conditions." Five of them were truck drivers who had been inadvertently involved in an incident in which a European American staff person had stolen meat from the storage locker.

For the first two weeks, I was housed in a tent and given only two army blankets and a cot, despite the winter snows continuously falling outside. In the mornings, the top blanket would be frozen with ice. Later, I was placed in one of the barracks that was part of the stockade. Soldiers stood posted as sentries outside the barbed wire fence at all times. I will never forget the hardship and degradation of being caged like an animal, the indignity of going to the latrine with a bayonet pointed at my back. The soldiers marched us to their mess hall by shoving us with the bayonets of their guns, their fingers on the triggers. There, we were fed their leftovers, such as fried chicken and beef stew. Weirdly enough, the food was much better than our normal camp meals of dry, tasteless meat, boiled potatoes, and smelly mutton stew. But I found it difficult to eat with a bayonet pointed at my back.

A security officer and policemen escort inmates to the stockade at Tule Lake. Photo by R. H. Ross, Wartime Relocation Authority, National Archives, Washington, D.C.

Although I was released after a month—when the camp officials realized that I was not involved in any conspiracy—I was still outraged. My anger blurred with sadness when my parents told me that the neighbor who had inadvertently broadcast Japanese music beyond the camp was sentenced to a prison outside of Tule Lake. I was sorry about the arrest of someone who was only trying to entertain the prisoners, but I still resented my own imprisonment. And despite my release from the stockade, I sympathized with the inmates, who now numbered two hundred, still imprisoned in this military jail. As the inmates' protests increased and they marched for better living conditions and treatment, the administration, rather than acquiesce to these demands, continued to use army tanks and soldiers with bayonets to quell the demonstrations.

After my release from the stockade, two of the young soldiers who had arrested me started to visit me, bringing me candy and other treats. They didn't say anything about my arrest, but it was obvious they felt bad that I had been unfairly thrown into the stockade. Due to their offerings of friendship, I actually started to enjoy their visits. We talked about the latest sports news from the outside world. "I'm a Yankee fan," I told them. Both of the soldiers were Dodger fans, and we engaged in heated debates about our favorite players, arguing the merits of Joe DiMaggio versus Pee Wee Reese and who hit more home runs. Since we were about the same age, we also talked a little about our dreams of going to college. I felt sympathy for these young men who told me, "We might soon be sent overseas to the battlefield." Like mine, their future was uncertain.

Soon other prisoners noticed the presence of these soldiers at my house, and even my best friends started to ask me, "Why are these soldiers visiting you?" I finally had to ask the soldiers to stop coming to see me. They had apparently noticed the strange looks their visits were causing from others and seemed to understand my request. During this time of protest against the camp administration, if I or anyone else was friendly to the authorities, we were suspected of being an *inu* (a "dog," or informant). I felt a mixture of relief and loss. While I kept my distance from my new friends, the soldiers, I missed them stopping by to see me. I look back fondly at our talks about baseball and college, and I wonder if they, too, made it home.

Author's note: In September 2008, my family discovered a letter I had written describing my time in the Tule Lake stockade. This lone letter was accessed through the Guy and Marguerite Cook Nisei Collection, which was donated to the University of the Pacific and is available online at the Japanese American Relocation Digital Archives: http://www.calisphere.universityofcalifornia.edu/jarda/. Excerpts of the letter are reprinted, verbatim, in "The Final Act: Burying the Past" (pp. 111–114) and the letter is also referenced in "Cleaning Up" (on p. 118).

THE QUIET SON

Soon after our family settled down in Tule Lake, I noticed a young man who never went to the mess hall for his meals. Instead, his mother always brought food to him in their room, which was next door to ours. He rarely left the barrack and only went outdoors on a few occasions when the weather was very hot, always wearing dark glasses. He was in his early twenties and a tall, good-looking fellow with wavy black hair. Apparently, he had no friends: I never saw anybody visit, and he never seemed to leave our barrack area. Since he was only a few years older than me, I tried several times to engage him in conversation. My everyday greetings—"Hi. How are you today?" or "Sure is hot out, isn't it?"—were met with silence. An obvious loner, he would not even look at me.

Soon after they moved in, I overheard his parents introduce themselves to my mother outside our barrack. They told her, "Our family, including our three daughters and one son, used to live in Washington State. Before the war, our son attended the University of Washington and had many friends." I'd noticed their son always wore a UW athletic sweater with two stripes, so he was probably a good athlete. A few months later, his mother told us, "My son hates living in Tule Lake and is anxious to leave and go to school."

One day, shortly after prisoners were allowed to relocate to the Midwest or the East Coast, I saw him leaving the barrack with a large duffle bag over his shoulder and a heavy suitcase. Although his parents and sisters stood outside watching him until he disappeared, he never looked back. I assumed he was leaving camp to work and continue his education. *Did they know where and why he was going?* I wondered.

Then one night the real story became clear. In camp, where the barracks were partitioned into four or five rooms—usually one room for each

family—the walls between the rooms consisted of only half-inch sheets of plasterboard, so we could easily hear the voices and sounds of our next-door neighbors. That night, my mother heard muffled, continuous crying, so she hurried next door to ask if there was anything she could do. She learned that the quiet son who had relocated had committed suicide. According to a letter he sent to his family, he could not find a job and his money ran out. The mother and three sisters sobbed uncontrollably,

A row of tarpaper-covered barracks at Tule Lake. Photograph by John D. Cook. Courtesy of the Bancroft Library, University of California, Berkeley.

the entire family devastated by the loss of their only son and brother. Pacing the barrack, the father blamed himself, "It's my fault. I should never have let him leave camp alone. But he hated being confined in Tule Lake, and we thought going back to college might help. We were wrong." The parents said softly to my mother, "We do not want anyone to know about the suicide," and then they closed the barrack door. Honoring this request, our family never discussed this incident with anyone in camp.

As time passed, the impact of the son's death seemed to subside into the daily routine of camp life. Yet questions kept gnawing at me, because I never knew what really led to this young man's suicide. Clearly, he had been despondent about being incarcerated in a concentration camp; he felt he was an American and did not belong there. What factors contributed to his death? Who were his friends? Did his passion for sports die in camp? Was he just another victim of the war and the "evacuation" order? We will never know.

A few months after the confusing Loyalty Questionnaire, the government designated Tule Lake as a segregation center, and all the prisoners from other camps who had refused to answer—or who had responded "incorrectly" to—the Loyalty Questionnaire were moved to our camp. The form included the following questions:

1. Are you willing to serve in the armed forces of the United States on combat duty, wherever ordered?

2. Will you swear unqualified allegiance to the United States of America and faithfully defend the United States from any or all attack by foreign or domestic forces, and forswear any form of allegiance or obedience to the Japanese emperor, or any other foreign government, power, or organization?

People who responded "no" to these questions were moved to Tule Lake; those who said "yes" were allowed to move to other camps. I never knew how my brother and sister responded, but as a family we talked it over and decided, "Let's stick together in Tule Lake, since we have many new friends here." I was relieved because I had answered, "no," and the fact that my family was staying in Tule Lake anyway meant I could remain with them. I wondered, *What would the quiet son have chosen this time? Would he have stayed with his family, not faced the dangers outside of camp?*

While it was a gift to remain as a family, we all still looked forward to our release. My older brother left first, jumping at the opportunity to join his girlfriend in New York City when the camp director announced at the end of 1944 that Tule Lake would close in one year. After the close of Tule Lake, my parents, younger sister, and I chose the West Coast and relocated to San Francisco. Here, in our chosen city, we would get a new start, a second chance. Unlike the quiet son, we could begin again.

THE ELDERLY ISSEI MAN

One day, an elderly, single Issei man came to the Relocation Office and gave me an address in Stockton, California, where he was going to resettle. He told me, "I have a place to live and there is a job waiting for me. I must go there as soon as possible."

When the administration announced that Tule Lake would close at the end of 1945, they established a relocation office and recruited prisoners with bilingual skills to interview camp residents on their skills, their preferred site for relocation, and the date of their planned departure. I was selected to be an "interviewer" since I was pretty fluent in Japanese.

"Do you have relatives or friends in Stockton?" I asked the Issei man, hoping he did. I was relieved when he responded, "Yes, I have friends in the area." The man appeared to be in his late sixties, was quite tall, and wore a beaming smile on his face. I wanted to make his big transition smooth, help him realize his vision of a new life outside of barbed wire. Quickly, I made out the application paper and issued a train ticket with his preferred date of departure from Klamath Falls, Oregon, the nearest train station. "Thank you," he said, his smile widening as I handed him his papers. Then turning around, he walked out the door.

Several days later, the superintendent of the Relocation Office called me to his desk.

"Did you pressure this man in any way to leave Tule Lake camp?" he asked.

"I have never pressured anyone to leave camp," I replied.

The superintendent then told me, "I received a letter from the Klamath Falls Police Department. The letter states that the Issei you processed to go to Stockton was found hanging under the high school football bleachers in Klamath Falls."

Stunned, I could not say anything for a long time. After this long silence, I tried to recall my interview with the Issei man. I told the superintendent, "He seemed happy to be leaving camp and assured me he had a job waiting for him." I returned to my own desk, trying my best to continue with the next interview and focus on the needs of the long line of people who were waiting to be processed.

After a long day, I finally allowed myself to reflect on the situation. I sat outside my barrack, the black sky dotted with stars. *What could have gone wrong?* I pondered. *Did he feel lonely after he left Tule Lake?* In camp, the bachelors lived together in barrack rooms just like mine, and some experienced leisure and companionship there for the first time. I saw many of the bachelors playing *go* (Japanese chess) and *hanafuda* (games played with Japanese "flower cards"), with the games apparently sometimes lasting for hours—an inference I made from passing them at random times outside and always seeing them playing. From these observations, I realized camp may have been the only time the Issei man did not live a somewhat lonely existence.

For many stress-filled days and sleepless nights, I relived my interview with the Issei man. *Was this a suicide due to my shortcomings? Had I missed something in our interview?* The high school football field was far away from the Klamath Falls train station. *Why did he walk away from the train station? Did an incident take place at the train station? Was his death due to theft or a hate mob? Was it really a suicide?*

I still wonder what really happened to the elderly Issei man. Whether he committed suicide or was a victim of foul play, I am still haunted by it: the noose tight around his neck, the cool air he breathed before he closed his eyes a final time.

THE FINAL ACT: BURYING THE PAST

Before leaving camp, I buried my diary, in which I had written about many bitter memories: the Loyalty Oath, the stockade, the renunciation of my citizenship, the segregation and separation from my friends. I even buried the good memories I had committed to paper: my first dance, the sweat and intensity of playing baseball and basketball games, the laughs and hopes I shared with the new friends I made from California, Oregon, and Washington. I wanted to bury my words in Tule Lake—my pages of frustrations, disappointments, anger, and fear of a life behind barbed wire. I put the diary in a metal box, put the box in a hole in the ground, filled the hole with dirt, and turned away.

Since my family left camp three months earlier than I, I had been living with some friends in their barrack. As I prepared to leave, I packed my clothing and a few personal belongings, including some photographs of classmates and some special friends. I stared at a photograph of three friends and myself behind the barbed wire fence (p. 98). My right arm is resting on the shoulder of Morgan Yamanaka. At the time I could never have known

Wayne with Miss Thomasina Allen, the bilingual missionary who was his partner in the Relocation Office at Tule Lake, 1945.

Morgan would one day become a sociology professor at San Francisco
State University and remain one of my best friends. I next looked at the
photograph of me standing next to Miss Thomasina Allen, her head tilted
toward me, wearing the bird pin she always wore, smiling vibrantly. I gazed
at her with fondness, warmed by the concern she showed for us, especially
the Issei. My bilingual coworker in the Relocation Office, she wasn't Japanese
but she spoke Japanese fluently because of her years as a missionary in Japan.
Her language skills and compassion allowed her to gain our trust.

With sadness, I placed the photographs in my suitcase and prepared myself
to say goodbye to the few remaining friends left in camp. We exchanged
addresses and said, "Let's stay in touch," but we all knew we would probably
never see each other again.

Finally, I went to see Mr. Guy Cook, the assistant principal of Tri-State
High School in Tule Lake. He always showed concern for me and interest in
my grades and academic performance. As we shook hands, he said, "Yoshito,
would you be willing to write to me about your experiences in Tule Lake?"
I was both surprised and touched that he asked, and even moreso when he
gave me his address and continued, "I've asked several students to write to
me and I would like to learn more about your recollections of the past four
years." I agreed to write when I got settled in San Francisco.

Although I would miss my friends and was grateful for Mr. Cook's gesture,
I was anxious to leave all other reminders of my life in Tule Lake behind me,
including my drawings of camp life—the sunsets, the panorama of desert
scenes. I left these drawings, along with an essay I had written in Japanese, in
the now deserted barrack room that had been my home for the past four years.
The essay, an assignment for a night class in the Japanese language, was titled
"Hope." I had not felt very hopeful at the time, so it was difficult writing a paper
on the required subject, and I was surprised when I received an "A". Sixty-two
years later, I still recall every word and have translated the essay into English:

Hope

I rushed out of the hot mess hall. Dinner was dried cod again. I
hated dried cod. Cod was smelly and had a bad taste. I spit out the
cod and washed out my mouth with a water hose.

I walked down the road to get away from the mess hall smell. As
I walked, I kicked the stones. In the distance, a softball game was
going on. I continued to walk down the road.

Soon, I found myself at the end of the camp. I lay on my back on the
green grass. I wondered how much longer the war would go on. The

guard in the tower looked down at me with sharp eyes.

I looked up and saw seagulls flying gracefully in the sky. They seemed to be saying, "Why do people fight against each other and cause death and hardship? We fly and just have fun with each other."

I wondered why people couldn't be friends and have fun rather than kill each other. I wanted to do something to bring peace to this world. I thought, I have to go to school and prepare myself.

I stood up on my feet with hope in my heart. At that moment, the bright red sun was slowly sinking into the horizon.

Editor's note: After returning to the West Coast, Yoshito (Wayne) wrote a series of letters he had promised to Guy Cook, the assistant principal of the high school in Tule Lake. In 2008, searching online archives, the Osakis were surprised to find, after over sixty years, one eleven-page letter dated June 14, 1946, from the Guy W. Cook Nisei Collection at the University of the Pacific. The following two excerpts from the letter illustrate the aftermath of the violence that inmates were subjected to at Tule Lake and the impact of the deplorable conditions they faced in the stockade.

GUY W. COOK
Assistant Principal

Guy W. Cook, assistant principal of Tri-State High School (Tule Lake). Photo from *Aquila 1943*, the yearbook of Tri-State High School, Newell, California, 1943.

The first morning when I went to the breakfast I was surprised and almost terrified when I took a look at the people I was eating with. There was a fat person sitting right in front of me and he had his eyes set right on mine. He had no white part left in his eyes. They were all blood shot. His long hairs were a mess & his face all swollen. He was certainly a gruesome and he just kept his eyes on me. Once in a while he took a deep breath and eat but soon he was watching me again. The others looked just as gruesome with bruises and scars on their faces but they were minding there own business. I looked around and wondered whether some of these people are Japanese. Some of them certainly didn't look like it.

It was just enough for us to drink so for six days, we didn't even wash our face or change our clothes. Later I begin to look just as gruesome as the rest of them were. I found this out when I went to the hospital as an interpreter for one Kibei fellow who had a head injury. I looked myself in the mirror and I couldn't even recognize myself. My face was all black with soot, my eyes blood shot & hairs all soiled. Our hairs were soiled because we often use to blow into the draft hole of our stove to get the thing going.

Excerpts (pp. 8 and 10) from a letter to Guy W. Cook from Yoshito Wayne Osaki, June 14, 1946. Courtesy of the Guy W. Cook Nisei Collection at the University of the Pacific.

A New View

I left the concentration camp with the seventy-six dollars I had saved from working at the Relocation Office during my final four months in Tule Lake. Once I was on the outside, I needed to find work quickly. Every day I looked through the want ads and made appointments for interviews in the commercial district, but the results were always the same: nothing. I was told, "The jobs advertised are for veterans," or "An earlier applicant has just filled the job." Most of the time I was told, "Fill out an application and you will be called." But I never received a follow-up phone call.

After several weeks of waiting, I began to feel frustrated: *Would I ever find a place in this changed world?* Desperate, I finally went to a Japanese employment agency, which could hire me out as a domestic servant or gardener, something many European Americans didn't seem to mind having. *What choice do I have?* I thought to myself as I filled out the application.

After searching the list of available jobs for a few more weeks, I was relieved to have finally found a position. An elderly European American woman who had lived in Shanghai for many years prior to the war and was now living in the exclusive Pacific Heights District of San Francisco hired me on a trial basis as a "houseboy" and chauffeur. Now that so many years have passed, I don't remember her actual name, but I do recall that "Mrs. A" already had a full-time Japanese cook and a Japanese cleaning woman who came once a week, so I had hoped she might treat me with some degree of cultural understanding. And I remember that Mrs. A's Pacific Heights residence was breathtaking: a three-story mansion filled with beautiful standing screens of Chinese landscapes, antique blue and white Ming vases, and Japanese scrolls of mountain scenes. My room on the third floor gave me instant comfort: nicely furnished, it contained an antique-looking mahogany bed and matching dresser and nightstand, its windows facing the scenic San Francisco Bay. From my window I could see Alcatraz, Angel Island, the Golden Gate Bridge, and across the water to Sausalito in Marin County. I could see large ships and many sailboats gliding through the sparkling water.

This room stood in vivid contrast to our barrack in Tule Lake, which had housed our entire family in one room, 404A. There, my father had constructed five six-foot wooden frame stands covered with cloth, which divided the twenty-by-twenty-foot room into a living area, kitchen, and three sleeping areas. From the windows of 404A, our only view was of the tarpapered barracks on either side of us. The frequent dust storms veiled these barracks in a haze of grit, and we coughed and choked on the dust that seeped through any crack. No matter how many rags we stuffed under the door and in the windows, the grains of dirt and sand covered us and every object in the room. In summer dust storms, we closed the doors and windows, which only made the air more sweltering hot in our barrack.

But in my room on the third floor of Pacific Heights, the air was cool, the view clear. Here, I could see everything. From this spot, I stood mesmerized by the Battle of Alcatraz, the infamous escape attempt by six prisoners in May 1946. For three days, sirens sounded and plumes of smoke drifted over the prison. In the end, two guards and three prisoners died, and fourteen guards and one inmate were injured. As I looked out the window and listened to the news reports, I wondered, *What is it like to be locked in an island prison with a view of one of the most beautiful cities in the world?*

The smoke over the area carried me back to the riots in the concentration camp. In the haze of Jeep dust, soldiers fired over the heads of demonstrators at Tule Lake. They marched prisoners to the stockade, all the while shoving them with rifle butts and pointing bayonets at their backs.

Beyond the barbed wire of the concentration camp, we could only look at miles and miles of barren desert, no glimmer of the sparkling waters of the Bay; San Francisco and its views existed only in our imaginations. The Alcatraz inmates had, of course, been convicted of the most heinous crimes, but we Japanese Americans had been imprisoned only on the basis of our ancestry. In the dust bowl of Tule Lake, some young men vented their anger through protests and demonstrations against the camp administration, which then responded by imposing martial law and rolling out army tanks. Armed soldiers took those believed to be the leaders and placed them in the camp stockade, where they were jailed for many months without trials. I myself had been arrested for no justifiable reason, only that my mother had let her friend borrow some of our Japanese records. In contrast, even the murderers at Alcatraz could count on the basic legal rights that we camp prisoners were denied.

Such injustice made me unsure of my real status in this first job after my release from the concentration camp. My primary job as a houseboy was to serve breakfast, lunch, and dinner, and clean the bathrooms. Though it was an undistinguished existence, I liked the job because it paid $160 a month plus room and board. Furthermore, I was delighted to drive Mrs. A's big car, a Lincoln Continental.

After I secured the job, I took every step to assure I would retain it. I rushed down to the Department of Motor Vehicles to get a driver's license, I bought and studied a map of San Francisco, since I was not familiar with the city, and I tried to find out Mrs. A's schedule ahead of time so I could figure out the best routes. Despite my preemptive measures, however, the first time I drove the big car, I stepped on the gas pedal too hard, causing a jerking motion. Exhaust fumes spewed from the tailpipe. When Mrs. A berated me, saying, "What are you doing? My previous driver never drove like this," I felt defeated.

After working for a short time, I started to feel uncomfortable with the presumptuous manner in which she treated me, in the way the master of the house would demean an Asian servant in prewar Hollywood movies. She would constantly yell at me in a very superior tone. I overheard her criticizing me to her friend and laughing about mistakes I made. "Can you believe that he put the mayonnaise on top of the artichoke instead of serving it on the side of the plate?" I had never seen an artichoke before that day. Once, when I drove her to a hotel, she ordered me to park in the red zone, which was against the law. I couldn't take it anymore. After that incident, I told her, "I am going to start looking for another job because I am concerned I might lose my driver's license." Suddenly, her attitude changed, and she didn't yell at me again. Instead, she told me quietly, "Drive me to the Palace Hotel tomorrow for lunch."

Her transformation appeased me, but only for a while. Although the work itself was easy and the pay was good, Mrs. A's personality mirrored the disrespectful attitude of some of the administrators of the concentration camp. Yes, her attitude had changed, but I knew it was insincere and only temporary—a desperate move to ward off my threat to leave. What she did not know was that, for almost five years, I had longed for freedom from authoritarian orders, tanks and protests, and miles of barbed wire. Throughout the ordeal of incarceration, I had tried hard to maintain the pride and dignity she seemed willing to put at risk, and now that I was free, no longer confined to a tarpaper barrack room with grains from dust storms in my clothes, nostrils, and mouth, I didn't want a job where I was humiliated by her or anyone else. I arrived at my decision: I did not have the proper personality to be an "Oriental houseboy." Unlike the Alcatraz prisoners, I could now make my own choice. Instead of being inside looking out, I could view the island prison of Alcatraz from afar while walking along the Bay and go wherever I wanted to on the streets of San Francisco.

Cleaning Up

I left my abusive and demeaning job as a houseboy in San Francisco and searched for a job in which I would be respected. Within a couple of weeks, I had answered a newspaper ad and found work as a live-in dishwasher at a restaurant in Orinda, a town across the Bay. Now, my desire for respect clashed with my need to earn a living. For here, I did not simply wash dishes.

I got up early to clean the dining room, kitchen, bar, and restrooms before the restaurant opened for business. Then I washed the vegetables for the cook. After a short lunch break, I scraped mounds of caked-on food off of plates and washed mountains of dishes, cups and glasses, and pots and pans in hot, soapy water. By the time this chore was finished in mid-afternoon, my shirt, pants, and apron were drenched in sweat and soapy water. I was exhausted and, at times, resentful by the time the dinner customers arrived, when I would have even more dishes, pots, and pans to wash until 2:00 a.m. I rarely had time to clean myself up or was too tired to do so. I worked in this "sweatshop" for over fifteen hours a day, with only part of Sunday and all of Monday off. After only a week of drudgery in this hot, humid kitchen, my job with the arrogant Pacific Heights lady and my nice cool room with the view of the Bay looked pretty good.

My hope for a better life was further blunted by the hot, stuffy, crowded storage room where I slept. Behind the restaurant, this room barely housed me and another fellow, a Kibei from Hawaii and fellow prisoner from Tule Lake. A former dishwasher, he now worked as the restaurant's salad chef. Two sleeping cots were squeezed into our room, which contained one small window up high and otherwise stored canned goods and other nonperishable restaurant supplies. On summer afternoons, with Orinda averaging about 100 degrees, the kitchen and the storage room became a sauna, and no bathtub or shower was available to cool us down. The Kibei, my ingenious

Wayne (right) and a coworker pose in front of the restaurant where they were employed. Orinda, California, 1946.

and wiry coworker, filled the dishwashing tub with cold water and half-soaked himself in it. I too was eager for this luxury, but I couldn't fit inside the tub. All I could do was wipe a wet towel over myself after work. I was jealous of my new friend as he bathed, even as he talked about his difficult situation: "Me and all other Hawaiians imprisoned at Tule Lake have to earn our own fare back to Hawaii, since Hawaii is still a territory and we are not U.S. citizens." He sat back into the water and continued, "I never even knew why I was picked up by the FBI and sent to Tule Lake."

His experience soaked me in a past that weighed heavy on me. "I was thrown into the stockade in Tule Lake for a month and then released with no explanation, so I can understand what happened to you," I responded, only able to dip my towel into a bucket of water so I could wipe away the beads of sweat.

When my bitterness about Tule Lake surfaced, I would sit down and write letters to Mr. Guy Cook, the assistant principal of the high school in Tule Lake, who had asked me to write about my experiences there. Whenever I found a few minutes between shifts, I tried to chronicle the events that had taken place in Tule Lake. Each letter took many days to finish since I had so little free time. Writing about my experiences was, however, worth it because, to some extent, it quelled my anger.

In due time, the Kibei returned to Hawaii, and I was "promoted" to salad chef. The pay was better, and I was relieved of the cleaning chores. But the tub was still too small. And I felt no relief when a Mexican teenager was hired for the dishwashing job. Recalling the hopelessness of my teenage years in Tule Lake, I encouraged him, "Finish high school and go on to college." He looked at me skeptically and just smiled, telling me, "This job is better than any I had in Mexico, and I just want to save a few dollars to send home to my family." Still, I didn't want to see his spirit darken or for him to be sullied by the injustice he would encounter due to his skin color. After I left that job to begin my own college education, I frequently wondered how that Mexican fellow was doing and wondered if he was "promoted" to salad chef himself. Somehow, I doubted it.

Although I sometimes regretted leaving my previous job in Pacific Heights, I believe that this job in Orinda, with its hardships and discomfort, made me strive for a better life. The promise of Sunday nights carried me through the struggle. On Sundays, the restaurant served brunch, so we didn't finish our chores until 3:00 p.m., but after that I headed back to the city for my day off. The bus took an hour to reach San Francisco, and when I got home I immediately turned on the hot water and filled the bathtub. I stepped in, sat down, and leaned back until the water reached my chin. All week while I had washed stack after stack of dishes in steamy, soapy water, I dreamed of soaking for a long time in a warm tub. By the time my bathwater had turned from hot to lukewarm, dinnertime had arrived. I stepped out of the tub to a delicious Japanese meal of rice and meat or fish prepared by my mother. After eating well and sleeping on my own bed Sunday night, then sleeping through the next day, I returned to Orinda Monday nights to repeat the same routine again. Although this weekly trip home to San Francisco was always too short, my Sunday night bath and meal cleansed me of dirt, pain, and hunger, renewing my body and spirit for the coming week.

Wayne standing with a surveyor at UC Berkeley's School of Architecture, c. 1949.

Regaining My Citizenship

On April 29, 1948, I heard on the radio and read in the *San Francisco Chronicle* the news that I had waited to receive for almost three years. That day, Federal District Judge Louis E. Goodman had ordered the wholesale restoration of citizenship to those Americans of Japanese ancestry who had renounced it during their imprisonment at Tule Lake. He upheld the claims of the Japanese Americans, who said they had signed the renunciations under duress. My joy and relief at this successful end of the ongoing litigation was indescribable.

For those three years, I had also been working to graduate from the City College of San Francisco and preparing to enter UC Berkeley's School of Architecture. For three years, I had gone about the everyday tasks of living and going to school, but my life still felt unsettled and my future uncertain. For three years, I had lived in the country where I was born and raised yet been stripped of the rights and privileges of citizenship. Now, with this announcement, I felt some measure of closure to the events at the Tule Lake concentration camp. I felt ready to put the bitterness of my experiences behind me, including my imprisonment in the infamous stockade. *I can now get on with my life,* I thought.

My relief was short-lived, however, as on March 1, 1950, I learned that the government had appealed the decision. For a while, what seemed certain became uncertain again. Thankfully, the issue of renunciation was finally ruled in favor of us renunciants in August 1955. In a letter dated August 29, 1955, I received the long-awaited news from Attorney Wayne M. Collins, who informed me that the U.S. District Court for Northern California "forever cancels your renunciation and declares you to be a native born citizen of the United States." Years of anxious waiting were now over and I thought, *I can now really get on with the rest of my life.*

We renunciants of Tule Lake will never forget the invaluable legal assistance provided to us by Attorney Wayne M. Collins, who was one of the few Americans willing to champion the principle of justice on behalf of those imprisoned at Tule Lake. We will never forget the litigation initiated by Mr. Collins on behalf of us—over five thousand renunciants in all—which stopped our forced deportation and enabled me and others to be released from Tule Lake camp six months after the end of the war. I was grateful to contribute the three hundred dollars that Mr. Collins asked to represent each of us. For the many who couldn't afford this fee or were repatriated to Japan, Mr. Collins worked essentially for free. I was and am grateful for the faith Mr. Collins had in us, the five thousand people for whom he campaigned mostly pro bono for twenty years, advocating tirelessly on our behalf. I am grateful for his hard work, for he even succeeded in getting citizenship restored to Nisei who were deported or repatriated to Japan, thereby making it possible for them to eventually return to the United States. Finally, I am grateful for the opportunity I had to meet personally with Mr. Collins so I could tell him, "Thank you for believing in us when no other attorneys in California would take our case."

Sometimes, I still open and unfold the letter from Mr. Collins informing me of the restoration of the full rights of my citizenship. I read it with the younger eyes of a man who had almost lost hope.

Editor's note: The following are the opening and closing statements of the four-page letter from attorney Wayne M. Collins, dated August 29, 1955, explaining the restoration and rights of U.S. citizenship.

WAYNE M. COLLINS
Attorney at Law
1701 Mills Tower
220 Bush Street
San Francisco 4, California

Telephone GArfield 1-1218

AUG 29 1955

Dear Mr. Yoshito Wayne Osaki:

Enclosed find a certified copy of the "Final Order, Judgment And Decree" in mass equity suit entitled Abo, et al., v. Brownell, etc., et al., Consolidated Number 25294, in the U.S. District Court for the Northern District of California, Southern Division, which forever cancels your renunciation and declares you to be a native born citizen of the United States.

The original judgment of the district court was in your favor. The defendants appealed and the Court of Appeals for the Ninth Circuit ordered the case re-opened as to you and certain other plaintiffs. My appeal to the U.S. Supreme Court to review and affirm the district court's decision as to you was denied on October 8, 1951. Thereafter, pursuant to an agreement I entered into with lawyers for the Justice Department, an administrative procedure was agreed upon which provided that in the event you were successful therein a final judgment as to you could be entered in your favor in the U.S. District Court. Inasmuch as you were successful in the administrative procedure the lawyers for the Justice Department and defendants, pursuant to the said agreement, stipulated that a final judgment be entered in court in your favor.

The entry of this conclusive judgment brings to an end the litigation I commenced on your behalf to cancel your renunciation and to have you declared to be a native born citizen of the United States. The judgment cancels your renunciation from the beginning. This means your renunciation was void from the time it was made and, in consequence, you always have been and still are a U.S. citizen.

The conclusive judgment is against the Attorney General of the United States, the U.S. Attorney for the Northern District of California, the Commissioner of Immigration, and the District Director of the U.S. Immigration and Naturalization Service for the Northern District of California.

You now are free to exercise and enjoy all the rights, privileges and immunities of United States citizenship. You now may register as a voter and vote at elections. You can purchase and lease land and buildings, hold public office, obtain civil service positions and public employment on the same basis as any other citizen. You now can obtain licenses on the same basis and at the same rates as other citizens. You now can obtain a U.S. passport to travel abroad and to re-enter the United States without filling out the special affidavit form which is required of renunciants whose status has not yet been completely determined. In States where old age pension laws provide pensions only for citizens you will, in course of time, become eligible for such old age pensions because you are a citizen of the United States. You can be taxed only on the same basis as other citizens. You cannot be classed or treated as an alien. You cannot be required to register as an alien or to apply for an alien registration card.

If you are in Japan you can apply to the nearest U.S. Consul for a U.S. passport. There you can use the enclosed certified copy of the conclusive judgment in your favor to prove your renunciation has been cancelled and that you are a native-born citizen of the United States.

-4-

You need not be ashamed of the fact that you once renounced citizenship. You did so because the government took advantage of you while it held you in duress and deprived you of practically all the rights of citizenship. You had no opportunity to make a free choice in the matter. Inasmuch as your renunciation is declared by the conclusive judgment to have been void you do not have to reveal to anyone that you once renounced citizenship. The records of your voided renunciation in possession of the Attorney General of the U.S. are not open to public inspection. My records are confidential and are not subject to examination. The only other records of your renunciation are those of the Court and consist chiefly of pleadings.

I am delighted that this litigation has terminated successfully for you. It is my hope that finally all those still in the mass suits likewise may have their renunciations cancelled by court judgment and their citizenship recovered.

You should keep the enclosed certified copy of the conclusive judgment in your favor as a memento of the ordeal you have undergone and also as a document which demonstrates that you are a citizen of the United States.

Very truly yours,

Wayne M. Collins

Toru Saito singing at the Topaz National Historic Landmark designation ceremony. Photo by Ashley Franscell, *Daily Herald* (Provo, UT), June 30, 2007. Courtesy of Ashley Franscell/*Daily Herald*.

TORU SAITO

Toru Saito was born December 11, 1937, in San Francisco's Japantown. At age four, he and his family were imprisoned at the Tanforan Racetrack and then at the Topaz concentration camp, in Utah. Toru was eight when the War Relocation Authority released his family and moved them to the Hunters Point shipyard neighborhood in San Francisco. Less than a year later, they were transferred to a federal housing project across the bay in Richmond, California, where they lived from 1945 to 1955, at which point the family moved to Berkeley, where Toru still resides with his wife, Bessie Masuda, a former camp singer.

After twenty years as a clinician at the Berkeley Mental Health Clinic, Toru retired and now spends time on his two passions: gardening and music. From Seattle to Las Vegas to Hawaii, he still performs professionally as a singer/ bandleader of his Shanghai Bar Band. He sings Broadway standards from the 1930s, '40s, and '50s.

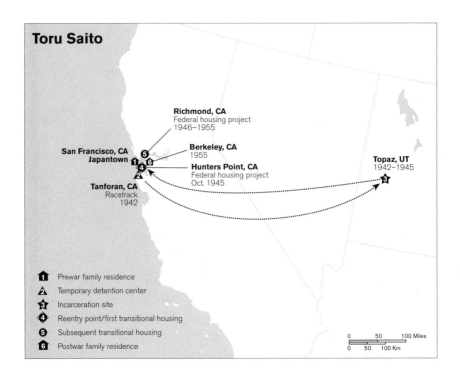

Toru Saito

Richmond, CA
Federal housing project
1946–1955

Berkeley, CA
1955

San Francisco, CA
Japantown

Hunters Point, CA
Federal housing project
Oct. 1945

Topaz, UT
1942–1945

Tanforan, CA
Racetrack
1942

🏠 Prewar family residence

🔺 Temporary detention center

🚩 Incarceration site

④ Reentry point/first transitional housing

⑤ Subsequent transitional housing

🏠 Postwar family residence

0   50   100 Miles
0   50   100 Km

STRANGER

It's early morning. It's chilly. Everything's wet, as if it had rained. It's a little past eight but still dark. It seems the sun's not going to make it today. Just beyond the end of Third Street, I see the San Francisco waterfront and the tall gray battleships waiting restlessly for orders. Behind the ships, an old foghorn moans through the mist like a dying sea creature. After four long years, I expected a warmer welcome from our beloved hometown, San Francisco, but this Hunters Point Navy Shipyard feels more like a cold slap in the face. What a contrast from the comforts of my own bed, our real home, Japantown, which is just over the hill. If I could gaze at the Golden Gate, would even that be hidden by fog? We are no longer prisoners, but are we really free?

My younger brother Jiro and I are up at the light of day, and nothing can keep us under our covers. We peer out our window, and for the first time in four years we see cars and pavement, our view no longer framed by barbed wire and guard towers. For four years, we've made unthinkable adjustments to changes in location and climate and living conditions. We have become tempered like high-strength steel; our hardships have galvanized our inner strength. Back in the fall of '42, we were just kids. Imprisoned in Topaz, we grew up fast. We left our childhoods in the desert sun and winter ice and snow. We learned our ABCs and our rights as free citizens in an elementary school as, ironically, prisoners with loaded guns aimed at us. All this for our own good? Well, that's what they said.

Jiro, which means "second son," is my sidekick who always tags along. We step out of the dormitory, once housing for the shipyard workers, and walk down Third Street, away from the heavy cranes of the waterfront looming over us and toward the flashing signs of stores. After a few blocks we feel caught, trapped by the harsh stares of *hakujin* (white) strangers on the streets. We run into a grocery store where we peer at the shelves. Our pockets empty, we gaze at bottles of Coca-Cola and 7Up, our lips smacking at these and other items we'd never seen in Topaz. Strong hands suddenly grab us by the backs of our necks, pull us to the front door. Here, the storekeeper lets go of us and points to a sign that reads "NO JAPS ALLOWED." "You Japs get the hell out of here!" he yells.

Walking toward home, the pain still fresh in our hearts, we see our first *kokujin* (black) man, our eyes wide with shock and wonder. He is tall, twice our size, facing down the street to our right, with a dark green T-shirt and jeans and brown shoes, waving both arms above his head at someone a block or two away. The sight of this young, dark-skinned man horrifies us. We stare in disbelief. We have never seen a man with such features. His chocolate-brown face and arms, his black woolen hair—they scare us to tears. He glares at our confused faces.

Now, many years later, I realize he must have been offended by our reactions, at how we ran away as fast as we could. I wish I could tell him this: That day I saw you, I was a frightened young boy who had been isolated for four years in Topaz. There, we were denied not only the freedom to move about the country but also the benefits of an open society with multiple cultures and differences. In Topaz, like Japantown, we all stuck together, we all looked the same. I ran because you were unfamiliar. Did I hurt you that day or have you forgotten? I know I haven't. Can you forgive me? Before you do, I can't feel real freedom in my heart. It is a lonely place to be. Please forgive me. I know a stare can make you feel unwanted and a stranger. I meant no harm.

FROM THE FIELDS TO HOME

Late summer, 1955. School's out, rock-and-roll is in, and the beat's here to stay. After three long months in a rural work camp as a migrant fruit picker, I

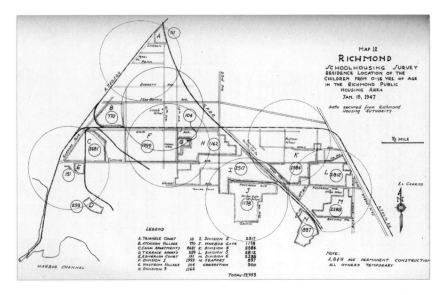

Above: A 1947 map shows the numbers of school-aged children at the Richmond housing project. Most of the Japanese American families lived in M section, near Fall and Gordon Streets.

Right: A group of Japanese American youth play baseball at the Richmond housing project. Toru remembers playing on a dirt lot with a concrete slab as home plate. "We all have scars on our legs to prove we slid into home plate many times," he said. Richmond, CA, 1947. Courtesy of the San Francisco Public Library.

rest my sunbaked face and huge mop of hair against the window of a musty-smelling Greyhound bus. We are speeding westward from the Suisun Valley, about an hour's drive north of Berkeley. It is my first time away from home, but it feels like three lifetimes without Mama's steaming pot of rice and *okazu* and our family conversation at the table.

The bus is racing me back to my own bed and the comforts of our very first single-family house. I'd spent my first four years in San Francisco's Japantown, my next four years in Topaz, and the next decade in federal government housing projects, where we were thrown together with the white working class from the South. Daily they told us, "Go back to Japan, you dirty Japs."

The bus is crossing the Carquinez Bridge, and I look down at the water, the breeze from the bay beginning to cool us. I am halfway home from the fields, thirty minutes from Berkeley; I am moving away from my years in the projects, where we were packed together like rats, and heading toward the promise of the first house we own. I am still exhausted from the summer, when I labored alongside the *braceros* brought up from Mexico to work in the fields with us. Although our English clashed with their Spanish, we grew close from working side by side in rows at subminimum wage; from the aching ten-hour days, toiling from dawn to dusk, toting a heavy ten-foot ladder; from our harvest of peaches and pears that were canned and placed on shelves at prices we couldn't afford.

The bus is taking me farther away from the valley of trapped heat where we sweated like hell and kept our shirts buttoned up against the peach fuzz that otherwise would cling to our wet skin and make us itch. I am going farther away from the signs—*Warning, Do Not Enter, Poisonous Sprays*—and the foreman who told us to ignore the signs: "That's for the other people."

The bus is getting cooler—relieving as the steel can of water we gathered around—and our gulps quenched our thirst, carrying us to the end of each day and the reward of balmy evenings.

We are turning off the highway, rounding the bend, slowing to the end of this ride. I have traveled years, survived barracks of barbed wire and overcrowded stucco tenements. My shoulders and back ache from hauling ladders and buckets of fruit. We are circling streets, nearing the depot. Instead of groves of trees, I see miles of houses. At last, one of them is ours.

THE NEXT HURDLE

I took a shower and got dressed in my Sunday best, an old dress shirt and pair of khaki pants that I had carefully ironed. I would have worn a suit if I had owned one. I shined my shoes and took off early, so I'd be the first one when the office opened. The seven-block walk to Herrick Memorial Hospital took about fifteen minutes, but I was sweating all over because I was so nervous. This was my very first job interview, and my palms clammed up as I neared the entrance.

"Be sure to show up on time," Helen had told me the previous Sunday at church. Helen Nishiyama was a Stanford graduate and the head dietitian at Herrick. "Toru, there's a dishwasher job where I work," she'd told me. "Go to the employment office on the first floor first thing Monday morning."

I reached the building, ran up the granite stairs, and pulled open the thick double-glass door. At the rear of the first floor, just beyond the elevators, I found the wooden door with a sign marked "Personnel." To the right of the door were racks of time cards next to a time clock, its slot worn from use. I opened the door and found a young, well-groomed brunette sitting behind the counter who looked up and smiled at me.

"I...I...I would like to apply for the dishwashing position in the kitchen," I stammered.

The woman's smile faded away as she looked me over, then said, "There are no dishwasher jobs."

I was speechless and confused. I couldn't believe my ears. I stared her in the eye, wanting to argue, but I stopped myself. I didn't want to do anything to threaten Helen's job.

"There are no jobs in the kitchen," the woman continued, this time with emphasis.

I turned around and walked out, brokenhearted. What was I to tell Mama? She was so excited about the prospect of my income helping the family. She stretched every dollar to put food on our table and clothes on our backs. Then my thoughts turned back to Helen. How could this office lady tell me there was no dishwashing job when Helen clearly had told me that they needed somebody? I spent the next week avoiding Mama, feeling like my life had caved in.

The next Sunday I spoke to Helen about my disappointment. "You go right back there and tell her I sent you," Helen said, seeming upset at me.

The following day, I made the walk to Herrick again, entered the personnel office, and found the same woman sitting behind the desk, applying nail polish to the tips of her long, slender fingers. ·

"I would like to apply for the dishwasher position," I said again.

The woman glared at me, apparently annoyed that I had interrupted her personal grooming. She did not say a word or smile at me but flicked an application sheet across the counter. My hands were trembling, and I looked down to avoid eye contact with the glaring woman, trying to keep focused on the form as I filled it out. When I was done, I handed her the form. She made a call, then said sternly, "Report downstairs to the kitchen and see Mrs. Sylvia Mitchell. She's the head dietitian."

As I walked down the flight of stairs, I felt dazed, my pace slowing as I anticipated the next hurdle I would have to jump. At the swinging doors to the kitchen, I hesitated. Turning around or leaving was not an option. I needed this job. I could give the money to Mama, fulfill what I had promised her: "Mama, I will do my best to help out."

I paused. Then I crossed the threshold and stepped on to the waxed granite floors, overwhelmed by the clean, white space. After years of tarpaper barracks and the housing projects with flimsy walls and cramped rooms, I was entering a new world. I made my way past the stainless steel counters and cauldrons of soup and found my way to the correct office. Through the window of her door, imprinted with the black letters "Sylvia Mitchell: Head Dietitian," I could see her behind a desk. Taken aback for a moment by the combination of the clean, white hospital walls and the white uniform and chalky white complexion of Mrs. Mitchell, I fought my distrust of everything white, the years of my own skin color setting me apart. I was facing another hurdle. I knocked on her door. She looked up and motioned to me. When she smiled ear to ear, I felt relieved.

"Who referred you to the hospital?" she asked.

"Mrs. Helen Nishiyama," I said with pride.

She stopped smiling as she read my application. My heartbeat quickened, my face turning hot. Then she glanced up and the smile reappeared. "You can start next week on Monday," she said before explaining the hospital policy for part-time students. "You can only work four hours a day. Tray line begins at 4:30 sharp," she impressed upon me. "You may come earlier and eat your supper; that's free." I thanked her.

I walked home elated. I had finally gotten my first real job. I would no longer have to suffer the hot, dusty groves of Suisun Valley, the long days of my migrant farmworker's life. I thanked God and Helen for this opportunity. My pace quickened as I looked forward to sharing my good news with Mama and my seven siblings. "I won't let you down," I promised Helen and Mama, looking toward the sky.

THE TRAY LINE

At 3:00 p.m., when my day at El Cerrito High School ended, I stood at the bus stop, waiting for the 72P. The bus arrived and I put in my token and took the nearest seat. On the twenty-minute ride to Berkeley, I kept checking my watch. I needed to be on time. "Never be late for work," Mama had warned me over and over in the kitchen while she cleaned and ironed our clothes. Her face beamed with joy and pride, but I detected concern in her eyes. My biological father had gotten numerous part-time, temporary jobs—as a cook, janitor, and porter—but had been laid off many times. My mother said nothing then, but I later learned that she was worried: she feared I would have the same fate as him, a grown man with five kids who still worked as a houseboy and who, as a Japanese, was only given menial work.

As we neared the corner of Grove Street and Dwight Way, I pulled the cable to signal the driver to let me off. It was only a one-block walk to

Herrick Memorial Hospital, where I proudly ascended the granite steps to the front entrance and the two giant swinging glass doors. I had entered them just the previous week, when I was awarded the job by Sylvia Mitchell, but as I walked through the front doors now, I couldn't have seen ahead to next week, when the top administrator would confront me, saying, "You will enter through the back door from now on," pointing to where the garbage cans were lined up on the loading dock. Instead, on this first day of work, my enthusiasm was undeterred as I arrived at 4:00 p.m. upon Ms. Mitchell's recommendation, so I could eat supper before the "tray line" started promptly at 4:30. Used to meals of rice and *okazu,* I stared in wonderment at my plate, at the most gourmet meal I had ever encountered: onions and calf's liver. In the coming weeks, I would also get to try beef stroganoff and other foods we associated with wealthy *hakujins.* Before Herrick, I ate only Japanese and Chinese food, and we couldn't afford to dine out.

I gobbled down my meal, then headed downstairs to the tray line, a conveyor belt that ran about twenty feet from left to right. Sarah, an attractive African American woman, placed each tray, with its menu ticket in a holder, on the end of the belt. As the soup man, I read the ticket and added either clear broth or the soup of the day. The person to my right would then read the card and place the appropriate entrée on the tray, which continued to the vegetable person, to the dessert and beverage person, and to the end, where one of Sylvia's staff dietitians checked each tray and placed it in a heated cart. Charlie, an African American man in his sixties, rolled the cart to the elevators for delivery to one of the three other floors: pediatrics on the second floor, OB on the third, and the locked psychiatric unit on Four North. Due to my naïveté and movies that depicted the mentally ill as dangerous, I was scared to enter that last unit to retrieve the cart. When I finally got up the courage to step inside, I learned that, contrary to my stereotype, the patients were actually docile and nonconfrontational.

Before long, I discovered the racism that existed at Herrick. Minority staff like myself, who had no support or influence, were treated as inferiors by Sylvia Mitchell and others in charge. It wasn't fashionable to be the only Japanese on a staff in which whites were the majority.

The hospital hired me and other college and high school students for certain part-time positions in the kitchen. We cleaned up the mess at the end of meals, emptying the trays from the carts, scraping the food off the plates, and placing the plates on a rack that we ran through the steaming dishwasher. Then we removed the hot dishes, stacked them, and put them away into steel wells for the next day's tray line. Of all the students, I was the only non-white.

The only janitor we had was Jessie, a hulking African American man with bulging arms. At 7:30 p.m., I was supposed to check out with everybody and go home. Some days, however, Jessie would call in sick, and I'd be asked to fill in for him, which I resented. "Toru, you're going to have to do the janitor's job tonight," Sylvia would tell me. I was the only one she asked; she never asked any of the white kids to stay. But I had no choice; if I refused, I would've been out of work, and I didn't want to lose my job. I was still thankful to at least have one, and so I accepted that as a high school kid I would do Jessie's grown-man job, straining as I rolled up the heavy wooden slats to scrub and mop the floors beneath until one or two in the morning.

Other times, when William, the pot-washer from UC Berkeley, failed to show, Sylvia would inform me, "William didn't make it tonight. You'll have to do his job." Standing in for him, I washed all of the pots and pans, including the floor-mounted stainless steel cauldrons, some of them four feet tall and four feet in diameter, in which the soup was cooked. Then I cleaned the grills and ovens caked with grease and oil from the day's cooking. Trying to follow the long list of tasks and keep the kitchen spic and span, I became overwhelmed. The first time I filled in for William, I stayed until 4:00 a.m., crumbling to the ground in tears from sheer exhaustion and lack of sleep. Even though I did get paid for my extra effort, and eventually learned a few shortcuts, the job never got easier. These late nights, I would walk home in a daze, crawl into bed with my homework untouched, and set my alarm. Then, I would wake up for school the next morning at six, begin my routine again, feeling like a guinea pig in its spinning treadmill, a tray on a conveyor belt that never seemed to end.

A COUNTRY DRIVE

Midafternoon in the middle of summer. I'm driving between Stockton and Lodi on a lonely backroad in the countryside, which the Japanese call *inaka*. A brilliant blue sky opens to the piercing sun. It's T-shirt weather as a lazy July breeze sweeps slowly down the San Joaquin Valley, its grasses yellowed and dry. It's the Year of the Ox, 1972. The landscape here is free of buildings except for a crumbling, sun-bleached barn nestled within the scrub oaks that soften the view of the rugged countryside. Along the edge of the pavement, the ever-present barbed wire fence curves like the meandering road I drive as I look out at the foothills.

I round the bend to a lush green meadow. It fades into the darkness of a distant thicket of dogwoods, an ideal backdrop for an old Dutch master's painting. Just beyond the fence, where the grass is greener, a herd of cattle stands frozen, noses to the ground. Captured by the scene, I press softly on the brakes and coast slowly off the pavement onto the bumpy yellow shoulder. I roll to a dusty stop, my car teetering dangerously to the right. Reaching over the passenger seat, I crank down the dirty window of my VW Bug for a cleaner look. In the pasture below, about fifty head of cattle ignore me as they graze peacefully in the sun. They seem content in their barbed wire confinement. Trying not to spook them, I step out cautiously and push the door closed, careful to avoid my usual slam.

Immediately, I detect the absence of pollution in the air; the sweet fragrance of the moist, fertile earth and the wild grasses consumes my senses. It's an organic sensation, something you miss in the smoggy city. This barnyard impression takes me back to my early childhood, to the stables at Tanforan, where we were first imprisoned. Thrust from Japantown into there, we had filled up bags with hay and made them into mattresses; we woke up to the smell of manure. At four years old, I looked for horses in vain.

But here, I can see what I couldn't back then: the animals, whom I move toward as I stumble down the embankment to the fence, wanting a closer look. Tiny bugs buzz sluggishly about me as if wondering why I'd bothered to stop. I feel safe and content. Up close I see the pasture is semi-flooded, water pooling in the large hoofprints sunken in mud. A lone steer swings its head slowly in my direction. Curious, it stops chewing and stares. Its large velvet brown ears turn to me, opening like large pouches. I'm awed by its big brown eyes and gorgeous long lashes. Its eyes fix on me without blinking. It hesitates, then labors cautiously toward me, step by step. When we're almost eye to eye, this gentle animal pauses. Then we stare face to face at each other, just a few feet apart. I see the innocence in its eyes. It appears so vulnerable and unaware of its fate. Its gaze seems to ask, "Are you here to feed me or free me?"

Only I realize its fate awaits at the slaughterhouse. I know it has no clue what lies ahead. I want to pet its face and brush off the grass stuck between its eyes, but I know that is wishful thinking. I want to do something to spare or even prolong its life, but I know that is just a dumb thought.

Staring at each other through that barbed wire fence takes me back. I am standing in the middle of the desert in Topaz, a youngster behind barbed wire looking out, not in. We didn't know what fate lay ahead for us either. *What a switch,* I think to myself.

This curious animal hesitates, unsure of my intentions. We are at a standstill. I notice its mouth, shiny and dripping wet. For a moment, its overwhelming size concerns me. But I know how looks can deceive us: up close, I realize this animal doesn't have horns or any intention to hurt me. Suddenly, the thought strikes me: *I can't take part in eating these animals, killed with violence, anymore.*

I can easily cut open this barbed wire fence and set all these animals free, but what will that accomplish? The authorities will be called and in no time the animals will be rounded up and herded right back behind that fence again. Is there no hope for their freedom? Where can I take them?

I drove away that afternoon. I was a changed man, innocent faces flashing repeatedly in my mind's eye. I stopped eating meat from that day forth.

Today, whenever I see animals behind a barbed wire fence, I see a concentration camp where prisoners await their fate. A feeling of guilt comes over me and I ask, "What am I doing to stop the slaughter?"

WITHOUT WARNING

I sit up in a cold sweat. My heart's pounding through my chest like a bass drum. I can feel the thumping with my hands. I'm choking for air, scared. It's pitch dark except for a dim light down the hallway. Then I realize I'm in bed. The clock's glaring, 3:30 a.m., 3:30 a.m. Was I dreaming again? I rub my face to make sure, but that doesn't help. My grip on reality's slipping.

Where did this dream begin? Decades ago, in 1945, near the end of our imprisonment in Topaz. I remember listening to Mama and Arthur's mother and Ukata's mother and Hiromi's mother, all of the mothers questioning each other at the mess hall and the latrine and the washhouse: "Where can we go now that we are being kicked out of camp? Where are you going? No one wants us back—the *hakujins,* that is. They do not want us back in our real hometowns. We are a people without a country. Without a home. Without a promise of help. Without a plan. Without a helping hand."

Their concerns were fueled by "anti-Jap" sentiments expressed by our neighbors back home in California who had signed petitions with the heading "WE DON'T WANT ANY JAPS BACK ON OUR BLOCK" and then sent us copies while we were in camp.

Then one day it was time to go. The guards weren't watching anymore. The gate was wide open and the guard towers were empty as the latrine on a winter's night. All we had was a little hope and faith in some god, a little candle in the immense darkness.

* * *

It's a dream I have had over and over my whole life: I am looking down from above, my pockets bulging with marbles. I'm wearing my blue straw hat and my favorite yellow shirt with Roy Rogers on the front. I'm almost seven, but everyone says I look older because of the permanent worried look on my face. It's hot as hell and dusty, too. I focus in on a crowd of terror-stricken faces. Frenzied, they grab on to each other, scream out panicked questions in disbelief. They are in the open field of Block 4, between the men's latrine and the washhouse, right next to buildings One and Two, where Toby the dog lives, where the sunflowers grow like trees against Barrack One.

I have grown up here since the age of four. We have played marbles here every day. I know every inch of this place. I can smell the dust and the familiar odors drifting from the latrines. This place is home to me, this place where I find myself again and again, Block 4, Topaz, Utah.

The crowd is made up of the frantic mothers of Block 4. They are gathered behind the washhouse, in the large open field where the bigger boys play baseball. Mrs. Hoshiga is asking Mrs. Uchida, "Is it true? Is it true?" Mrs. Uchida replies, "Yes, that's what I heard." Another voice asks, "So, is that what you heard?" Mrs. Uchida's reply: "Yes, Mr. Ogi told me." More voices: "Oh, did you hear that? So, it is true? Oh, my God, it can't be true, it can't be true!"

"*Honto? Honto?* Who told you that? Who? Who?"

Mrs. Ogi bursts in, "Who told you that? Oh, that can't be true. Oh my God, oh my God. Where's the block manager? Oh, where's Mr. Takahashi? Anyone see Mr. Takahashi?" She fights her way through the crowd.

"I don't know the answer. Don't ask me. I don't know," a mother says.

"Where's my big sister Akiko?" I ask. "Where's my mother?" I ask. I can't find them among the bustling crowd.

Mrs. Okada breaks in, "Oh, did you see Mr. Takahashi? Oh, we have to find Mr. Takahashi. Oh, my goodness. He would know? Oh my God. This can't be true. Did you hear that? Did you hear that? They are going to kill us all? Oh my God. This can't be true."

"This must be a mistake," says a Kibei lady. I hear someone say, "They are going to hang us like criminals." No, they can't stop it now, and I'm going crazy with fear. I'm searching for Mama. Suddenly, the crowd parts as two *hakujin* army officials come to make an announcement. "The process has begun and cannot be stopped," they say. Dressed in military brass, the two *hakujins* walk toward the Block 4 crowd, who part to allow the men through. The soldiers, here from Block 2, where they and the other *hakujins* lived, continue their announcement. Yes, they have already built the gallows. They have already started the mass killings. They have already hung all the people from Blocks 1 and 3. They are going to start on Block 4.

That's when I snap. That's when I scream, "No, oh no!"

I sit up in a cold sweat. The clock shows 3:30 a.m. In the dark, I've relived this nightmare. The dream centered on the question I heard again and again: "Where can we go?" At six years old, I had never seen my mother panic before. Unlike most kids, I didn't have an aunt, an uncle, or grandparents to come to my aid or rescue. Still, sixty-three years later, the dream continues, reveals my mother's—our community's—pain. The dream is the panic we felt, the outside world not wanting us back. Where the hell could we go after camp? Even those of us who could afford to own property had to depend mostly on rentals for shelter. How were we going to pay the rent with job discrimination and without employment? Is it any wonder that, without the help of the mental health intervention available today, our self-esteem suffered catastrophic harm? Is that the reason why we repressed our shame and guilt and pushed the damage to ourselves to the back of the closet? Or has our pain gone so far underground that we most often fail to see or acknowledge it ourselves? Every one of us knows of malfunctioning members of our community, but we look the other way, to give affected families their own privacy and to honor their pain. Or we try to deny it ever happens.

Yes, survivorship is a dark and twisted road. My own journey begins late at night, in the dark, when the dream begins. Each time I wake in a sweat, I am reminded of the words of my friend Doctor Takagi: "We are all damaged goods." How correct he is. Most of us are good actors and magicians and can fool scrutinizing onlookers. Or we simply use the closet to tuck away our injuries and handicaps. We all have our hidden wounds. Mine is the dream that comes without warning, the inner pain, the heat and dust and crowds in camp, my mother's face of panic, the voices screaming, "If we had a home, they couldn't kill us. What can we do? Where can we go?"

Voice Lesson

"I will learn how to breathe," I repeat to myself. My hands sweat and my knees tremble as I sit in the waiting room of an old white Victorian on Bancroft Way. I'm here for my first voice lesson with Ms. Claire Zellerbach, a renowned teacher with famous former students to her credit. Her sessions aren't cheap; this is costing me a fortune. Nonetheless, I have finally decided to move forward. I've put off these lessons for forever it seems. I can't remember just how long it's been since I was first urged to find a trainer. "Hey, you've got a good voice," my friends kept telling me after my gigs: parties, dances, and other get-togethers where I was asked to sing. "You should develop your talent. Take voice lessons. There, you'll learn how to breathe."

At first I didn't really believe them, or believe that I had any real talent. I had never thought I was worth the time or the money. What would others say when they heard I had the nerve to consider voice lessons? "Who the *hell* does he think he is?" they would say.

I look down at my watch: 4:55 p.m. Five more minutes before I meet Ms. Zellerbach. I peer out the window at the fog creeping slowly across the San Francisco Bay into Berkeley, spreading uphill through the campus. I can hear the Cal band practicing across the street on the football field for the Big Game, this Saturday's 1982 edition. I am beginning to dream of lofty heights: *How far can this voice lesson really take me? Will I ever make the big-time?* Then, I am brought back to earth: *Who am I kidding anyway? I'm nobody.*

"I will learn how to breathe," I repeat again, trying to center myself. Suddenly, the door opens, and I look up from my watch at Ms. Zellerbach, a tall, elegant woman with graying hair, a kindly smile, and gracious blue eyes. "Come with me," she motions, and I follow her into a small library, catching a whiff of her expensive perfume. I take a seat in a black leather chair that smells brand new.

"Now, Mr. Saito, how long have you been singing and what kind of songs do you like?" she inquires.

"Uh…uh…I like folk songs and uh, old standards," I stutter. *Jesus Christ! Why did I have to say "folk songs"? She's going to think I'm some dumb-ass unsophisticated Japanese. I can't believe I'm screwing up like this already. She's not going to take me seriously. She'll think I'm some stupid, wannabe idiot.* I feel like a real *bakka.* A tingle of shame runs up my back as I try to compose myself.

Hey, what the hell? I scold myself. *I am not that big of a dummy. I've been paid to sing for some years now…Well, nothing to write home about, money-wise that is…just a few bucks…But I can hardly call myself a "professional"…*

I was always embarrassed when others asked me if I was a professional singer. I've been asked that so many times, yet I never felt comfortable addressing the question. Sure, I've been paid for singing, but do I make a living at it? Surely not.

My internal discussion comes to a halt when Ms. Zellerbach asks, "Mr. Saito, what are your thoughts before you go up to sing?"

I'm caught off-guard; I didn't expect such a question. My answer arrives out of nowhere. "I say to myself, *I'm no good. I'm nobody. I'm going to make a fool out of myself, and people will say, 'Who the hell does he think he is?'*"

A long pause follows. I am shocked by my answer, and so is Ms. Zellerbach, whose smile turns into a look of concern.

"My God, why do you think such negative thoughts of yourself?" she asks softly.

I'm at a loss for words. I stammer, "Uh…uh…I guess…because I'm Japanese?"

"That's interesting," she replies. "You think because you're Japanese you're no good?"

"Why, I never thought of it," I respond, "but that's what I say to myself every time I go up to perform. Besides, all the famous singers I like are either white or black—like Nat King Cole and Perry Como and Bing Crosby. None of them are Japanese," I think out loud. I feel backed into a corner. Here, I came to learn how to breathe, and instead I am with Sigmund Zellerbach, who seems to know me better than I know myself.

"How can you expect to perform as a singer if your self-image is so negative?" she implores.

That really hits me between the eyes. *Why do I think so little of myself? How can I expect to perform with such negativity? That's a real handicap. Yeah, Mrs. Z. is really on to something.*

Then I hear it hit: the voice—not my own, the voice of someone else. "Hey you Japs, get the hell out of here! Go back to Japan," a giant *hakujin* man screams at me. Moments before, we had been spinning our tops on the sidewalk, the smell of dried fish and sweet pork drifting across the streets from Mr. Ogi's market in San Francisco's Japantown. "Don't go playing past that garbage can," Akiko, our big sister, had warned, pointing to Mr. Kami's overflowing bin by the curb. Out of nowhere, this man had driven up, stopped his car, got out, and screamed at us at the top of his lungs. For a moment, I stood frozen, scared to death of his bulging eyes and yellow-stained teeth. Then I turned, ran, and flew up the front stairs of our house, slamming the door shut behind me. "Mama, Mama, a big *hakujin* man just called us a Jap! What's that?" I asked, gasping for air.

Mama said nothing, but hurried to the door and locked it. "Stay inside," she warned. "Don't go outside anymore, because it isn't safe." *Anymore? Don't go out anymore?* That gave me goose bumps. It was December 1941. A few days after Pearl Harbor. The seed had been planted. The outside world was no longer safe.

Even though that happened forty-one years ago, I realize: nothing has changed. I am still the little boy in front of his house, unwelcome in his own country, the voice of the man stuck in his head. *If I'm not allowed to have a place here, who the hell am I at this age to think I deserve the spotlight? If I'm Japanese, how can I become a whole person, a worthy human being? How can I find my voice?*

"Here's a trick you might consider," Ms. Zellerbach declares. "If being Japanese is such an obstacle for you, why not try to imagine yourself as a white singer performing instead?"

Instantly, a huge weight lifts off of my shoulders. Being Japanese has been such a heavy burden. I look across the room at Mrs. Z., the smile returning to her face. Her blue eyes sparkle with satisfaction—she's gotten through to me.

I get up from the chair, grab my jacket, and write her a check. She pats me on the back and sees me to the door. As I step out into the cold fog, I hear the band louder now. The trumpets are screaming the Cal fight song. *Yes, this trick will work for now. But who knows? Maybe one of these days I'll really make it. Not as a Japanese who pretends to be white but as a proud Japanese who can let go of the trick and be his own singer.* I thought I'd come here to learn how to breathe. Instead, I learned the real lesson: how to value myself and my voice.

Toru singing during the 2006 Tule Lake Pilgrimage, at the Ragland Theater, Klamath Falls, Oregon. Courtesy of Satsuki Ina.

Uyeda family, 526 43rd Avenue, San Francisco, c. 1947–1948. Back row: Daisy, Annabelle, Doris, Florence, Kaye, Roz, Nancee. Seated: Juneko, Mitsuzo (Papa), Matsuye (Mama), Elsie. Center front: Meiji Marshall. Photo by Robert Laing.

DAISY UYEDA SATODA

Daisy Uyeda Satoda spent 1942 through 1945—her entire high school years— imprisoned in the Central Utah War Relocation Authority concentration camp at Topaz, Utah. Upon their release from camp, her family resettled in San Francisco, across the bay from Oakland, their prewar home. Daisy has since been actively involved in the four Topaz camp reunions as well as in the thirty-two reunions of the Topaz High School Class of 1945.

Daisy believes the story of the unjust incarceration of 120,000 innocent Japanese Americans during World War II should never be forgotten and remain forever in our history books so that this miscarriage of justice never befalls another group of people. To tell this and other stories, she has participated in Brian Komei Dempster's Internment and Resettlement Writing classes and has been a member of the Senior Asian American Women's Writing Workshop at the Japanese Cultural and Community Center of Northern California for more than ten years.

Her writings have appeared in From Our Side of the Fence: Growing Up in America's Concentration Camps *(2001) and* Blossoms in the Desert: Topaz High School Class of 1945 *(2003), both of which were granted major funding from the California State Library's California Civil Liberties Public Education Program. She was also the editor of the Topaz anthology* Return to Topaz '93: Recollections, Reflections, Remembrances.

Daisy is married to Yone Satoda, and together they have three children and five grandsons. She remains actively involved in several community organizations.

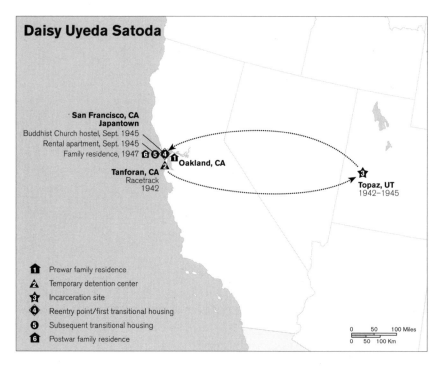

Daisy Uyeda Satoda

San Francisco, CA
Japantown
Buddhist Church hostel, Sept. 1945
Rental apartment, Sept. 1945
Family residence, 1947 **6 5 4** **1** Oakland, CA

Tanforan, CA
Racetrack
1942

Topaz, UT
1942–1945

1 Prewar family residence

2 Temporary detention center

3 Incarceration site

4 Reentry point/first transitional housing

5 Subsequent transitional housing

6 Postwar family residence

0   50   100 Miles
0   50 100 Km

THE RED COAT

The eerie wail of foghorns welcomed us as we disembarked from the ferry.
We stepped into the soft, swirling fog of a typical summer evening in the City
by the Bay: windy, bone-chilling, and misty. The strange foghorns intensified
my loneliness and fear, and I buttoned up my bright red, all-wool overcoat,
the fabric enveloping my body in a cocoon.

We had been released from the Topaz concentration camp—our home
during World War II—two days earlier, on August 29, 1945. I had recently
graduated from Topaz High School after having spent my entire three years
of high school in this desert town in central Utah. Topaz was a self-contained
and self-governed city where we had lived in isolation and had no contact
with the world beyond the barbed wire fence that had imprisoned us.

When Topaz was going to close, my parents had to remain behind to
clear out our barrack rooms. Papa asked me, "Can you please take Nancee
and Elsie with you to San Francisco? That way they will be on time for you
to register them for the fall semester." School was scheduled to start the
following week, and I nodded "yes" as I continued with my packing. Inside
my open suitcase, I folded my coat and placed it carefully over my other
meager personal belongings—clothing, toilet kit, diary, album with photos

of my schoolmates, the Topaz High Class of '45 yearbook, address book, and precious letters and postcards from friends who had left camp earlier. Then I closed my suitcase, both scared and excited about the prospect of freedom. Where would we live? Could I take care of my sisters?

Now hundreds of miles away from Topaz and frightened by the cacophony of myriad noises in this bustling city, my little sisters, Elsie and Nancee, ages eleven and thirteen, clung to my arms, their grip softened by the sleeves of my new coat. I pulled them along while feeling the weight of their shock: we had not had streets, sidewalks, cars, traffic, or outdoor lighting of any kind in Topaz. This chaos was uncomfortably new to us.

Elsie began to hyperventilate as she peered nervously into the street, hoping to catch a glimpse of my sister Kaye, who was scheduled to pick us up and deliver us to the hostel at the San Francisco Buddhist Church. The church was a temporary haven for those of us resettling in San Francisco after our incarceration in various camps. "Where is Kaye?" Elsie whimpered. Tears trickled down her face and she pleaded, "Can't we go back home to Topaz?"

To distract her younger sister, Nancee put her arm around Elsie and gently said, "Just look around you and take in the sights." We stood in awe at the passing parade of sleek automobiles, streetcars, buses, motorcycles, and taxicabs that whizzed by us at alarming speeds.

For the last three years, we had not seen any type of vehicle except for the army trucks that delivered food and coal to the mess halls in Topaz. Since we had no transportation of any kind, we had to walk to get anywhere within the one-mile-square boundary of our camp. We traveled on dirt roads past open ditches and nary a street sign. On our walks, we did not pass stores, movie theaters, hotels, or restaurants because Topaz had none.

It almost seemed surreal here in San Francisco: our footsteps on pavement, the bright lights of matinee shows on movie billboards, the vivid-colored dresses displayed on shining steel racks in shop windows, the smell of grease wafting from skillets where eggs and bacon were being fried in a nearby café.

As we took it all in, we grew more comfortable and forgot about our long wait for Kaye. Soon we were mesmerized by the electric traffic lights that alternately changed from green to amber to red. The towering heights of the skyscrapers overwhelmed us. Our necks swerved in huge arcs as the street lights turned on, almost blinding us with their brightness. We covered our ears with our hands to blunt the deafening noises of a bustling metropolis, the constant honking from seemingly every vehicle on the street.

We must have resembled displaced persons from a war-torn country, self-conscious as we fingered our unfashionable homemade dresses, gawking at every incredible sight: the towering office buildings, the variegated exotic flowers in storefront planters, the white boats in the bay.

In contrast, Topaz was one-dimensional: everything was flat, drab, dry, and colorless. There was very little greenery—no trees and only some scattered vegetable gardens. Our house was a bare army barrack shared by several other families, furnished only with cots and a cast-iron potbelly stove. Black tarpaper covered it all—the barracks, communal bathrooms, latrines, laundry rooms, and mess halls.

Our routine, like the landscape, was monotonous: get up, eat breakfast at the mess hall, go to school, return for lunch at the mess hall, back to school, play a bit, have dinner, and then go to bed. Details like what we wore ceased to matter as much because we all dressed the same—in G.I. (government-issued) black mackinaws, which were surplus items from World War I. These short, heavy coats weighed about five pounds and were distributed campwide. Since we had been uprooted from our homes in the moderate climates of the West Coast, we did not have warm clothing of our own to withstand the minus-zero-degree winters of Utah. In our camp clothing, we couldn't fully express ourselves and our individuality. What we wore was extremely limited, and even when we tried be unique, so many of us ordered similar clothing from the Montgomery Ward mail-order catalogs, which served as our fashion bibles. Placed under so many restrictions, we had become numbed by life in Topaz.

Here in San Francisco, the world stood in vivid contrast to Topaz. As we looked around the Ferry Building area, we noted that the majority population was no longer us but white people who were stylishly dressed in whatever they wanted: the men in suits and hats, carrying briefcases, and women who were so chic in dresses, suits, coats, hats, and gloves.

Suddenly, I wanted to look like them and be a part of the city's scene. I wanted to claim the streets as my own, without the stares or hushed whispers of each passerby who must have heard that we Japanese Americans had been released from the camps and were resettling in the western coastal states. Just then, I turned around and saw the enormous floor-to-ceiling windows of the Ferry Building; in the center of the middle window, I saw my full-length reflection. I was crestfallen. My beautiful red coat, the one I cherished as my most prized article of clothing, now looked like a bargain basement "hot sale item."

I don't think anyone had a floor-length mirror in Topaz. There, just a few months earlier, I had pored through the Montgomery Ward catalog to select this coat as my graduation present from Papa. I had proudly worn my red coat to the senior prom even though it was about 110 degrees that evening. I had felt so grown up and elegant. I treasured that coat, especially since it cost more than one-half of my father's monthly pay of sixteen dollars as a dishwasher in our mess hall.

I glanced at myself in the next window, and to my disappointment the mirror image remained the same. I unfastened the top button of my coat, turned up the collar around my ears, threw my head back, and struck a model-like pose. The sounds and sights of the city receded as I stared at myself in the window, my reflection blurred by passing cars and the lights at the foot of Market Street.

I was startled from my trance by Nancee excitedly shouting, "Look, look! Kaye is finally here!" Kaye was honking the horn and signaling for us to rush into the car since she was double-parked.

Only as we were pulling away from the curb did it dawn on me that my red coat really was not a fashion statement. No, it looked exactly like what it was: an inexpensive $8.98 coat from a mail-order catalog. Beautiful when I wore it in Topaz, here in San Francisco the coat looked like a cheaply made piece of clothing that no one even noticed.

410 AUSTIN ALLEY

"Can I stay over this weekend? I just got evicted from my apartment," Reiko asked plaintively. Reiko had lost both her parents and had no living relatives. She loved sharing time with our boisterous family, and we often referred to her as our "lost" sister.

"Of course," I replied. "We always have room for you, although you know you will have to share a bed with two of my sisters." Our family of thirteen traditionally slept three to a bed, except for my parents and two brothers.

It was early 1946, and our family was living in San Francisco after having spent three and a half years in Topaz. Resettlement was difficult for all of us, but especially for those like Reiko, and most difficult was finding a place to live.

My family was fortunate to have our ever resourceful mother, who found a very old, rickety three-bedroom rental house soon after our arrival in San Francisco. The address was 410 Austin Avenue (actually, it was an alley), right behind the San Francisco Buddhist Church. The exterior of the house was quite shabby; it needed a paint job and perhaps a crane to keep the house from collapsing onto the adjoining building.

The house had only one bathroom and one toilet, so naturally we all developed strong bladders and were constipated most of the time.

The rent was fifty-five dollars a month, and our house was like Grand Central Station for the friends who gathered there every weekend. Even now, after sixty-plus years, old friends laughingly refer to the house as "Goofy

The Department of Justice required all "enemy aliens" to carry a "Parolee's or Internee's–at–Large" document. C. 1945–1946.

Village," because most of the crooked steps that led up to the front door were broken. Back then, we worried that one day someone would crash through the well-worn wooden staircase, which became especially precarious when the overflow of people in the house forced newcomers to hang out on the tiny five-foot-square porch. Our regulars learned to step gingerly between the broken slats and to tread knowingly onto the reinforced sections of the stairway.

Although the Austin Alley house was not fancy—actually it was slum-like—it was a place where we gathered to reunite with old friends and out-of-town visitors, to greet soldiers who were far away from home, and to welcome others who were friends of friends. Even more importantly, 410 was a haven for finding prospective matrimonial partners, especially on Sundays, which was the traditional day off for domestic workers. Many of our friends, like Reiko, could not afford to support themselves and had very few employment skills, so they often found jobs as live-in domestic help in fancy homes in the city. Papa, patriarch of our large family, was keenly aware of the isolation and loneliness of these young people and always reminded us, "We are lucky to have a home, and we should invite your friends and other young people for dinner." Papa saw 410 as a unifying place, where we could meet up with other Nikkei who were alone in the city.

For these Sunday open houses, he made special dinners for our friends. On weekdays, they either attended college or worked at entry-level jobs, returning in the evenings to the residences where they earned their keep—room and board and, in some cases, small stipends—as maids, housecleaners, gardeners, cooks, and mothers' helpers. Papa always cooked them a roast of some kind: pork, beef, lamb, or corned beef on St. Patrick's Day or ham on Easter—food he could stretch to feed an additional ten to twenty drop-in guests if necessary. Papa had an uncanny skill for carving seven- to eight-pound roasts into paper-thin slices, which he then smothered in tasty gravies. A simple iceberg lettuce salad, loads of rice and mashed potatoes, and green vegetables usually accompanied his hearty main dishes.

The kitchen was a whirlwind of activity as Mama and Papa plated the dishes and my younger sister Roz and I served, cleared, and washed the dishes—the one twelve-piece setting of china and silverware we owned—between the several shifts of dinner.

Our roast lamb dinners were shunned by my sister Flo; they reminded her of the prewar days when Papa cooked mutton quite often, as it was a very inexpensive cut of meat. Flo, the original "drama queen," would turn up her nose and gag when she sat down to eat the dish. Once she even blurted out, "Yuck! I hate lamb. Lamb smells like dirty armpits!"

Papa, in contrast, was very quiet and self-effacing. When there was no meat left over, he ended up eating *ochazuke*—hot tea poured over rice—with *otsukemono,* pickled radishes or Napa cabbage. He insisted that it was "much healthier to eat vegetables and to eat meat only sparingly," but we secretly knew he was mostly just making sure everyone else got their share.

Mama, on the other hand, a four-foot-eight, roly-poly 165-pounder, never missed a meal. A social butterfly, she always seated herself at the middle of the table, ate through all three shifts of dinner, and regaled the young people with her endless litany of hilarious experiences and escapades. Her stories often related unsuccessful attempts to con her way into jobs that she could not handle and then the firings that were automatic because of her general ineptitude.

One night she told the table, "Mrs. Kimi Handa once asked me to cover for her at a housecleaning job, and the lady of the house asked me if I preferred to be called Mary or Matsy." Mama, whose first name was Matsuye, bristled at both suggestions and said very sharply, "My name is *Mrs.* Uyeda." Needless to say, at the end of the day the employer told Mama she worked too slow, then paid her the going rate of $1.50 per day and added, "Your services are no longer needed as Kimi will be back to work at the end of the month."

Still alive with my mother's voice and my father's dinners, this old building is home to memories for many of us who passed through the front door during the uncertainties of the resettlement years. Here, we gathered on the stairs and in the crowded dining room where we made connections, laughed between bites of Papa's succulent roasts, and were endlessly entertained by my mother's outrageous stories. Names and faces have dimmed with age, but 410 is still home, the lively place where we struggled to build a life from what had been torn asunder by our imprisonment. Together, we turned the harshness of our wartime past into tender scenes of our communal strength.

PAPA'S HOME-BAKED BREAD

"There's going to be a bread strike," Papa said as he wearily unloaded his bag of groceries onto the kitchen table of our house at Austin Alley. "The shelves at Safeway are already bare. It looks like people are starting to hoard again."

He knew we needed to stock up; with nine lunches to make every day plus eighteen slices of toast to cook and butter for breakfast, the three loaves he was able to grab at the store were not going to last for more than two days.

I did not realize until years later the full extent of what Papa, the self-appointed cook of the family, was facing during the postwar period of 1946, when America was still on rations, and supplies for civilians were limited. Even though we were a large family, we were able to stretch our ration coupons since we did not need too many severely restricted items, such as butter, sugar, flour, and meat, which were used only minimally in Japanese cooking—the only type of cuisine that Mama cooked.

After putting away his grocery items in the kitchen cupboard, I found Papa with a worried look on his face as he pondered this dilemma. Then, he put on his hat and coat again and said, "I am going back to the grocery store." He returned home an hour or so later, huffing and puffing, lumbering into the house. In his arms, he carried a ten-pound bag of flour and several packages of Fleischmann's yeast cakes, plus bologna, ham, cheese, and lettuce, but no bread.

"What are you up to?" asked my oldest sister, Doris, as she and the rest of us checked out his purchases.

Mitsuzo Uyeda (Papa), Sacramento, California, c. 1915.

Papa replied, "I'm going to make bread for sandwiches for the family to take to work or school."

Doris rolled her eyes and said, "Papa, you've never made bread before, and it'll probably turn out to be dry and tasteless like hardtack."

"Don't worry," assured Papa. "I know how to make bread. It will be easy. It's just like making biscuits, but I have to use yeast instead of baking powder."

Papa then reminded us of the time he had made soap when we were in Topaz. He said, "I used ashes from the potbelly stove in our barrack room, got some used fat from our mess hall, had the block manager buy me some lye and glycerin from the drug store in Delta, and I added leftover slivers of scented bath soap. I cooked this mixture on the hot plate in our room. The people in our block laughed at me when I undertook this experiment but were so grateful when I later passed out the homemade soap to them."

Prewar, Papa also had to be resourceful, as his extremely limited earning power was already strained beyond the breaking point. But now we wonder: How did he manage to feed and clothe his family of thirteen through all those lean Depression years? To his credit, his pride kept him from divulging to the family his shame over the abject poverty in which we were forced to live. Poor Papa must have had many sleepless nights.

Only years later would we children fully appreciate Papa's self-taught culinary talents and creations. As a child, I vaguely knew that he had owned several restaurants in Watsonville that had failed during the Depression and on up to the time of our incarceration. Then, before the wartime government rationing of items like meat, sugar, and butter, Papa cooked for his restaurant customers only American and Mexican foods, which was a mystery. I have often wondered how he had learned to prepare other ethnic foods when we could only ever afford to eat in cheap Chinese restaurants.

Many hours later, Papa came out of the kitchen and asked Doris to see what he had placed on the table. Reluctantly following Papa, Doris did a double take as she saw four loaves of gleaming golden bread on the cooling rack. "Wow, Papa, you outdid yourself; the bread looks wonderful—just like store-bought bread. The aroma is heavenly—smells as yummy as Eagle Bakery. I know the bread will be every bit as tasty as it is beautiful."

Papa sliced up the bread and passed the first piece to Doris, who promptly slathered her portion with butter and Mama's strawberry preserves. "Oh, Papa," she exclaimed, "this is sooo good—a thousand times better than the cottony Wonder Bread you buy." Stuffing her mouth with bread, she mumbled, "I want another slice, and make it quick!"

Papa kept his silence as was his usual wont; rarely did he acknowledge the barbed remarks uttered by us—the nine sharp-tongued "Doubting Thomas" Uyeda sisters—who now hurried into the kitchen upon hearing the excited commotion between Doris and Papa. After sampling the bread we, too, were amazed at Papa's inventiveness and yelled out, "Good job, Pop!" as we hastily devoured the first loaf. Meanwhile, Papa took a step back and, not saying a word, smiled with a knowing nod. Now, as I recall this long-ago, almost forgotten kitchen scene, I try to compare our current favorite five-dollar artisan breads from the French bakery to Papa's homemade concoction. The new breads may include fancier ingredients like organic flour, dried figs, olives, walnuts, or cheese, but I am certain those gourmet additions do not evoke the same nostalgia that we feel sixty years later when remembering Papa's bread. Thinking of it now, I am warmed by the love Papa showed as he passed out the steaming bread we savored, the melted butter lingering in our mouths.

KING CAFÉ

One afternoon, my sister Elsie, who was attending Lowell High School, dropped a coin in the jukebox of the King Café and played, for the hundredth

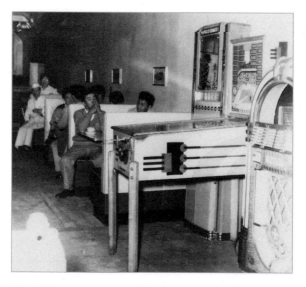

The jukebox was a prominent fixture at the King Café on Webster Street in San Francisco's Japantown, and friends Eddie Hitomi and Gary Toji (front booth) were frequent patrons. In the background, Papa in a chef's hat is seated while Mama in her apron stands. 1949.

time, her favorite song: "Gloomy Sunday" by Billie Holliday. Elsie sang and swayed to the music as a tall and attractive woman came up, stood behind her, and said, "Um, do you like that song?"

Elsie, snapping her fingers and swinging her hips, said, "Oh, yes, this song is sooo good."

The lady added, "Did you know that's me singing on that record?"

In the fifties, this part of San Francisco was the jazz center of the West. All the famous black musicians and performers, including some of the biggest names in the music world, congregated there, with Holliday, Lionel Hampton, and Duke Ellington jamming at the nearby after-hours nightclubs.

At the time my mother had opened the King Café, in 1948, she couldn't have known it would become a hangout for Holliday and others in the jazz world. After resettling in San Francisco following our three-and-a-half-year imprisonment at Topaz, Mama had made the daring decision to open this little restaurant in the Fillmore District. Begrudgingly, we supported Mama's venture; once we completed our day jobs, we sisters had to pull evening shifts as waitresses and dishwashers at her restaurant. During this time, I came to see a different side of Mama as she interacted with her larger-than-life and sometimes non-paying customers. Even though she lacked financial acumen, I grew to learn the real meaning of this place to her.

Mama's café was like a second home to her, a melting pot where people of different races and backgrounds could mix. Meeting place for musicians and popular hangout for Nikkei of all ages, the King Café also was home to society's misfits or, more correctly, the derelicts of this famous ghetto: the pimps, prostitutes, "homos," drunks, felons, and dope addicts. Mama had an engaging knack for being able to cadge rides from some of her more infamous customers, some of whom dealt drugs, pimped women, and gambled. The neighborhood residents feared these African American gangsters, but to Mama these deal-breakers—big-time, conniving wheeler-dealers—looked good, dressed sharply, and always had huge, long, black limousines with drivers. They were on to her wily ways but never hesitated to drive her to doctors, dentists, beauty salons, department stores, and other appointments whenever she asked.

Mama enjoyed the attention, teasing, and bantering of these regular customers, but she did not tolerate trouble. In order to get rid of the troublemakers, she used to call the cops so often that the cops became regular

Family and friends gather at the King Café in 1949. Left to right: Roz, Nancee, Mama, Papa, and friend Gary Toji.

customers themselves. The cops would first confiscate the guns, knives and shivs, brass knuckles, and other weapons the customers hid in their pockets or strapped to their legs. They would then tell the drunks, "Cool off and wait in one of the booths," while they had their lunch or dinner at the counter. Sometimes they would take leisurely refills on their coffee before snapping on the handcuffs and hauling the bums to the cooler.

Mama's steadiest customer was Harry, the beat cop. He looked in on the restaurant several times a day, feeling that his uniformed presence would prevent any unwholesome disturbance or action. Harry was a very handsome African American, a little on the round side and with a huge grin. Before the war, there was only limited interaction between African Americans and Japanese Americans. Now, after the war, they coexisted in this small area of San Francisco, not just as neighbors but as friends.

One day Harry came in with a long face.

Mama looked at Harry and, noticing something amiss, said, "Harry, how come you have on a different uniform?"

Harry replied that he had been fired from the force and was now a member of the "Special Police," who was paid by various merchants to protect them from vandalism in the Fillmore.

Knowing that policemen did not get fired from their jobs without a good reason, she asked him what had happened.

I am sure Mama was concerned about Harry. The Fillmore was proud of him, as he was only the second African American policeman to join the San Francisco Police Department, in the 1940s. He was a hero in the community and everyone respected him because he was smart, honest, kind, gentle, and soft-spoken.

"Well, Mom," said Harry meekly, "I got busted for pimping."

"What's pimping? You don't have pimples."

Harry explained that he got busted for hustling women for Marshall, Frank, and other big-time guys who hung out down the street at Jimbo's Bop City.

Mama got excited and asked, "Why you do such a dumb thing? Everybody knows that Marshall is a big-time dope dealer. Besides, his lady friend looks cheap like a prostitute." Mama disliked the woman's bright red dyed hair, the theatrical makeup, and tight dresses. "Why black guys like white women anyway?"

Mama had recently suspected that Marshall and his girlfriend were shooting drugs in the restroom of the King Café. Earlier that day she had banged on the door until they came out, and she told Marshall she was going to report him to the police. She also said she was going to tell Harry.

Marshall laughed and said, "Mama, it won't do no good. Harry won't be arresting anyone anymore." Now she understood why Harry had on a different uniform.

"Harry," she said, "I'm surprised you dumb enough to take money from them. They not good people, and you know that. How come you so crazy?" She shook her head and polished the counter extra hard as if trying to rub some sense into Harry's head.

Harry looked down into his coffee cup. "I just wanted to do something special for the family. I wanted my wife to have a beautiful fur coat to wear to church." He had gotten Gladys a real mink for nothing from Frank, who had repossessed it from one in his stable of women. Gladys refused to wear the coat, saying it was bought with blood money.

Realizing that Gladys had already dressed down Harry, Mama lightened up and commiserated with him. "Harry, you made one big mistake."

Harry admitted, "I just wanted a little bit of the fast action enjoyed by big shots like Marshall and Frank with their five-hundred-dollar suits and big bankrolls. I know what they did was illegal, but it all looked so easy. I just wanted a little take to buy Gladys a mink and used cars for Shirley and Junior."

Patting Harry's back and straightening his tie, Mama told Harry that everything was going to be okay because he was paying for his stupid mistake by getting kicked out of the police force. She added, "Harry, you brought big shame on your family. The only way you can make it up to them is to be honest, work hard, and not be tempted again by money that you don't earn."

Harry knew what everyone else did—that anyone at anytime could come to Mama and confide in her. She let everyone in through the doors of her café. Not only did her place house those like Harry, who protected the law and broke it, but it was also a destination for people like Lois, who simply broke the law. Lois was an African American prostitute who worked the neighborhood and was also a very kind woman who liked to help out by waiting on tables and doing the dishes. She would not accept any pay from Mama. We were fascinated by her red-lacquered, curved, two-inch-long fingernails. She was not pretty, but she had an animal magnetism. Men loved her. She was living with George, a suave, middle-aged Nisei bartender/musician. A relationship between a black woman and a Japanese American man was unusual in the late 1940s, and Mama told George that his older brother, who had passed away a short time ago, would not have approved of it. George just shrugged and said, "Mama, you don't understand. I hang out with the 'black cats' and I still get very lonely, and the Nikkei girls won't go out with me. Lois is a very nice woman and she does not pressure me for marriage, although she does proudly introduce herself as 'Mrs. Lois Sasaki.'"

Lois never hustled any of the customers, but she later seduced a young soldier into marrying her, so she could get his army allotment. The naïve and innocent eighteen-year-old Private Green was in love with Lois, who admitted to being ten years older, although twenty years would have been more accurate. We never saw Lois after she left San Francisco to join the private when he was transferred to an army base outside of California. Very odd bedfellows.

No matter how crazy her customers acted, though, Mama still accepted them. Indeed, Mama didn't care what others thought, and she did what *she* thought was right. Older than most Issei women, she was a Nisei anomaly as someone who looked past the superficial barriers the world created. We can never forget "Frankie Kitanai (Dirty)," a "flaming homo," as he labeled himself. Frankie was an old family friend and member of a wild Nikkei gang from the prewar days, and he was the palest white man I had ever seen. Tall, blonde, and nice-looking, he always wore his trademark bright-red-framed eyeglasses. Frankie held court practically every evening in one of the booths at the King Café. He told risqué jokes and loved shocking people with hilarious tales of homosexuality. In his saner moments he would often ask Mama to make him his favorite *saba zushi* (marinated raw mackerel sushi).

King Café was open for about three years. In that short time, Mama's charisma and her zany restaurant attracted scores of steady customers: singers, cops, outcasts, the invisible, and the forgotten. Mama treated them all equally. She epitomized the courage of the Nisei who forged ahead after resettlement. Though she was a lousy businesswoman and at times fell prey to her own naïveté, I can proudly say that she was truly color-blind, a woman who embraced everyone and everything with open arms.

Matsuye Moriyama (Mama), Sacramento, California, c. 1915.

Top: Looking down the row of barracks westward at the Minidoka War Relocation Authority Center, August 1943.

Bottom: A panoramic view of the Minidoka concentration camp. Photo by Francis Stewart, August 18, 1942. War Relocation Authority Photographs of Japanese-American Evacuation and Resettlement, WRA no. G-413 (top) and D-108 (bottom). Courtesy of The Bancroft Library, University of California, Berkeley.

Harumi Iwakiri Serata was born on April 14, 1931, in Fife, Washington, a suburb of Tacoma. After the December 7, 1941, bombing of Pearl Harbor, her father was detained by the FBI and interned at Fort Missoula Internment Camp in Montana; her mother and the family's four children were forcibly removed to Puyallup Assembly Center outside of Seattle and later imprisoned in the Minidoka concentration camp in Idaho, where they spent three years.

Harumi left Minidoka in April 1945 to resettle on a farm in Eden, Idaho, where her father was employed as a farm laborer. The rest of the family worked on neighboring farms weeding and harvesting vegetables. Once they had saved enough money, they returned to their home in Fife, Washington. There, Harumi met and married Walter Kenbo Serata, and together they moved to San Francisco in April 1954.

After thirty-four years of service, Harumi retired from the State of California's Department of Social Services. She has since volunteered at many nonprofit agencies, and in 1997 she received the Kay Okamoto Volunteer Award.

Harumi has attended writing classes for the past thirteen years. She has written the Iwakiri family history for the benefit of future generations, and her stories and poems have been published in the anthology From Our Side of the Fence, the newspaper Hokubei Mainichi, and various newsletters. She has also been interviewed by AsianWeek, along with other members of her writing group.

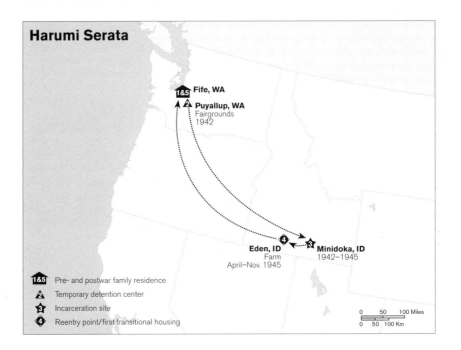

Harumi Serata

Fife, WA `1&5`

Puyallup, WA `2`
Fairgrounds
1942

Eden, ID `4`
Farm
April–Nov. 1945

Minidoka, ID `3`
1942–1945

`1&5` Pre- and postwar family residence

`2` Temporary detention center

`3` Incarceration site

`4` Reentry point/first transitional housing

0   50   100 Miles
0   50   100 Km

THE DESERT

We looked at the desolate land as we got off the train and boarded the bus.
The desert was so hot and dry, over 100 degrees, covered with sagebrush
and tumbleweed. As we looked out the windows, no one spoke a word. I
thought, *Where are we going?*

The bus stopped at Block 3, a cluster of tarpapered buildings, and we
were told to get off. This would be our home—the Minidoka concentration
camp—for the duration of the war. Papa was busy talking with the advance
organizing group, who helped him get assigned to a room and find cots,
mattresses, and blankets. With six of us in one room, it was very cramped
when we set up the cots; we barely had enough room to walk between the
beds. But we were tired from the trip, so we went to sleep early.

The next day, as we inspected our surroundings, we noticed the grounds
of the camp were level and stripped clean of vegetation. A barbed wire fence
surrounded the camp, and a guard tower had been erected to assure no one
would escape. We looked at the desert on the other side of the fence, and
it looked so forbidding. With its blanket of sagebrush, the desert floor was
flat as far as our eyes could see. We came from the Northwest, a land full of
greenery with tall trees and rolling hills. In Minidoka, we could not see even

one tree that could give us shade from the hot sun. Mama warned us, "Never go near the fence. It's dangerous. There's a guard tower and soldiers with rifles patrolling along the fence."

After a year, the official camp restriction was lifted, and we were encouraged to leave camp and wander into the desert. As children, we discovered many treasures out there, such as beautiful rocks, plants, and flowers. We saw cactus flowers, little bluebells that smelled like onions, and the twisted, gnarled branches of the bitterbrush that the men sculpted into figures. We saw trails snakes made as they slithered across the desert floor, many rabbit droppings, and tumbleweed that rolled across the landscape with the wind. Young people fished and swam in the canal. We began to see the beauty of the desert; it was not so desolate after all.

We children stayed close to camp, but the Issei men would wander far into the desert looking for rocks, plants, and branches to be used in their gardens. They also discovered the many trails probably used by the camp construction crew. They must have enjoyed the freedom of being away from the prison camp, if even for just a short time. Occasionally, one of them became disoriented and would get lost in the desert and a search party was sent out to find him.

As the winter of 1944 ended, we were told, "The camp will be closing and you will have to make plans for your departure." We had been incarcerated for almost three years. In April 1945, Papa decided to move us to a farm in Eden, Idaho, where he got a job as a farmhand. When my family relocated, my nineteen-year-old sister-in-law, Chiyo, was left behind in camp with her baby. Her husband—my brother George—had been drafted into the army, and her parents and younger sister had decided to return to Japan when the war ended, which meant they were relocated to Tule Lake Segregation Center in Northern California for the time being. She felt abandoned by her own family, and since we were all she had left, she depended on us to include her when we moved out of camp. We told Chiyo, "We need to work and save money before returning to our home in Fife, Washington. It will be difficult to find a job or resume the produce business. We want you to stay in camp until we move back to Washington." We all had to work to make ends meet, and we knew she would be unable to do such hard labor, especially with a baby.

On Sundays, we would take Chiyo out of the camp to spend the day with us. Driving out with her in the daytime was easy because visibility was good, but returning was difficult since we had to drive in the dark. The desert was teeming with thousands of jackrabbits with large ears, and their eyes shone in our headlights before they scampered away. We would drive to Chiyo's block and let her off at the fence. It was very dark, and Chiyo would have to walk to her barrack with only a flashlight while carrying her baby.

Chiyo became more and more unhappy as people left the camp and Minidoka became a ghost town. On one Sunday we went to pick her up, she was even refused permission to leave the camp; the War Relocation Authority no longer granted any special privileges, as a way of trying to force people out of camp permanently. Chiyo would tell us, "My friends are all gone. I feel alone, afraid, and isolated." The mess hall was closed down and the water was shut off in her block. She had to walk to the next block to eat her meals and take showers. Toward the end of summer, she asked, "Can I move in with you in Eden?" But there just wasn't any room for another person with a baby in the small house. We told her, "Go to Seattle and we will meet you there in a few months once the harvest is over." Chiyo decided instead to move to Minneapolis, Minnesota, to be near her husband's army base. She and her husband, my brother George, stayed in Minneapolis until his Military Intelligence Service course was completed and he received orders to be shipped overseas to Japan.

By November of 1945, snow was on the ground. The harvest was over, and we knew it was time to return from Eden to our home in Fife, Washington. We thought about going to see the Minidoka camp and the desert one last time before leaving. Mama said, "Why bother? Everybody is gone, and the camp is closed." Looking back, I wished we could have gone. In this place where we spent three years of our lives, we met many others whose friendships made our incarceration tolerable. Maybe we could have revisited our barrack room once more to see the items we had left behind: table, chairs, and cabinets that Papa had made with scrap lumber. Maybe we could have found my doll with the many outfits I made for her, or even the electric hot plate we used to cook in our room. Maybe we could have brought closure to our long odyssey.

LEAVING CAMP

One day in late fall of 1944, our home-class teacher, the motherly, middle-aged Mrs. Frost, said, "You can go home now to the West Coast. You no longer have to stay in camp." Mrs. Frost thought it was wrong that we were imprisoned, and she had therefore felt compelled to teach us in camp even though she herself was not incarcerated.

We looked at her blankly and said, "The war is still going on; isn't it dangerous to leave camp?" In the past, teachers had told us, "You are in camp for your safety, and there are people who want to harm you." We had heard rumors of harassment faced by those of us trying to relocate. Some were even forced to return to the camps when their houses were shot at or their cars were run off the road.

Despite the anxieties we harbored from hearing these stories, the teachers were quite persuasive in convincing us why we should leave camp. They said, "There is housing and financial aid available for you," and they wanted us to relay this message to our parents. Little did we know that the housing was in hostels or consisted of cots in church basements, or that the financial aid was only twenty-five dollars per person and a train ticket. Little did we know that many families had to apply for welfare.

One girl's family did leave camp immediately after the War Relocation Authority announced that the West Coast was no longer a restricted area. Her wealthy father was concerned about his many properties and anxious to know his losses. We were concerned for her safety, but she wrote a letter that stated, "I'm all right and reacquainted with my old school friends, who welcomed me back." The teacher read the letter to the class and reassured us, "See, it is safe to leave camp."

When the restriction on the West Coast was lifted, Papa and a group of men from camp traveled to the Tacoma area to assess the situation. In the rural community of Fife, Washington, where we had lived before the war, he inquired about job opportunities and then walked to our old house. Papa asked the current tenant, "Can I stay overnight? There are no motels nearby." The female tenant, whose husband was in the navy, was alarmed by my father's presence—local residents who had spotted Papa walking along the highway made a threatening phone call telling him, "Leave or you will be harmed"—but the tenant's uncle and aunt, who were living with her, said, "Don't let them bully you." Papa stayed the night and left the next day, returning to Minidoka to rejoin the family.

After that experience, our family did not return to our home in Fife directly from camp since Papa knew he would be unable to find a job there and we needed to save money to see us through the lean winter months. Instead, Papa got a job on a farm in Eden, Idaho, a few miles from camp.

We left camp around April 1945, before the school year ended. We loaded our few possessions on the back of a truck. "We can't take everything. Take only the essential furnishings we need on the farm," said Papa. Mama said, "I don't want to take anything we made in camp. Leave the table and chairs made with scrap lumber." She probably did not want to be reminded of our stay there, but against her wishes we did take the chest of drawers Papa had made along with one army blanket. We felt relieved and happy to finally leave camp even though we were disappointed we couldn't return to our house in Washington.

From Minidoka we drove to the farm of Kenneth and Eileen Roberts who had three children: a teenage son, a younger boy, and a baby girl. John, the older son, had chores to do, so we did not speak with him. But Dickie, the second son, always came to our house, and we had fun playing with Velda, a happy baby. Looking back, I can see they were very kind to take in a Japanese American family from camp. They lived in the large house in front of the property with tall shade trees, and we lived in a small white house in the back with three small rooms and a screened porch. The house had no bathroom or running water, just an outhouse twenty feet away and a water pump fifty feet from the house. As we hung our curtains from camp we noticed the numerous nail holes already in the window frames, a sign of the many people who had hung their curtains here before us.

The farm had about 130 acres, with beans and hay and a pasture with a herd of cows and some horses, which came quite close to our house, expecting the treat of a carrot, especially when we stood near the fence. They would stare at us and we would look at them. We had never seen horses so close before. One day we noticed a bag hanging from a horse's rear end, and a baby horse was on the ground nearby, still wet. Another horse tried to get close to inspect the baby, but the mother mare fought it off. My sister, Tatsie, and I became scared, and she said, "I'll tell Mrs. Roberts what happened," and ran to her house. I stood by the horses, afraid the baby might get trampled. Mrs. Roberts, a petite woman, took a stick and whipped the intruding horse away. The horse reared on hind legs, and we marveled at Mrs. Roberts's bravery.

Papa worked on the Roberts family farm, milking the cows and controlling the irrigation of the crops to make sure the water flowed through the rows of plants. Mama and we three sisters got jobs working at various farms, where we weeded, picked onions and cherries, and harvested potatoes. All the chores we did by hand in those days are now done by machines. My younger sister and I had never worked before and found it hot, dirty, and backbreaking. We were still children and learned the hard way of life for transient farmworkers.

In August 1945 Mrs. Roberts told us, "School will be starting." *How strange to start so early*, I thought; I learned later it was because we would take time off in the fall for the harvest season. We went to the nearby grammar school, a small brick building with an outhouse in the back. I had the sixth, seventh, and eighth grades in my room; one teacher taught all three grades, so we got only a third of the attention, and I knew I wasn't learning much. The children attending were a mixture of locals and children of transient workers from the Southern states. My sister and I were the only Japanese Americans from the camps.

Our male teacher drove the yellow school bus to pick up the children in the morning and return them home in the afternoon. I took the bus to school, but on the way home the route had too many stops, so I usually walked. That way, I could return sooner. Sometimes one student would ride his horse to school when he missed the bus. He tied the horse to a tree during the day.

One time our teacher was called out of class to drive his bus to pick up the German prisoners of war who were working on nearby farms and to take them back to their prison camp. On the way, he stopped by the school to check on us, his students. When our class looked outside the window and waved to the prisoners, our teacher became angry and said, "Never do that again." But I could relate to the Germans our teacher drove to and from their jobs on the farms. They, too, were prisoners. I was confused. Why was the teacher so angry? Was it because the prisoners were our enemy? Many of the prisoners were very young, probably teenagers, and I thought, Weren't we Japanese Americans considered the enemy, too, since we had lived in a camp?

After we attended classes for about a month, the school closed for harvest season. We all had to go into the fields to pick potatoes in rows so long we couldn't see the ends. We filled bushel baskets with potatoes and dumped them into sacks—each weighing around sixty pounds when full. We were paid by the sack for this grueling work in the dusty field where we were hunched over all day.

Left to right: Harumi, her sister Tatsie, and friends Betty Osada and Janie Otsuka gather at the Buddhist Church in Tacoma, Washington, the center of social activities, including dances, parties, and shows. C. 1947.

We returned to school in the middle of October for our Halloween costume party. The teacher created a haunted house, and I dressed up as a Hawaiian girl with a flowered dirndl skirt and a flower pinned to my hair. I attended the event with my best friend, Betty Lou, who was my same age but more mature. Although I can't recall her costume, I remember certain other things about her well: she wore makeup, had a grown-up figure, and lived in a very shiny house with flattened tin cans used as shingles.

The war in Europe and the Pacific ended that fall while we lived on the farm in Idaho. A holiday was declared, and we stopped working for the day. Papa dropped by the store to pick up a few items, and the local men gathered there to celebrate invited Papa for a drink. My sisters and I were happy the war had finally ended; it was a day we had anticipated for a long time. "We can finally go home," we said to each other. In contrast to our excitement, we noticed Mama and Papa were quiet and went to bed early that night. Now, I can gather they were probably sad to see their homeland defeated and humiliated, but at the time we didn't understand why they weren't also happy about the end of the war.

Winter came, and we returned to our home in Fife, Washington. We had to say our goodbyes, and I remember my teacher had tears in his eyes when he said, "Good luck to you." I think he knew we would have some hard times ahead.

We anticipated our next steps. We would have to enroll in a different school, and my older sister Chiyo and Papa would have to find jobs. Feeling both relieved and anxious, we were finally on our way home. It had been three years and seven months since we had left Fife, and again we would have to swallow our pride in the struggle to reclaim our lives.

LETTERS FROM JAPAN

During World War II, my parents lost all contact with their relatives and friends in Japan, since communication between Japan and the United States had come to a halt. While imprisoned in Minidoka, my parents must have worried and thought about those close to them—were they safe? When we returned to our home in Washington after the war ended, they were finally able to write letters to their families and friends.

Five years had passed since their last contact with Japan, and much had happened during the war. My parents wrote to their loved ones about being incarcerated in a concentration camp in the desert of Idaho. They also wrote about how they had lost their business and had to start over. "We are healthy and working hard to regain our lives and business,"

Harumi (center) plays cards and listens to music with friends at the Hashimoto residence, a frequent Saturday-night gathering place. C. 1949.

they wrote. "Please reply and let us know how you are and if you need anything."

After the war, Japan was in despair. We heard about the severe food shortage, about their country being occupied by U.S. Armed Forces, and about how the Japanese people had to rebuild their country with their own strength and will combined with the assistance of the U.S. government. Most of all, our family wanted to be in touch with their relatives to make sure they were okay.

The relatives wrote back, chronicling all of the events of the past five years, including who had died and who was still alive. Luckily, living in Shikoku, they were not bombed and had enough food to eat. They had a garden for vegetables and fished in the Inland Sea. "Please don't worry about us; we do not need anything," their letters said. There had been quite a few deaths in the family, though: two of Mama's sisters had died of tuberculosis, and also her mother had died, Papa's father had died, and some young men in the family had died fighting in the war. Mama locked herself in the bathroom, the only place where she had privacy, and here she read over the letters and cried.

My parents also received letters from friends who had returned to Japan before the war. "Please send us sugar, coffee, cigarettes, hard candy...," they

Harumi, her sister Tatsie, and Mary Nomura prepare for the Hana Matsuri (Buddha's birthday celebration). C. 1952.

wrote. "Isn't it strange they would ask for things when our family doesn't, even though we are also in need?" said Mama. We sent packages only to learn that half of what we mailed was stolen. Our family and friends wrote back thanking us and reporting that the packages they received were opened and half of the contents were missing. Mom heard about the "black market" and said, "At least they didn't steal all of it."

One lady wrote to us that she would like a box of Hershey's chocolate kisses. "I haven't eaten any chocolates during the war and I remember how wonderful they were." Another person wrote, "The cup of coffee you sent was the last thing my husband drank before he died."

Papa received a letter from a friend, Hiroshi Yamamoto, requesting a suit, and he included his measurements. "I need the suit for a job as a translator and need to look presentable," he had written. Mama was suspicious and said, "They sell suits in Japan. Why does he need one from us?" "We were good friends when he lived in America," said Papa. "We should send it to him." Papa purchased a dark suit with a shirt, tie, socks—the complete outfit—and sent it to Hiroshi.

Hiroshi's wife received the package and wrote, "I was shocked to see the suit. I didn't know Hiroshi had requested it from you, and I apologize for my husband's deception. Hiroshi works as a caddy at a golf course for the American army. He is a broken man and has taken to drinking and has a mistress young enough to be his daughter. They have moved into my house, and I have had to take care of them. Please do not send him any more packages."

Papa wrote a letter back to Hiroshi: "I am very disappointed with you. I learned that the suit you requested was not for a job as a translator. I could not afford to spend the money, and it was a sacrifice for me since I have a family to feed." He never heard from Hiroshi again.

But not everyone took advantage of us like Hiroshi had. I remember we received packages of tea and *nori* (seaweed) from people in Japan who appreciated the care packages we sent to them. They wrote, "Our home was damaged, but we have survived the war and your package has given us hope for the future." To them, the words of encouragement and empathy we gave them from far away in America meant more than the material items.

TRICK OR TREAT

Author's note: After World War II ended in the Pacific, Nisei and Kibei (born in America but educated in Japan) soldiers were sent to Japan to be interpreters and translators during the time of U.S. occupation. Japanese American civilians were also recruited by the military to work in Japan in various capacities. In all, over five thousand Japanese Americans were in Japan to help the country recover from the war.

My brother, George, was a Military Intelligence Service (MIS) soldier assigned to work as an interpreter at a bus station in Tokyo, Japan. The following is a story I wrote for his children about their father's service during this period.

"This box is much too large," said my sister-in-law, Chiyo, with a laugh. She was sending a wallet as a Christmas gift to her husband, George, who was stationed in Tokyo, Japan. She had to use a regulation military-size box (approximately 12x8x2 inches) and the wallet rattled loosely inside of it.

"Why don't you put in some boxes of raisins to fill up the extra space?" Mama suggested. "That's a good idea, since we don't want to eat them," my sister, Tatsie, replied. The raisins were left over from Halloween, when we had been disappointed that Papa had come home with this dried fruit instead of chocolate candy bars to give to the children. We giggled as we helped pack the small raisin boxes, thinking we were playing a trick on George. We visualized the surprised look he would have on his face when he opened the regulation box.

After a few weeks, we received a letter from George written in Japanese thanking us for the raisins. Mama was surprised and pleased that George still remembered how to write in Japanese, because in high school he had skipped Japanese classes to play football and hang out with friends. Now he was in the army during the U.S. occupation of Japan, working at a bus station.

Mama read the letter to us: "I gave a few raisins to the children hanging around the bus station. They no longer have homes since Tokyo was heavily bombed during the war, setting the city on fire. Many lost their parents. Most of the buildings and homes were destroyed, and the people took refuge in any public building."

Word got around that George was giving out raisins, and a long line formed. "The line got so long that I had to ration the raisins, giving just a few to each person. One boy begged for an extra raisin to share with his siblings," wrote George.

Mama's eyes welled with tears as she thought about the homeless children. She said, "See, there are children in the world who are grateful for the raisins." We learned then that our Halloween trick was really a treat and that our life here was much better than those who were less fortunate.

GREYHOUND BUS: 1946

"Can I sit in that seat?" I asked the man. He didn't look at me or move. Some of the passengers observing the incident wore smug looks on their faces. Feeling uncomfortable, I moved toward the front of the bus.

"There's a seat back there. Why don't you sit down?" said the bus driver.

"I asked the man if I could sit down, but he won't move. It's all right, I'm getting off soon anyway," I said.

Living in the suburb of Tacoma, Washington, we would take the Greyhound bus going into downtown. Most of the time I didn't experience any incidents, but on this day the bus was full except for one empty seat next to a white man who sat near the aisle. He was in his late thirties or forties, and I was still a child in the eighth grade.

The tall, large *hakujin* (white) bus driver didn't say a word but stopped the bus on the side of the road. "Come with me," he said and walked down the aisle toward the man who remained sitting in the aisle seat. "Move over," he told the man, then turned to me and said, "Now sit down." The bus driver had a stern look on his face. He returned to his seat and resumed driving. I felt guilty for causing this commotion and sank down in my seat.

Nearby passengers watched me silently, and I felt uncomfortable sitting next to a man who was obviously a bigot. Will he say or do something bad or mean to me? I observed him discreetly and sat as far away from him as possible, feeling annoyed and harassed. As I got off the bus, some of the passengers stared at me through the windows. Did they feel sorry for me? Or did they not care at all?

I should have felt grateful to the bus driver for doing the right thing, but I was embarrassed and did not want to draw attention to myself. I felt sadness and anger that we had to endure discrimination for who we were and the way we looked. I got off the bus and walked slowly home, down the narrow, tree-lined country road, quietly and with a heavy heart.

The Tashiro family sends off sisters Chiyo (far left) and Sumi (fifth from left) as the two depart from the Amache concentration camp for Denver, Colorado, in 1943.

MICHI TASHIRO

Born a farmer's daughter, Michi Tashiro grew up in the city of Turlock, California, until the bomb fell on Pearl Harbor in 1941. Along with her parents and nine siblings, she was forcibly removed from their home to the Merced Assembly Center and eventually incarcerated in the concentration camp in Amache, Colorado, officially known as the Granada Relocation Center. After World War II ended in 1945, she returned with her parents and four of her siblings to the farming community of Cortez, California. There was no future in farming for her family, so the following year they moved to San Francisco, where she has lived ever since. Recently retired from the California State Health Department, Michi spends her leisure time dabbling in art, hiking, and writing.

Author's note: Some of the historical facts and quotes in these stories are indebted to the following sources: Amache, *by Robert Harvey, and* Farming the Home Place, *by Valerie J. Matsumoto.*

The Swing

I wander out into the October heat, heading toward the playground next door, anticipating a good ride on the swing. Fine powdery sand clings to my clothes and filters into my shoes, cramping my toes. No hint of a breeze exists, and the sand lies silent, still. Kicking, batting, tossing of balls, shouting, and the laughter of rowdy games—all of these are gone.

Who will mend the tattered makeshift basketball hoop, awkwardly dangling on the washhouse wall? Where has Harry, a lifetime ball player and

173

Michi Tashiro

San Francisco, CA
Seventh-day Adventist hostel; ❻◄⋯
family residence, 1947 ❼

Cortez, CA
Tent camp, Oct. 1945; then
one-room shack in orchard

Turlock, CA ❶❺❹◄⋯⋯⋯⋯
Ⓐ

Merced, CA
Fairgrounds
1942

Amache, CO
1942–1945
⋯❄

❶ Prewar family residence
Ⓐ Temporary detention center
❄ Incarceration site
❹ Reentry point/first transitional housing
❺ Subsequent transitional housing
❼ Postwar family residence

0   100   200 Miles
0 100   200 Km

our athletic director, gone? He was always on the field shouting, "Play ball," keeping us out of mischief during idle times.

I glance beyond the swing, across the field at the deserted high school, and think, *Why did they have to close it?* Through sweat and brawn, the folks in Amache made it—in the words of War Relocation Authority head Dillon Myer—the "most famous high school in the United States." Now that the beehive of activity within the school is gone, will everything else follow? Will its innards be gutted and the print shop equipment, garage shop tools, craft shop materials, and science lab glassware be repossessed by the government or sold to the grabbing hands of outsiders? Even the furniture made in the shop may be taken away.

It was like a queen bee abandoning her hive and taking the drones away with her. As the sweetness of the honeycomb evaporates, I shudder.

As I make my way toward the swing, I see my younger sister Chito, who, at age seven, is four years younger than I, standing in front of a huge stack of books heaped outside the elementary school nearby. She stiffens and shrugs her shoulders, puzzled, undoubtedly wondering if they are going to trash this pile of books. While rifling through the stack, her eyes widen in surprise, as though she has discovered a gold mine. She snatches up a tattered tome and continues scrounging.

Unlike me, Chito enjoys school and reminds me of the time it was a safe haven during a turbulent sandstorm when she and Shigeru, our barrack neighbor and playmate, were the only ones in school that day. Hurricane winds whipped around, crashing sand and debris against the building. Chito tells me, "I guess Miss McGovern, my teacher, didn't want to send us home in the storm, so she kept us in class. With a broom and dustpan, I swept up sand all around the room." Finishing her story, Chito laughs and continues to sift through books.

Still intent on reaching the swing, I leave Chito only to see Papa and Mama, who are returning from the Administration Office. Passing by the high school, Papa picks up a couple of gypsum boards off the ground while Mama waves pieces of paper in her hand, urging him to hurry home. As they approach me, I hear snatches of their conversation.

"*Got-ten,*" swears Papa. "They don't want to keep us in Amache, so they keep shoving us to leave," he mutters. His five oldest—George, Keita, Sumi, Chiyo, and Frank—have already left, because there was no future for them behind the barbed wire fences of camp. In 1942 George and Keita had come to Amache first to complete building our barrack home, and then they, like our athletic director, Harry, had immediately left camp under the WRA's Leave Program and resettled on farms in Colorado. Sumi and Chiyo had left for Denver in 1943, and then moved to Chicago the following year, later joined by brother Frank, who left camp in 1944, during his senior year of high school.

This identification card for Sumi Tashiro provides clearance from the WRA for her to leave camp in 1943.

Since George and Keita hadn't lived with us in Block 11E and their stay in camp had been so short, I hardly noticed when they left. But the day was a downer for me when my sisters Sumi and Chiyo left Amache. We gathered by our garden gate, anxiously waiting for the truck that would take them to the train station in Granada, a mile from camp. A few of the neighbors came to say goodbye. Mama, her hair appearing whiter to me that day, pressed her index fingers to her lips and solemnly advised, "*Ki wo tsuke*, be careful, and watch your manners." Sumi and Chiyo, dressed in their finest suits, silk stockings, and high heels, grinned and nodded their heads.

"No *shim-pai*, not to worry, Mama," Sumi reassured her. "I live at Governor Carr's home in Denver while I go to school. He is no longer our governor, but he helped us a lot when he was." Glancing over at Chiyo, Sumi continued, "Chiyo staying with a family. She find a job in town…maybe at a big hotel they call the Brown Palace Hotel."

Papa dug deep into his pants pocket, pulling out his wallet, saying, "Here, not much…but for food." Chito kept close watch over their suitcases, one apiece. Chiyo and Sumi left camp just as they had entered: with only what they could carry.

Our family was slowly breaking up. "Who's going to help me sew my dirndl skirt?" I cried while dabbing my eyes with the back of my dirty fist. I didn't understand why they had to leave us. Mama and Papa did, but they bit their lips and kept mum. "Goodbye and good luck!" we shouted, waving as the truck bumped across the athletic field and disappeared out of camp. "Where's Denver, anyway?" I yelled at the trailing dust.

As I near the swing now, Mama and Papa pass by, heading for home, now in muffled conversation. I am unaware that Mama and Papa, who are middle-aged and stuck with us five underage children, have had to file and get approval for their own "Plan of Relocation" to get a "WRA Alien's Travel Permit."

Idle thoughts keep rumbling through my mind as I finally reach the swing and grab a hold of its rope. *Could the papers that Mama was waving at Papa have anything to do with us leaving camp? I wonder where we'll end up?*

Unbeknownst to me at the time, Mama and Papa had already made arrangements with our friends in Cortez, California, to return to that state. After months of planning and meeting with caretakers of their farms in Cortez, community leaders developed a well-organized course of resettlement that would allow us to return there. "We lucky they let us go home with them," Papa would tell me later with Mama standing by, smiling appreciatively.

But now, Papa is still within earshot as he glances toward me, shouting, "Come home…time to pack! We leave Amache pretty soon!" Mama and Papa walk farther off, disappearing behind our garden fence. Assuming they will

WAR RELOCATION AUTHORITY

_____Granada_____ Relocation Center

ALIEN'S TRAVEL PERMIT

(To be used only in cases of Terminal Departure)

This is to certify that the travel of M rs. Yukino Tashiro_____, Alien Registration

No. _____4166319_____, to _____Denair, Calif._____ has been permitted by

the Department of Justice. Any travel thereafter may take place only with the permission of the United

States Attorney in the judicial district of the destination shown above.

_____Sept. 14, 1945_____
(Date)

J. Donnega

_____Leave Officer_____
(Title)

U. S. GOVERNMENT PRINTING OFFICE   16—45180-1

The 1945 "Alien's Travel Permit" for Michi's mother, Yukino Tashiro, which was required by the WRA prior to leaving camp.

do all the packing for us kids, I dally and scoot onto the seat of the swing, burnished with age and use. I dig the toes of my shoes into the ground and shove off into a mesmerizing slow-motion arc.

I am going to miss this swing that Papa and his friends had made for us young kids. Harry had also gotten the older kids to construct the baseball diamond and basketball hoop, and the old men on our block were always scrounging for more materials that might be used in this way. With their ingenuity and hard work, they not only built the swing, but they transformed Amache from a desolate plot of desert into a thriving community.

We made everything from scratch: the hospital, the farm, the schools, the churches, the playgrounds, the fire department, and the press. Although the WRA censored and dictated the type of news to print, the Amache newspaper, *The Pioneer,* was one of the best of the ten camps. All of the good things about camp are gone now, since the government started in earnest to close down the community early this year, months before Japan surrendered.

I pump the swing hard, looking out at our ghost town, flying high enough to almost see the roof of the mess hall just beyond the washhouse. If I crane my neck to look behind me on the upswing, I might get a glimpse of the abandoned hospital, where Papa used to bake pies for the sick. Now that the hospital doors are closed, Papa cooks at our mess hall for the few of us still remaining in camp.

"*Got-ten,* no can make toast," Papa complains as the electricity flickers. "No food delivery anymore either. I go to office to pick up canned beans myself." It is catch-as-catch-can to get food on the table. No wonder those who come from other blocks to eat at our mess hall complain. As the swing slows down, I think of Papa's home-baked apple pie, and my stomach grumbles.

I pick up speed on the swing again. But as high as I go, I cannot see what lay beyond the fence, other than the cemetery. *Are the hogs, the chickens, and the cattle still there? Who will harvest the sugar beets that Papa and others spent days farming? Who will get all the farm equipment? What's going to happen to the irrigation ditches? Will the fields be overrun by jackrabbits and rattlesnakes?* From my high vantage point, I can see that the flowers in Mama and Papa's garden around our home are wilting. Only prickly cacti stand erect and cottonwood leaves mournfully shimmer.

Church doors are closed, and I feel the spirits carried by the wind from the cemetery. Many who died in Amache are no longer buried here. Their families, resettling out of camp, took them away. I think only twelve remain, mostly infants. *Who would want to take those dead babies from their resting places?* I always hear Mama chanting, *"Namuamidabutsu, namuamidabutsu, namuamidabutsu,"* a prayer for the dead.

When my forward swing gets as high as the washhouse roof again, I let go of the ropes and slide off of the seat into free flight. With both legs stiffly outstretched, I land hard on the ground.

While measuring the distance flown from swing to landing, I blurt out, "Betty, pal of mine, where are you?" We were constant companions before the war, climbing peach trees, batting balls, and trying to stay upright on two-wheeler bikes as we pedaled the short distance from my house to Main Street. In camp we vied to be the best in jacks, pick-up sticks, and shooting steelie marbles. We shouted the loudest, ran the fastest, and laughed the hardest when tossing the rubber ball over our barrack, playing "Annie, Annie, Over." *Hey, Betty, where'd you go this summer?*

Dejected, I shake out the legs of my overalls, then go to fetch Chito, who clutches her prized volumes. When Chito and I reach home, Mama and Papa are scurrying about in our cramped quarters, sorting clothing, tools, and toys that are scattered about on three of the four cots lined against the far wall. Teru, the youngest, sits on the other cot, hugging her favorite stuffed clown doll suited in green and white stripes and a white ruffled collar. Both seem oblivious to the clammy heat and scratchy wool army blanket beneath them. Teru yawns and slowly rolls over onto the bed, then falls asleep. The clown slips from her grasp and lands in a heap beside her. Its wobbly head, topped with a pointed cap, bends slightly askew on a threadbare neck. Its black cross-stitched eyes peer at Mama and Papa as though asking, "What's going on here, anyhow?"

I think of running back to the swing for a quick ride, but Papa bristles. "Amache closing October 15," he tells me. "No one here to help. I shut box with nail. I ship it myself." I quickly toss my majorette boots and baton into the box, right alongside Chito's books. "Fifty dollars from government not much. But they give us free ride on 'California Special' train to Cortez," he says, swinging his hammer like the seasoned melon crater that he is.

Mama sighs, relieved that we will be returning to California even though there is no home to go to. "Kajioka-san says we can stay at the Presbyterian Church and work on his farm. He longtime friend and so *shin setsu* (kind)," Mama says.

"Yes, it is he and our Cortez friends who are getting us back to California," Papa replies. "Maybe that's what freedom means, huh, Mama?"

In spite of the heat, I shiver as we drag the heavy box out the front door. From our stoop, I stretch tall and strain my eyes to look back at the athletic field, where the swing is now quite still. I long to ride it a final time, but I can't. It's time to leave it, the playground, and Amache, to surge forward into our new, waiting life.

TRAIN RIDE FROM AMACHE

Already trying to forget Amache, I look the other way as I pass by the swing to scamper aboard the waiting army truck. Gagging on dust and tightly hugging my rucksack, I stare out the rear of the truck as the wavering desert mirage of camp—the gate, the barbed wire fence, the guard towers, the athletic field, and our barrack home—disappears. "Hate to leave," I softly murmur, sniveling. We bump along on the dusty road to Granada and the waiting "California Special" train.

Scrambling aboard the old rickety train, I drag Chito to a window seat and remind her, "Don't want to get train sick again." The train—ugly military brown on the outside, hot and stuffy inside—rumbles at a snail's pace, as it did three years ago when we were thrown into camp. The rocking motion, metallic clacking of wheels, and shrill whistle of the coal-burning train make me sick to my stomach. Teru, my three-year-old sister, fidgets while Mama cools her off with a damp towel, and Papa has to ride herd on the boys, my younger brother, Tochi, and my older brother, Tok.

This time there are no soldiers aboard, and we are free to move about the train. As my stomach settles, I sit up and stare out the window at the passing desert, transfixed. The sand seems to glow warmer than it did in Amache.

Indian paintbrush sparkles brighter and yucca spikes appear less prickly. When we pass by an occasional ranch, the barbed wire fence is a good thing: it keeps the herd in and the coyotes out. *Which side of the fence do the ranchers live on?* I wonder.

On the second day of our trip, the train briefly stops in Albuquerque, New Mexico. Our friend Nis-san goes off to have a smoke, and he doesn't get back on the train before it leaves the station. As Papa assures us that we haven't lost Nis-san forever and that he will get to California somehow, I wonder if we'll ever see him again blowing his smoke rings for us. While we chug along, my anticipation about returning to our old town, Turlock, grows.

On the third day, when the train finally jolts to a stop, I jump up, grab my bag, and expectantly hop off. Instead of town, we have landed in the middle of a peach orchard. "Where's our store and boarding home, anyway?" I ask, disappointed. Mama and Papa don't tell me what I will come to later know: the boarding house was razed in our absence, and our store was taken over by a local merchant who no longer carried Japanese goods. For now, Mama and Papa ignore me. We pile our baggage onto Kajioka-san's pickup truck and bump along to our new home.

THE TENT CAMP

The only house I see is a packing shed on the edge of the orchard. Opposite the tracks, post-harvest grapevines, their leaves turning yellow, sparkle like topaz. The earth smells fertile, and lugs are piled high with golden Thompson grapes that hint of good years to come. My new life as a farmer's daughter doesn't seem so bad to me now. *Guess I wouldn't mind living in a church,* I muse as Kajioka-san turns into the driveway of the Cortez Presbyterian Church. I hurriedly scoot out of the truck.

The clearing around the church is filled with a cluster of large circus-type tents, an encampment of some sort. Mama calls and waves to a lady cooking at a crude brick barbecue pit, "Yoo-hoo, *konnichiwa* (hello), Nishi-san." They warmly greet each other, then Mama immediately asks, "Did you get your lost baggage yet? We get your postcard in Amache, asking where it was. Papa find it at Granada train station. He put on next train…should be here soon."

Mrs. Nishi is about to respond when Kajioka-san, seemingly anxious to get back to work, interrupts and says to Papa, "The church and the other camp by the Social Hall are full. You can use that tent, the one over there." He points to the last unoccupied tent in the lot, adjacent to the one of the two tents being used by the Nishi family of ten. I glance behind Mrs. Nishi and gawk at the sea of white tents.

What? My heart is crushed that we left our barrack home in Amache for this. Whereas in camp we had two rooms for nine of us, we are now downsizing to one tent for seven of us in the middle of the church courtyard. "Where's the mess hall, the washhouse, the bathhouse, the school? Where will we play ball?" I mutter under my breath. *I'll be so embarrassed when I return to Lowell Elementary School. I'll have to tell my friend Janet that I live in a tent with no running water.* Before I can verbalize my thoughts, Mama and Papa thank Kajioka-san and hustle us off to the tent. *Golly, why did Papa lead me on?*

We are cramped together in one large canvas tent with two wrought-iron army cots—one for Mama and one for Papa—and a large lumpy mattress for us kids covers the floor. I cram my small hand-carried bag under Mama's cot, the only space available. I jump onto the mattress, tussle with my sibs for the softest spot, then grouse, "Should'a left Amache on the first Cortez train. We would most likely be living indoors now if we had." I whine on, "Why'd we give up the comfort of our barracks for this?"

Papa, tiring of our raucous play and my complaining, yanks us off the pad and proceeds to lay down the law. "Tent not for play...only for sleeping. We live here until we find a house. We work on Kajioka-san's farm...pick *budo* (grapes). Mama cook outdoor on open fire pit. Some days we cook inside... in church kitchen. We eat outside on wooden table. Kajioka-san says we can get food from his ranch, if we no can buy. We wash our face and clothes in washhouse...over there. If we no can use church toilet, we go to outhouse... by the peach trees. Cortez Committee work hard to give us roof over our heads, dishes to eat from, and bed to sleep in."

Mama, nodding in agreement, glances at us kids and adds, "You go to school...already late...it start last month. Mrs. Yokoi write me that...even before we leave Amache." Teru isn't old enough to go to Ballico Elementary School with Tochi, Chito, and me, so Mama and Papa have to take her to work with them. "When school done for the day come help pick *budo* and watch Teru," Papa interjects emphatically. Tok rolls his eyes, crosses his fingers behind his back, and nods his head. I'm flabbergasted at the thought of all work and no play, especially in the hot sun, so I protest. "*Shikata ga nai* (it can't be helped)," Papa replies, "so that's the way it's going to be."

It's a long three-mile hike along the Santa Fe Railroad tracks to Ballico. *Wonder if we'll ever get a school bus,* I think to myself when I hear an old Santa Fe freight train rumble by. We play games, kicking ripe melons or squashing pennies under the wheels of passing trains. "Chicken, chicken," I scream as Tochi jumps out of the way of an oncoming train, and I recall how he once got burned playing "chicken" over a fire pit that was dug at the end of our barrack in camp. *What a daredevil.* Mama treated the blisters with her own miracle cure. *I didn't know that his burn would clear up with his own* shi shi (*urine*), I thought as Mama worked her magic.

I'm disappointed that I never reconnected with prewar school chums in town, and eventually even Janet Harding becomes only a fondly remembered name. She had been my best friend before the war. We made cacophonous music together in our school band, with me striking the triangle and she leading us. Whenever I think of Janet, I reread the letters that I got in camp from my third-grade classmates back at Lowell Elementary School. "Dear Michiko," Janet always wrote at the beginning. Next to me, she had the neatest handwriting. *Has she been appointed class recorder in my absence?*

Betty is my best friend now. She, like us, came from camp to this same temporary housing. When we are of no help at the packing shed, she and I sneak down to the mom-and-pop store in Ballico to get some treats. When we open Kool-Aid packets, we take out miniature plastic dolls. What a collection I have now. All the Kool-Aid crystals we have sucked on seem that much sweeter.

In our new home, we live communally, sort of like in Amache, all helping each other out. If Kajioka-san is too busy, one of the other farmers takes Mama or Papa to shop for groceries or a new sharp pruner in Turlock. On those trips Mama and Papa visit our old neighbors Mr. and Mrs. Gailey, inquire about prospects of getting a new store or home in town, and thank them for having stored some of our large household items during the war, including our upright piano, Zenith radio, Mama's big steamer trunk, and an old family samurai sword. "As soon as you find a home, you can take your furniture," Mrs. Gailey always says at the end of their visits. But when Mr. Gailey hints that returning to Turlock might not be a viable option because "some white folks won't want you back here," Papa bites his lip and silently returns to Cortez.

As winter approaches, the days get shorter, the nights chillier, and the clouds darken, threatening rain. Our farmwork switches from picking fruits and nuts to pruning dormant peach trees, making grapevine cuttings, and digging up roots of turnips, carrots, and potatoes. I worry. Mama and Papa work long hours, barely having any time to think about what tomorrow will bring or the long laborious road that stretches before them. We have been living in the tent camp for a couple of months now, and life is settling down into a routine.

One day when I return home from school, the tent camp is eerily quiet. My friend and playmate, Betty, has disappeared with hardly a goodbye. Her family and others in tent camp had been waiting for the leases of tenants to expire so they could, one by one, finally reclaim their own properties. Betty has moved way over to the other side of the railroad tracks, farther than I am allowed to venture by myself. The other families scattered in all directions, miles from our campsite.

Staring into our cluttered tent, I think enviously of Betty now sleeping in her own bed, eating in a dining room, and taking a bath indoors. I couldn't have known her house had been trashed by the tenant farmers who lived there while she was in camp. Years later she showed me her Papa's letter, written to attorneys, that described the damage done to their ranch, including the loss of an acre of Thompson seedless grapes that he had planted just before the war broke out. He returned to his farm in 1945 expecting his first crop of grapes, but the vines were gone, and all he had was an acre of barren ground.

Now that Betty has moved, I don't see her very often, because when not in school, she's busy cleaning up her family home, replanting the grapevines, or gathering eggs from their chicken coop. Our evenings become increasingly lonely as we cook and eat by ourselves at the outdoor fire pit. "We need house before it rains," Mama desperately says while warming and massaging her aching legs in front of the fire.

In bed, I hug the army blanket that Mama was wise enough to have packed when leaving our 100-degree desert home in Amache. Papa picks up his pack of Lucky Strike cigarettes off the top of an orange crate and slowly shuffles outside for a smoke. He must be thinking about all the other Cortez families, about one hundred and fifty parents and children, who are now resettling into their own homes while we are still homeless. In the stillness of the moonless night, dying embers from the cooking pit cast eerie shadows of the tent camp against the church wall. Papa studies the floating, flickering images for a while. I imagine he wants to make our stay in tent camp as short as possible. "*Gambare*, stick with it," he resolves.

THE SHACK

That following week, we roll up our bedding, dismantle the tent, discard the old mattress, and leave our tent camp for good. As we were in Amache, we are last to leave. I tote my bare-bones belongings and my majorette outfit—baton and boots—from the campsite to the one-room shack on the other end of the peach orchard. It isn't exactly the Palace Hotel, but at least it has four wooden walls, a sturdy roof, and a slatted wooden floor. "Pretty neat," I whisper while wondering if it measured up to Betty's home. *Yeah, we don't have indoor plumbing, but now I get to sleep on a cot,* I think to myself. Drawing an imaginary circle above the floor with my outstretched arms, I immediately claim one corner of the room. *Shouldn't leak,* I assure myself while craning my head toward the rafters.

I think we've "made it," and this step up from tent life is going to be a breeze. But in reality we are already faced with our first test of survival in independent living. *Why does everyone live so far away now...alone by themselves, in their own homes? Who will take Papa to town to get a new hoe, work gloves, or a pack of cigarettes? Will Mrs. Suzuki still bring her garden goodies*—nasubi *(eggplant),* gobo *(burdock root), Armenian cukes—to Mama? Will I have to walk to school by myself now? When will we see our friends? Who will I play with now that Betty lives on the other side of the tracks?* Puzzling questions bombard me.

"Everybody work. No *monku*, no complaining," says Papa, demanding full cooperation from all of us kids. We divvy up the chores, fighting for the easy ones. When the dust finally settles, Tok, the oldest at age fifteen, gets to build fires, both for the *ofuro* (bath) and the potbellied stove in the house. "It's fun," he teases, duping me into doing all the hard work for him: chopping fallen trees, stacking cords of wood, scrounging for kindling, and shredding pages of Sears catalogs that will serve as fire starters.

Tochi and Chito, playing games, count the pumps of water until we fill the *ofuro*. As we watch the water slowly wobble through a wooden trough

A drawing of the *ofuro* by Frank Akio Tashiro (Michi's brother), 2005.

from the pump to the bathtub, about twenty feet away, we marvel at Papa's cleverness.

"He makes filling the *ofuro* almost fun," Chito mumbles, pursing her lips and pumping real hard.

"Better than slinging buckets around," Tochi says while grunting and pumping.

"Tub full," chimes in Teru, who's watching us from the back stoop of the shack.

Along with taking on these new chores, we must learn to survive by living off the land more. We eat fallen nuts from Mr. Kajioka's walnut trees and overripe melons lying beside the railroad tracks. Who could fault us for picking the fruit off of the church *jakuro* (pomegranate) tree? "Here it is," I scream at Papa when I spot a cluster of brown velvety fungus hanging on a rotting tree stump. Papa is the only one who knows which mushrooms are okay to eat. "*Chiri chiri* (sautéed mushrooms) for dinner," he says. I snip off the fungus with a grape-cutting knife and toss it into my gunnysack.

As the days get warmer, the air gets drier and the mushrooms disappear. Mustard greens begin to flower and go to seed. We pull up grasses that we call "Indian spinach." "Wash Indian spinach good before we cook," Mama tells Chito the first time we have it for supper. Chito picks a pan full of spinach, then washes the living daylights out of it, shredding the leaves like confetti.

I seldom see Betty or my other friends except at school or at special get-togethers at the Cortez Social Hall. The hall was the Japanese language school before the war, but I guess the farmers are too busy putting their lives back together now to even think about offering Japanese language classes. So instead we use the hall for special things, like weddings, funerals, and festival celebrations. "That's fine with me," I mutter, recalling the shellacking I got for playing hooky on my first day of Japanese school. The Japanese language teachers used to live in the house between ours and the social hall, but I don't know who lives there now.

Only years later would I realize that I shouldn't have been complaining back then, because I heard others had it worse than we did. The Andows' home was damaged three times in drive-by shootings, probably by townspeople who resented our return. Mr. Kishi's home, Morimoto's tankhouse, and even the Presbyterian Church were targeted too. At the time, Mama and Papa never told us about these incidents, but I suspect they discussed them with Betty's papa and Mr. Kajioka. Lucky for us, these community leaders were released from the segregated camp when the war ended and became an integral part of the "Amache Cortez Committee" that orchestrated our return to California.

I still wonder why, when the first Cortez families came back, their homes were shot at and their farms vandalized. "Why didn't the local police or the federal government come to their aid?" the Resettlement Committee asked, but their pleas fell on deaf ears. *This was a lot more serious than trick-or-treat pranks,* I thought. *Lucky those bullets didn't kill anyone. And look at all the painstaking work and ton of paint it must have taken to patch everything up.*

There are times when I see just the farmers congregate at the social hall. Apparently, the farmers have pooled their resources and are being hassled with red tape as they try to retrieve their property and, once they do, to get their big equipment, like tractors, back into working condition. They also plan to plant crops that will bring in the most money. I hear Papa say that the price of veggies is high now. *Maybe they'll plant carrots next,* I figure. One day, when the farmers file briskly out of the hall with satisfied looks, I think they must have made some progress.

With the winter rains comes the muddy muck. We are thankful for the roof over our heads, but we are housebound, each in our own private space in our cramped one-room home. Papa, in his workshop corner, rifles through pieces of lumber. Mama, seated near the stove, reads letters that are in a box on her lap and studies her English grammar book, lying on the table beside her. I sit on a stool, trying to perfect my sock-darning technique. My brothers and sisters are all over the shack, mostly jumping up and down on the cots, playing king of the hill.

The roof rattles with pelting rain, and the kerosene lantern hanging from the rafter flickers like an old silent movie. "Gosh, haven't seen a movie ever since Camp Amache," I blurt out unexpectedly. Mr. Goto used to bring the latest Hollywood films to our mess hall every week. Even before the war, Mr. Sato, a traveling entertainer, had brought *chanbara* (Japanese samurai movies), to the Turlock Hall at least once a month. It's weird that in camp the movies came to us, but now we have to go to the movies. The closest theater is in Turlock, seven miles away. My heart races as I ponder, *Would Mama and Papa let us go to town to see a movie some day? Bing Crosby and Bob Hope in* The Road to Rio? I look up at Bing's autographed photo, tacked on the wall above my cot, and his face dims in the lamp's ocher glow.

A REAL HOUSE

When spring rolls around, we finally find a real house to rent on the other side of the railroad tracks near the Social Hall and, even better, close to Betty's place. *Gosh, we've moved out of the boonies. There's so many houses here,* I marvel.

In May 1939 the Cortez baseball team beat Lodi, 6-0. The Cortez Wildcats were the only team in a league of six Japanese American teams to own its own ballpark. Posing after the Cortez-Lodi game are, front row, from left: George Tashiro, George (Cobby) Kajioka, Ernest Yoshida (manager), Nobuhiro (Nogi) Kajioka, Henry (Hank) Kajioka, Yukihiro (Yuk) Yotsuya. Back row, from left: Keichi (Deacon) Yamaguchi, Yeichi Sakaguchi, Fred (Pinto) Kajioka, Shizuma (Shiz) Kubo, Kaoru Masuda, Kaname (Ben) Miyamoto, Bill Noda, and Minoru (Min) Yenokida. From *Farming the Home Place: A Japanese American Community in California, 1919–1982*, by Valerie J. Matsumoto. Photo courtesy of Yukihiro Yotsuya.

It's kind of like homecoming when Tok tells me, "See the baseball field out back? That's where brother George used to play before the war. Cortez Wildcats beat the living daylights out of Lodi once, six to zero." Tok starts ticking off the names of other families living nearby: Sugiura, Miyamoto, Morofuji, Morimoto, Asai, Sakaguchi, Taniguchi…

As Tok rambles on, I step back and admire the house we want to call our own but cannot because we are just tenants. It's in pretty good shape, with white walls and canary yellow window trimming. *Jeepers, it's real paint. Needs a little touch-up, though.* I run my fingers over the weathered windowsill, which is pocked where the paint has chipped and peeled away. I finally cut off Tok so we can go inside. We walk into the front room, pass by an overstuffed sofa, a kitchen table, and a couple of wooden chairs. *Wow, two bedrooms, a kitchen, and a parlor! Kind of like one of Chito's fairytale castles, I* decide. *No, it's probably more like my friend Betty's home just down the road. Can hardly wait to see her again.*

We not only get a new home but a new school bus that picks us up directly in front of our house. As the days get warmer, the one-armed ice cream vendor parks his cart at our bus stop, ringing his bell. I miss our adventurous walks to school each day when we lived in the tent camp and the shack, but I am excited when I hear the rumbling of the bus and tinkling music of the ice cream man. One day Tok, the only one with money, buys a quart of vanilla ice cream, then quickly disappears behind the house to gobble it all up. Chito, Tochi, and I never forgive him for that, but we laugh whenever we are eating ice cream and the story comes up again.

Since we are living in a real house with a little more room now, Mama asks Papa to retrieve our furniture that has been kept for us by our friends, Mr. and Mrs. Gailey. Along with Tok and some neighbors, Papa goes to Turlock to load the truck with our household goods—the radio, piano, steamer trunk, and boxes of Mama's huge aluminum pots and pans, Japanese cooking tools, and her favorite cast iron skillet. Due to the weight of all our stuff, the tires in the truck lose air and the whole vehicle lists and drags its tail the entire seven miles back to Cortez, finally jostling to a stop at our front door.

"Put the piano near the front door," I beg. I want to be sure that anyone passing by will hear me play it, off-key or not. We place the Zenith radio on the table between the parlor and kitchen, so everyone can hear it. Mama stacks her pots and pans in the kitchen, then immediately drags her steamer trunk into her bedroom. *Wonder why she's so possessive about that trunk? Got some important stuff in there?* I ponder as I see her drape a doily over it. *I guess she's planning to use it as a dressing table.* Mama pats the doily smooth with her stubby hands.

After the sweltering autumn in a tent and then the wet, muddy winter in a one-room hut, this springtime four-room house is a real home to us. I bounce on the sofa and feel its comfort.

JULY FOURTH

Papa grimaces, knowing that he has to find a permanent home for us before another winter arrives. He jabs the windmill that he had crafted back in our shack days and had stuck into the ground by his blooming *kabocha* (pumpkin). "Keep crow away," he mumbles. Then Mama steps into the garden, undoing all of Papa's hard work—she over-waters, over-prunes, over-transplants, and definitely under-weeds. *"Got-ten,"* swears Papa. Water from the draining *ofuro* swirls around his boots.

I'm not aware of it at the time, but looking back I suppose we are living as "model" Americans. I pledge allegiance to the flag every day at school, just as I did before and during the war. Although the war has been over for almost a year now, I still collect tin foil off of gum wrappers and Papa's cigarette packs. Don't know where to donate it, though. I also help Mama make care packages of coffee, sugar, and Hershey's candy bars. I think she gives them to the Red Cross, hoping some of them might get to her family in Japan; we haven't heard yet if they survived the atomic bombings. We're still on gas and food rationing. We don't need gas without a car, but we sure would like to get some real butter instead of this gosh-awful make-it-yourself yellow margarine. Yellow dye sticks to my hand for days. Yuck.

I swell with pride as the Fourth of July approaches, wondering when we will be invited to participate in the parade in Turlock once again. In camp we paraded down the main drag in the center of the compound; Boy Scouts carried American flags, and girls in majorette outfits twirled their batons. Before the war, the Fourth of July parade was the only one that we ever took part in with the white folks. I even got to be Queen of the Harvest in 1941. All dolled up in a floor-length organdy gown, my lips painted ruby red, I sat on the float of the Horn of Plenty. I was proud as I rode the float and looked at the American flag propped in front between two watermelons. A large printed poster on the side of the float read PRODUCE FOR USA. My buddies Misao and Fred pulled the cart.

A float in the July 4 parade, Turlock, California, 1941. Left to right: unnamed young girl in kimono, Violet Kumimoto, Michi (on float), older sister Sumi, Misao Niizawa, and Fred Nakano.

I am disappointed that, this time, we are not asked to take part in the Turlock parade. *Are the townsfolk still mad at us for the war?* Instead, we spend our first Fourth of July as free citizens all by our lonesome, shooting flares in our front yard. I strut about in my majorette boots, twirling and tossing the baton a few times before the festivities begin. Tochi and Tok startle and scare us out of our gourds, flipping firecrackers left and right.

In between the popping, I think I hear Mama whisper snatches of the Declaration of Independence: "All men…created equal." Mama desperately wants to become an American citizen, even though the government won't let her. She seizes every opportunity to study the workings of our U.S. government. "Waste time," Papa says. "You never become citizen." I worry about Papa, who spends his days fruitlessly searching for a home of our own.

The boys then display their grand finale. They light a giant firecracker, toss it under an inverted tomato can, and duck for cover. Standing in frightened anticipation of the explosion, I cower with my eyes scrunched closed and hands cupped over my ears. *Boom! Ping!* The can explodes and shoots straight for the heavens, narrowly missing me.

"*Got-ten. Ki wo tsuke!* (Damn it. Be careful!)" Papa shouts. As I stand there in stunned silence, wondering where in the world Tok got these illegal fireworks, Papa rushes into the house. Coming to my senses and remembering something I had inside, I follow, making a beeline to my orange crate dresser. Papa returns outside with a package of safer sparklers and Mama's *osenko* (incense sticks) to be used as punks to light them. Scouring the house, I come out emptyhanded; I couldn't find the American flag I had made at school for this special day.

I amble to the tire swing that we hung on a tree beside the cesspool, nestle in, and slowly sway to and fro. As Mama and Papa clean up the fizzling fireworks, faint images of old friend Nis-san's smoke rings waft in the air. *Will we ever again see any of our friends we have lost touch with? What is Betty doing tonight? Will I ever be queen again? Will Mama ever become an American citizen?*

As the smoke dissipates, I think about our uncertain future, wherever we may find our new home. Maybe we'll end up in a wonderland—like one of those in Chito's fairytale books.

APPENDIX A: LESSON PLANS

The following set of lesson plans was designed primarily—like those in our first book, *From Our Side of the Fence*—as a guide for former camp prisoners who wish to document their experiences, but they can serve other groups and purposes as well. The assignments could, for example, be the basis for interview questions that younger generations can ask elder family members, or they can act as prompts for educators who want their students to imagine the resettlement experience. Over the years, we have hosted many presentations throughout the West, several of which included writing workshops, and we have been heartened to hear of the writing communities that have formed and the individuals who have been inspired as a result. It is our hope that this new material will encourage still more individuals to begin writing and will bring together new communities and breathe new life into existing ones. The stakes are high; time is running out. These stories need to be told before they are forever lost.

For this set of lesson plans, my process of creating the material was much different than it was the last time around. This time, since the writers and I had worked together so closely for such a long period and had built a rapport of trust and mutual respect, rather than impose a generic, limiting, or arbitrary set of writing topics upon them, I made the decision to gradually let the process of exchange—between teacher and writers, and among the writers themselves—lead us toward the formation of a curriculum.

During our first several months—roughly June to July of 2007—I provided a great deal of structure, offering topics derived from my own limited knowledge about the resettlement, but I also emphasized that they could choose their own paths and directions for any given prompt if they were inspired to do so.

As time progressed and we gathered momentum, I was no longer the sole generator of topics; instead, we were using the synergistic nature of dialogue and community to guide the class. The more I heard from the writers, the more I realized how much more there was to learn about the resettlement experience. The students became guides for me, teaching me about their personal histories through the lively conversations we had, powerful stories we shared, and useful feedback we gave each other. From these exchanges, and in reading and commenting upon their work, I gathered even more ideas for prompts, which in turn generated many of the topics that follow.

During our two-year period of focused writing, each student eventually took off in his or her chosen direction, writing about resettlement in a variety of ways. Some focused on a well-defined historical period, others covered a span of many decades. Either way was fine. While we agreed that resettlement was largely defined by each person's postwar experience, we also agreed to not limit ourselves with specific time periods or static definitions of the emotional and psychological process of resettlement. The following topics and lesson plans are based upon this pedagogical strategy of structured freedom: I offered specific topics that could be used for "free-writes," to spark new ideas, and to generate scenes and stories while, at the same time, I allowed room for the writers to explore and reflect upon whatever experiences might prove most relevant to them individually.

Although I originally structured the assignments to build one on top of the other, users of this guide can pick and choose from the assignments at will, and in any order. Moreover, for each of the following prompts, you might find it most useful and productive to compose an initial draft in the form of a focused "free-write," that is, automatic, nonstop writing on the topic without censoring your thoughts or worrying about grammatical errors. Once the free-write is completed, you can revise the piece on your own or in conjunction with others, picking out and developing the strongest passages, cutting away the weaker sections, and phrasing and structuring the material in the most effective way.

—*Brian Komei Dempster*

WRITING ASSIGNMENT #1: LEAVING CAMP

1. Describe your first memories of leaving camp. Was it the train ride home? The first meal you tasted beyond barbed wire? What images, tastes, and smells do you recall? What emotions? Fear? Uncertainty? Relief?

WRITING ASSIGNMENT #2: HOMECOMING

1. Describe your first experience or memory of home after your release from camp. Did you return to your original home? If not, what were the circumstances and where did you go? How did your new "home" compare with camp? How did it compare with your home *before* camp? Compare and contrast the similarities and differences. Describe the impact on you, your siblings, and your parents. Did you have any significant encounters? Did you experience prejudice and racism, or perhaps unexpected acts of generosity and kindness?

2. Focus on an object that you lost during the war or that you missed during camp and/or after your release from camp. What particular memories were and are connected to the possession you lost? After camp, did you try to replace the thing you had lost? Were your attempts effective?

3. Write about an individual or family from outside the Japanese American community who supported your family after the war. Show who this character or family is and your relationship with them through their actions toward you and your gestures toward them. Use dialogue, description, and scene development to dramatize this experience.

4. Write about any experience of revisiting the detention center(s) or camp(s) after the war. You can write this as a story, a poem, or in any other form you want. How did your experience of the past resurface in the present? How did the past and present echo one another? Were you able to feel a sense of closure?

5. Do a free-write based on repeating the phrase "Home is…" (or any other significant phrase from your experience after the war).

WRITING ASSIGNMENT #3: STARTING OVER

1. Describe your first day of school (or any other significant school day or event) after you left camp and returned "home." Create the setting, the mood, and your emotional state. Describe your teacher and classmates through their physical appearances, dramatizations of their actions and behaviors, and their interactions with you. How did this experience differ from your educational experience in camp?

2. Describe your first job interview after camp, or the challenges of a sibling or parent trying to find work. What job were you or they seeking and why? What did the process feel like, how were you or they treated, and what was the outcome?

3. Write about your first work experience during resettlement, focusing on a significant memory or set of events. Show the challenges and rewards of your job through details and scenes. What dilemmas did you face and how did you resolve them?

4. From the perspective of witness and observer, characterize the impact of the resettlement on the professional life and work of an elder, whether it be a parent or someone else. Create a scene or scenes that show them performing their work or telling you about their work. Reflect upon the way imprisonment transformed their work and their attitude toward their career. What did they lose? What, if anything, did they gain?

5. Demonstrate the impact of the incarceration and resettlement on your family's savings, livelihoods, and property. Did you leave your property in someone else's hands? Were you able to retrieve this property? How did the financial strain of imprisonment impact you and your family after the war?

6. Write a piece that shows the connection between your experience of incarceration and the education you sought and/or the profession you chose.

WRITING ASSIGNMENT #4: PREJUDICE AND TRAUMA, CONNECTION AND EMPOWERMENT

1. Write about a material object you desired and/or received after the war. What did this object mean to you and why? How did your experience of imprisonment influence your perception of this object? Describe how and why you obtained this object—or if you were unable to—and its significance to you.

2. Recount a specific story of prejudice you or a loved one faced at school, at work, in the neighborhood, or elsewhere. Be specific about the setting, characters, and details of this experience and dramatize any relevant internal conflict.

3. Create a story that centers around how the trauma of war affected you or someone else. You could write about a recurring nightmare or a specific event or situation that triggers memories of imprisonment. You could also look at how the incarceration and resettlement impacted your or someone else's physical health.

4. Write about the phenomenon of silence after the war and how and why you or someone else did not speak about the incarceration. Give examples of silence and its consequences.

5. Discuss the role of friendship and community during the resettlement. You could write a story about a close friend or a group you were involved in. What were your shared activities and interests? What support was provided? How did this friendship or group empower you?

6. Write about your or someone else's experience of dating or romance after the war. How did being released from camp impact your love life and your views of intimacy? What pressures, challenges, conflicts, and rewards were involved?

WRITING ASSIGNMENT #5: APPEARANCE AND IDENTITY, PERCEPTIONS AND EXPECTATIONS

1. Write about the theme of appearance and identity. How did your perception of yourself, your culture, your environment, and your surroundings change after you were released from camp and returned to the outside world?

2. Describe the instructions you were given by the War Relocation Authority and/or others right before you were released from camp. How did they expect you to act upon your return to the community? What was your response to their expectations? In what ways did you conform to them, rebel against them, or both?

3. Describe any encounter or experience with someone who believed the incarceration did not happen or was resistant to learning about your experience.

4. Write a piece about someone who returned to camp after his or her release, and explore their possible motivations for doing so.

5. Explore the issue of gender in relationship to resettlement. As a female or male, what responsibilities did you have? What pressures and expectations were placed upon you? What was the emotional and psychological impact?

6. Write a piece in response to any written materials or documents you have from during or after the war, including a letter, diary, or any other form of correspondence that has significance to you.

WRITING ASSIGNMENT #6: MEMORIES AND LEGACIES

1. Write about a time that your identification of a particular being, object, image, or place transported you back in time to the incarceration (for instance, a herd of cattle, a barbed wire fence, a prison). How did this thing serve as a metaphor? What connections do you make between the present and past?

2. Illustrate how your diet and the foods you eat were influenced by the incarceration and resettlement.

3. Describe any destruction or loss of property you witnessed during and/or after the resettlement. Describe the place that was lost or destroyed and what it meant to you, your family, and your community.

4. Compose a character portrait of an individual who died and/or was significantly impacted by the camps.

5. Create a story about a place where people gathered and came together as a community. You might also write about a group—such as farmers—who organized to empower themselves.

6. Write about the anniversary of Pearl Harbor or the Day of Remembrance. How do these events resonate with you now on an emotional and psychological level? Have you participated in any significant activities or had any memorable experiences related to these events?

7. Describe your experience of sharing your incarceration/resettlement story with others, whether in writing classes, at schools, or in other contexts. What questions were you asked? What did you gain and learn from this process?

8. Write about a time during the resettlement that you confronted a stereotype about being Japanese American and/or felt (or were treated as) inferior.

APPENDIX B: OVERVIEW OF MIGRATION: FROM INCARCERATION TO RELEASE

The writers in this anthology, most of whom are Nisei, offer an in-depth look at the Japanese American resettlement. Their emancipation from camp and subsequent migration odysseys form a powerful collective narrative that stands on its own yet is even more illuminating when considered in the context of the entire Japanese American imprisonment and resettlement saga.

The Migration Chart (on pages 200 and 201) provides an overview of the continual uprooting process of resettlement—from the writers' forced removal from their homes, to their incarceration, to their eventual release from the camps, to their return to transitional housing, and finally to their postwar residences.

The War Relocation Authority (WRA) table on page 199 helps us see their journeys through an even wider lens. The twelve writers included in this anthology were among the approximately 120,000 Japanese Americans who were under the control of the WRA from 1942 to 1946. Ten of the writers—along with more than 90,000 other Japanese Americans—were kept first in temporary WRA detention centers, usually hastily built sites located at racetracks, fairgrounds, and livestock exhibition grounds. We also see that more than 17,000 other Japanese Americans, like the Ohmuras and Osakis, were taken directly to WRA incarceration sites—in their cases, Poston I and Tule Lake, respectively. We see the equally harrowing experiences of others, including Kiku Hori Funabiki, whose father was among the approximately 3,000 "enemy aliens" arrested by the FBI and incarcerated at a Department of Justice internment camp administrated by the Immigration and Naturalization Service (INS).

By the end of World War II, anti-Japanese hostility in the West and elsewhere was still a real concern for Japanese Americans, and only about 45 percent of them returned to the West Coast directly after their release. Like six of the writers, many of those returning West were children, youth, and young adults who accompanied their Issei parents. Others, like the Hashizumes and Iwakiris (Harumi Serata's family), moved to locations in the interior of the United States, both because they had heard of employment opportunities there and because they had been instructed by the WRA not to congregate with fellow Japanese and Japanese Americans. According to various sources, more than 4,000 Nisei were sponsored to continue their education in the Midwest and East, due in part to efforts of the National Japanese American Student Relocation Council, as coordinated by the American Friends Service Committee and other church representatives, service groups, and educators (see Nisei Student Relocation Commemorative Fund, "A Short History," and Sutter, "American Refugees"). Receiving early leave clearance in 1945, Flo Ohmura Dobashi, Fumi Manabe Hayashi, and Kiku Hori Funabiki were among those who left the camps to attend colleges, in Ohio, Missouri, and New York, respectively.

Only four of the writers' families—the Iwakiris, Manabes, Horis, and Yoshimuras—had prewar family homes that they could eventually return to (in these cases in Tacoma, Washington, and in Berkeley and San Francisco, California). The Ohmuras and Okimotos returned to their church parsonages, assisting others in their congregations to resettle in their hometown communities of Riverside and San Diego. A number of the writers found temporary shelter in makeshift accommodations, church hostels, government housing, or shared homes with other returnees. *Making Home from War* reflects the varied journeys, in destination and time, of the authors and, by extension, all Japanese Americans, as they searched for places where they could resettle, places that they might one day call "home."

INPUT-OUTPUT DATA FOR WRA CENTERS, 1942–1946

FROM		TO	
90,491	assembly centers	54,127	returned to the West Coast
17,915	direct evacuation	52,798	relocated to interior and Hawaii
5,981	born in camp	4,724	Japan
1,735	INS internment camps	3,121	INS internment camps
1,579	seasonal workers (furloughed from assembly centers to work crops, then to camp)	2,355	armed forces
1,275	penal and medical institutions	1,862	died
1,118	Hawaii	1,322	to institutions
219	voluntary residents (mostly non-Japanese spouses)	4	unauthorized departures
120,313	Total population ever under WRA control	120,313	

This chart originally appeared in Roger Daniels, "The Forced Migrations of West Coast Japanese Americans, 1942–1946: A Quantitative Note," in *Japanese Americans: From Relocation to Redress*, edited by Roger Daniels, Sandra C. Taylor, and Harry H. L. Kitano. (Salt Lake City: University of Utah Press, 1986). Used with permission. Several figures have been corrected by Roger Daniels since this table's original publication.

MIGRATION

WRITER	PRE-WWII RESIDENCE	TEMPORARY DETENTION CENTER [i]	INCARCERATION SITE, 1942–1946 [ii]	REENTRY POINT
Florence Ohmura Dobashi	Riverside, CA	N/A	Poston I, AZ May 1942 [iii]	Brecksville, OH August 1944
Kiku Hori Funabiki	San Francisco, CA	Pomona, CA (fairgrounds) May–August 1942	Heart Mountain, WY	Manhattan, NY January 1945
Sato Hashizume	Portland, OR	Portland, OR (livestock exhibition grounds) May–September 1942	Minidoka, ID	Salt Lake City, UT July 1945
Fumi Manabe Hayashi	Berkeley, CA	Tanforan, CA (racetrack) April–October 1942	Topaz, UT	St. Louis, MO December 1944
Naoko Yoshimura Ito	San Francisco, CA	Pomona, CA (fairgrounds) May–August 1942	Heart Mountain, WY	San Francisco, CA August 1945
Florence Miho Nakamura	San Francisco, CA	Tanforan, CA (racetrack) April–October 1942	Topaz, UT	San Francisco, CA August 1945
Ruth Y. Okimoto	San Diego, CA	Santa Anita, CA (racetrack) March–October 1942	Poston III, AZ	San Diego, CA September 1945
Yoshito Wayne Osaki	Clarksburg, CA	N/A	Tule Lake, CA May 1942 [iii]	San Francisco, CA March 1946
Toru Saito	San Francisco, CA	Tanforan, CA (racetrack) April–October 1942	Topaz, UT	San Francisco, CA October 1945
Daisy Uyeda Satoda	Oakland, CA	Tanforan, CA (racetrack) April–October 1942	Topaz, UT	San Francisco, CA September 1945
Harumi Iwakiri Serata	Fife, WA	Puyallup, WA (fairgrounds) April–October 1942	Minidoka, ID	Eden, ID April 1945
Michi Tashiro	Turlock, CA	Merced, CA (fairgrounds) April–October 1942	Amache, CO	Cortez, CA October 1945

Notes

[i] The dates in this column refer to the dates of operation of the temporary detention centers.

[ii] This range of dates spans the opening of the first and closing of the last of the War Relocation Authority incarceration sites.

CHART

TRANSITIONAL HOUSING	POST-WWII RESIDENCE
Attended school in Brecksville, OH, for fourteen months, then returned to Riverside in September 1945.	Japanese Congregational Church parsonage, 3195 14th Street, Riverside, CA [iv]
Attended Queen's College in NY for one semester, then returned to CA to attend UC Berkeley, joining parents at Seventh-day Adventist hostel in San Francisco, where she stayed until fall 1947.	1725 Post Street, San Francisco, CA [iv]
Stayed in Salt Lake City for one year, then helped family members open the New Rose Hotel in Portland in July 1946.	New Rose Hotel, 1328 S.W. 3rd Avenue, Portland, OR
Went to school in Kirkwood, MO, for one year, then returned to Berkeley in fall 1946.	1616 Russell Street, Berkeley, CA [iv]
Helped family reopen the Hokubei Hotel in San Francisco in August 1945, providing housing for many returning Japanese American families.	Hokubei Hotel, 1570 Buchanan Street, San Francisco, CA [iv]
Shared home on Bush Street with other families returning to San Francisco.	2663 California Street, San Francisco, CA
Lived in parsonage shed for three months, then moved into parsonage in December 1945.	San Diego Holiness Church parsonage, 3042 Webster Street, San Diego, CA [iv]
Joined family at a rented "flea house" on Pine Street in San Francisco.	Pine Street, San Francisco, CA
Lived in Hunters Point government housing (San Francisco) for less than one year, then moved to Richmond (CA) federal housing.	2506 California Street, Berkeley, CA (from 1955)
Stayed at San Francisco Buddhist Church for two weeks, then moved to a rental on Post Street.	526 43rd Avenue, San Francisco, CA (from 1947)
Lived on a farm in Eden, ID, for seven months, then moved back to family farm in Fife, WA, in November 1945.	Route 6, Box 491-A, Tacoma, WA [iv]
Stayed in a tent camp, then in a one-room shack in an orchard in Cortez, CA, then moved to Seventh-day Adventist hostel in San Francisco.	Lyon Street, San Francisco, CA (from 1947)

[iii] This date indicates when a person was sent directly to an incarceration site, having bypassed a temporary detention center.

[iv] This address indicates the person returned to his or her pre-WWII residence.

BIBLIOGRAPHY

This bibliography includes relevant sources on Japanese American resettlement after World War II but is by no means exhaustive. For the sake of simplicity, we have chosen to include works that, for the most part, focus on the resettlement period and the immediate postwar experience. The material is separated into three categories: Scholarly Resources, Literature, and Film/Multimedia/Production. Our inclusion of works from a variety of genres and viewpoints underscores that resettlement is diverse, multifaceted, multigenerational, and ongoing. New sources will surely continue to emerge.

SCHOLARLY RESOURCES

Austin, Allan W. "A Finer Set of Homes and Dreams: The Japanese American Citizens League and Ethnic Community in Cincinnati, Ohio, 1942–1950." In *Remapping Asian American History,* edited by Sucheng Chan, 87–106. Walnut Creek, CA: Altamira Press, 2003.

———. *From Concentration Camp to Campus: Japanese American Students and World War II.* Champaign: University of Illinois Press, 2004.

Brooks, Charlotte. "In the Twilight Zone between Black and White: Japanese American Resettlement and Community in Chicago, 1942–1945." *Journal of American History* 86, no. 4 (2000): 1655–87.

Burton, Jeffery F., et al. *Confinement and Ethnicity: An Overview of World War II Japanese American Relocation Sites.* Western Archeological and Conservation Center. National Park Service, U.S. Department of the Interior, *Publications in Anthropology* 74 (1999).

Collins, Donald E. *Native American Aliens: Disloyalty and the Renunciation of Citizenship by Japanese Americans during World War II.* Westport, CT: Greenwood Press, 1985.

Daniels, Roger, Sandra C. Taylor, and Harry H. L. Kitano, eds. *Japanese Americans: From Relocation to Redress.* Seattle: University of Washington Press, 2001. First published by University of Utah Press, 1986. (The chart on p. 199 is based on information in "The Forced Migrations of West Coast Japanese Americans, 1942–1946: A Quantitative Note," by Roger Daniels, from this book.)

Fugita, Stephen S. *Altered Lives, Enduring Community: Japanese Americans Remember Their World War II Incarceration.* Seattle: University of Washington Press, 2004.

Fukuda, Rev. Yoshiaki. *My Six Years of Internment: An Issei's Struggle for Justice.* Commentary by Stanford M. Lyman, Ph.D. San Francisco: The Konko Church of San Francisco, 1990.

Harden, Jaclyn. *Double Cross: Japanese Americans in Black and White Chicago*. Minneapolis: University of Minnesota Press, 2003.

Harvey, Robert. *Amache: The Story of Japanese Internment in Colorado during World War II*. Lanham, MD: Taylor Trade Publishing, 2004.

Hasegawa, Susan. "Returning Home: The Post–World War II Resettlement of Japanese Americans to San Diego." *Japanese American Historical Society of San Diego*. Last modified September 26, 2009, http://www.jahssd.org/index.php?option=com_content&view=article&id=57:returning-home&catid=25:the-project&Itemid=37.

Hayashi, Amy N. *Japanese American Resettlement: The Midwest and the Middle Atlantic States, 1942–1949*. Philadelphia, PA: Temple University, 2004.

Hirabayashi, Lane Ryo, Kenichiro Shimada, and Hikaru Iwasaki. *Japanese-American Resettlement through the Lens: Hikaru Iwasaki and the WRA's Photographic Section, 1943–1945*. Boulder: University Press of Colorado, 2009.

Ichioka, Yuji. *Views from Within: The Japanese American Evacuation and Resettlement Study*. This brochure showcases art produced in the concentration camps; it accompanied an exhibit at the University of California, Los Angeles, in 1989.

Ito, Leslie. "Japanese American Women and the Student Relocation Movement, 1942–1945." *Frontiers: A Journal of Women Studies* 21, no. 3 (2000): 1–24.

———. "Nisei Student Relocation Commemorative Fund." Afterword in *Storied Lives: Japanese American Students and World War II,* by Gary Okihiro. Seattle: University of Washington Press, 1999.

Japanese American Historical Society of Southern California. *Nanka Nikkei Voices: The Resettlement Years, 1945–1953*. Los Angeles: Japanese American Historical Society of Southern California, 1998.

Kashima, Tetsuden. *Judgment without Trial: Japanese American Imprisonment during World War II*. Seattle: University of Washington Press, 2003.

Kitano, Harry H. L. *Generations and Identity: The Japanese American*. Needham Heights, MA: Ginn Press, 1993.

Kochiyama, Yuri Nakahara. *Passing It On: A Memoir*. Los Angeles: UCLA Asian American Studies Center Press, 2004.

Kurashige, Scott. *The Shifting Grounds of Race: Blacks and Japanese Americans in the Making of Multiethnic Los Angeles*. Princeton, NJ: Princeton University Press, 2008.

Leonard, Kevin. *The Battle for Los Angeles: Racial Ideology and World War II*. Albuquerque: University of New Mexico Press, 2006.

Linchan, Thomas P. "Japanese American Resettlement in Cleveland during and after World War II." *Journal of Urban History* 20, no. 1 (1993): 54–80.

Matsumoto, Valerie J. "Nisei Women and Resettlement during World War II." In *Making Waves: An Anthology of Writing by and about Asian American Women,* edited by Asian Women United of California. Boston, MA: Beacon Press, 1989.

————. *Farming the Home Place: A Japanese American Community in California, 1919–1982.* Ithaca: Cornell University Press, 1993.

Nakano, Mei. *Japanese American Women: Three Generations, 1890–1990.* San Francisco: National Japanese American Historical Society and Mina Press, 1990.

Nakasone-Huey, Nancy Nanami. "In Simple Justice: The Japanese-American Evacuation Claims Act of 1948." Ph.D. diss., University of Southern California, 1986.

National Japanese American Student Relocation Council. *From Camp to College: The Story of Japanese American Student Relocation.* Philadelphia: National Japanese American Student Relocation Council, 1945.

Okihiro, Gary Y. *Storied Lives: Japanese American Students and World War II.* Seattle: University of Washington Press, 1999.

Personal Justice Denied: Report of the Commission on Wartime Relocation and Internment of Civilians. Foreword by Tetsuden Kashima. Seattle: University of Washington Press, 1997.

REgenerations Oral History Project: Rebuilding Japanese American Families, Communities, and Civil Rights in the Resettlement Era. Los Angeles: Japanese American National Museum, 2000. Four volumes focusing on the regions of Chicago, IL; Los Angeles, CA; San Diego, CA; and San Jose, CA.

Robinson, Greg. "Birth of a Citizen: Miné Okubo and the Politics of Symbolism." In *Miné Okubo: Following Her Own Road,* edited by Greg Robinson and Elena Tajima Creef, 172–91. Seattle: University of Washington Press, 2008.

————. *A Tragedy of Democracy: Japanese Confinement in North America.* New York: Columbia University Press, 2009.

Robinson, Greg, and Toni Robinson. "Korematsu and Beyond: Japanese Americans and the Origins of Strict Scrutiny." *Law and Contemporary Problems* 68, no. 2 (2005): 30–52.

Sato, Dale Ann. "Resettlement History." *Japanese American Historical Mapping Project.* 2006; accessed April 3, 2010. http://www.jahmp.org/history.php?t=Resettlement.

Seigel, Shizue, ed. *In Good Conscience: Supporting Japanese Americans during the Internment.* San Mateo, CA: Asian American Curriculum Project, 2006.

"A Short History of the National Japanese American Student Relocation Council."
Nisei Student Relocation Commemorative Fund, Inc., website. Accessed
April 3, 2010. http://www.nsrcfund.org/history/history.html#h1.

Simpson, Caroline Chung. *An Absent Presence: Japanese Americans in Postwar
Culture*. Durham, NC: Duke University Press, 2002.

Spickard, Paul R. *Japanese Americans: The Formation and Transformations of an
Ethnic Group*. New Brunswick, NJ: Rutgers University Press, 2009. First
published by Twayne Publishers, 1996.

Sutter, Jack. "American Refugees: The Japanese American Relocation."
American Friends Service Committee website. February 2002; accessed
April 3, 2010. http://www.afsc.org/ht/d/sp/i/16080/pid/16080.

Taylor, Sandra C. "Leaving the Concentration Camps: Japanese American
Resettlement in Utah and the Intermountain West." *Pacific Historical
Review* 60, no. 2 (1991): 169–70.

Thomas, Dorothy Swaine, and Richard Nishimoto. *Salvage: Japanese American
Evacuation and Resettlement*. Berkeley: University of California Press,
1975.

Yakota, Kariann. "From Little Tokyo to Bronzeville and Back." M.A. thesis,
University of California, Los Angeles, 1994.

yamada, gayle k., and Dianne Fukami. *Building a Community: The Story of
Japanese Americans in San Mateo County*, edited by Diane Yen-Mei Wong.
San Mateo, CA: San Mateo Chapter of the Japanese American Citizens
League, 2003.

LITERATURE

Edmiston, James. *Home Again*. New York: Doubleday, 1955.

Hongo, Garrett Kaoru. *Yellow Light*. Middletown, CT: Wesleyan University
Press, 1982.

Houston, Jeanne Wakatsuki, and James D. Houston. *Farewell to Manzanar*.
Boston, MA: Houghton Mifflin, 1973.

Inada, Lawson Fusao. *Legends from Camp*. Minneapolis: Coffee House Press,
1993.

Kashiwagi, Hiroshi. *Swimming in the American*. San Mateo, CA: Asian
American Curriculum Project, 2005.

Kogawa, Joy. *Obasan*. Boston, MA: David R. Godine, 1982.

Kumata, Michelle Reiko. *Flowers from Mariko*. New York: Lee and Low Books,
2001.

Mirikitani, Janice. *Awake in the River*. San Francisco: Isthmus Press, 1978.

———. *Shedding Silence*. Berkeley, CA: Celestial Arts, 1987.

————. *We, the Dangerous*. Berkeley, CA: Ten Speed Press, 1995.

————. *Love Works*. San Francisco: City Lights Foundation, 2002.

Mirikitani, Janice, ed. *Ayumi: A Japanese American Anthology*. San Francisco: Japanese American Anthology Committee, 1980.

Mori, Toshio. *Unfinished Message*. Edited by Patricia Wakida. Berkeley, CA: Heyday Books, 2000.

Mura, David. *The Colors of Desire*. New York: Anchor Books, 1995.

————. *Where the Body Meets Memory: An Odyssey of Race, Sexuality and Identity*. New York: Anchor Books, 1996.

————. *Famous Suicides of the Japanese Empire*. Minneapolis: Coffee House Press, 2008.

Okada, John. *No-No Boy*. Seattle: University of Washington Press, 1979.

Rizzuto, Rahna Reiko. *Why She Left Us*. New York: Harper Collins, 2000.

Shigekawa, Marlene. *Welcome Home Swallows*. Torrance, CA: Heian International, 2001.

Sone, Monica. *Nisei Daughter*. New York: Little Brown, 1953 and 1979.

Uchida, Yoshiko. *The Invisible Thread: An Autobiography*. Englewood Cliffs, NJ: Julian Messner, 1991.

————. *Journey Home*. New York: Aladdin Paperbacks, 1992.

Yamada, Mitsuye. *Camp Notes and Other Poems*. Latham, NY: Kitchen Table: Women of Color Press, 1980.

————. *Desert Run: Poems and Stories*. Latham, NY: Kitchen Table: Women of Color Press, 1988.

Yamamoto, Hisaye. *Seventeen Syllables*. New Brunswick, NJ: Rutgers University Press, 1994.

Yamauchi, Wakako. *Songs My Mother Taught Me: Stories, Plays, and Memoir*. Edited by Garrett Hongo. New York: Feminist Press at the City University of New York, 1994.

————. *Rosebud and Other Stories*. Edited by Lillian Howan. Honolulu: University of Hawai'i Press, 2010.

FILM/MULTIMEDIA/PRODUCTION

After the War. Written by Philip Kan Gotanda. Directed by Carey Perloff. American Conservatory Theater, San Francisco. Performances from March 22 to April 22, 2007.

American Fish. Directed by Jesse Wine. 10 min. Center for Asian American Media, 1995. Based on the short story "American Fish" by R. A. Sasaki. Videocassette.

The Cats of Mirikitani. Directed by Linda Hattendorf. Coproduced by Linda Hattendorf and Masa Yoshikawa. 74 min. New Video Group, 2006. DVD.

The Chessmen. Written and directed by Kenneth Kokka. 18 min. Self-distributed, 2004. Based on the short story "The Chessmen" by Toshio Mori. Film.

Children of the Camps. Directed by Stephen Holsapple. Produced by Satsuki Ina. 57 min. Center for Asian American Media, 1999. DVD.

Civil Liberties in Times of Crisis: The Japanese American Experience. Produced by Dianne Fukami. 40 min. Bridge Media, Inc., 2005. DVD.

Crossroads in Nihonmachi: The Struggle for an American Community. 55 min. Urban Voice, 2007. DVD.

"A New Beginning: Japanese American Community in Chicago, 1944 to the Present." Online photographic timeline. *Chicago Japanese American Historical Society*. June 2007. Funding provided by Discover Nikkei. http://www.cjahs.org/timeline/timeline_flash.html.

"New Neighbors among Us: The Japanese American Resettlement." Oral histories with photos and historical documents. *Denshō: The Japanese American Legacy Project*. June 2008. http://www.densho.org/archive/default.asp?path=fromthearchive/200806-fromthearchive.asp.

Piecing Memories: Recollections of Internment. Produced by Dianne Fukami. 17 min. Bridge Media, Inc., 2001. Videocassette/DVD.

Rabbit in the Moon: A Documentary/Memoir about the World War II Japanese American Internment Camps. Directed and produced by Emiko Omori. Coproduced by Chizuko Omori. 85 min. 2004. DVD.

Resettlement to Redress: Rebirth of the Japanese American Community. Directed by Don Young. 54 min. KVIE Public Television, 2005. DVD.

Return to the Valley: The Japanese American Experience after World War II. Directed by Scott Gracheff. Produced by Christina Lim. 80 min. KTEH PBS, 2003. DVD.

Starting Over: Japanese Americans after the War. Produced by Dianne Fukami. 60 min. KCSM TV, 1996. Videocassette.

When You're Smiling: The Deadly Legacy of Internment. Directed and produced by Janice D. Tanaka. 60 min. Center for Asian American Media, 1999. Videocassette/DVD.

Who's Going to Pay for These Donuts Anyway? Directed and produced by Janice Tanaka. 58 min. Center for Asian American Media, 1992. Videocassette.

About the Editor

Brian Komei Dempster is a Sansei whose grandfather, Archbishop Nitten Ishida, a Buddhist priest, was taken by the FBI from the family's church home in San Francisco shortly after the December 7, 1941, bombing of Pearl Harbor. The archbishop was separated from his wife and children and interned at various Department of Justice camp locations; the rest of the family, including Brian's mother, Renko, an infant at the time, was first incarcerated at the Tanforan Assembly Center and then at the Central Utah Relocation Center (known as Topaz). Eventually, the Ishida family reunited at the Crystal City Internment Camp in Texas. After being released from camp, they lived in a housing project in Richmond, California, until they could return to their church residence in San Francisco.

Dempster received bachelor's degrees in American ethnic studies and English at the University of Washington, and he earned his MFA in creative writing from the University of Michigan. He is the editor of *From Our Side of the Fence: Growing Up in America's Concentration Camps* (Kearny Street Workshop, 2001), which received a 2007 Nisei Voices Award from the National Japanese American Historical Society. His poems have been published in the anthologies *Language for a New Century: Contemporary Poetry from the Middle East, Asia, and Beyond* (Norton, 2008), *Asian American Poetry: The Next Generation* (University of Illinois, 2004), and *Screaming Monkeys: Critiques of Asian American Images* (Coffee House, 2003). He has also contributed poems to various journals, including the *New England Review,* the *North American Review, Ploughshares, Prairie Schooner,* and *Quarterly West.* His work—as a poet, workshop instructor, and editor—has been recognized by grants from the Arts Foundation of Michigan and the Michigan Council for Arts and Cultural Affairs, the California State Library's California Civil Liberties Public Education Program, and the San Francisco Arts Commission. He is an associate professor of rhetoric and language and a faculty member in Asian American studies at the University of San Francisco. In 2010, he was honored with the university's Distinguished Teaching Award.